MAGNETIC NORTH

A Trek Across Canada

David Halsey
with Diana Landau

Sierra Club Books | San Francisco

Copyright © 1990 by the Estate of David Halsey

Sierra Club Books paperback edition: 1991

Library of Congress Cataloging in Publication Data
Halsey, David, 1956–1983.
    Magnetic North: trek across Canada / by David Halsey
    with Diana Landau.
        p.   cm.
    Includes bibliographical references.
    ISBN 0-87156-566-8
    1. Canada—Description and travel—1951–1980.   2. Hiking—Canada.
3. Halsey, David, 1956–1983—Journeys—Canada.   I. Landau, Diana,
1950–   . II. Title.
F1016.H35   1990
917.104′644—dc20   90–32056
                                                            CIP

Cover design by Paul Bacon
Book design by Abigail Johnston
Maps by Ronna Nelson
Set in Trump Mediaeval by Classic Typography
Production by Lynne O'Neil

Printed on recycled acid-free paper in the United States of America
10 9 8 7 6 5 4 3 2 1

Contents

Prologue

Fort Langley, British Columbia

On May 4, 1977, a group of four young men shouldered backpacks at the edge of the Pacific Ocean in Vancouver. They might have been setting forth on a lighthearted weekend hike into the Coast Mountains, but this was a more ambitious outing. The modestly equipped quartet called itself the 1977–78 Trans-Canada Expedition, and its final goal was Tadoussac, a village on the St. Lawrence River in Quebec—4,700 miles from Vancouver and the Pacific. If successful, they would be the first in modern times to traverse Canada coast to coast by a wilderness route and using only essentially primitive means: foot, snowshoe, cargo toboggan, and canoe.

All four were in their early twenties; their leader, David Halsey, at twenty, was the youngest. Dave Halsey had conceived and planned the journey while a sophomore in college, scrutinizing hundreds of maps and historical documents to create a route based on the historic paths of explorers, traders, and trappers, with some detours to avoid now-urbanized areas. It was neither the most difficult way across Canada (a route through the Far North, he recognized, would exceed his capacities) nor the easiest. Besides its awesome scope, the expedition promised plenty of thrills and hardships: backpacking through rough bush, canoeing and portaging rivers notorious for rapids, cross-country skiing across frozen lakes in the dead of winter, navigating the treacherous tidal shoals of James Bay.

In pitching the trip to his teammates, Dave dwelt long on the thrills and short on the hardships. He spiked his original proposal for the expedition and his many verbal presentations with parallels to the careers of the great explorers he idolized: Antarctic pioneers Robert F. Scott, Richard E. Byrd, and Ernest Shackleton; and Alexander Mackenzie, who charted the first waterway to the Pacific for his Northwest Fur Company. Visionary and persuasive beyond his years, Dave had already accomplished much to get his dream journey under way—most notably winning the interest and encouragement of the National Geographic Society, which provided some seed money and photographic equipment and offered to consider the story for publication later on.

His attraction to wilderness and its challenges was compelling. "To me," he wrote in his proposal, "the exhilaration of crossing a five-mile stretch of open water with nothing but the thin shell of a canoe separating me and all I own from that icy expanse is unequalled. . . . I feel sorry for anyone who has never known intense cold that cannot be escaped, or the exasperating fatigue of an impossible climb." More than anything, it was Dave's contagious excitement about his expedition that had carried it so far.

A mere four days after it began, however, the expedition almost ended. On May 8, after hiking fifty-seven miles up the Fraser River from Vancouver to Fort Langley, the teammates stood divided on the river's north bank, with Dave witnessing the collapse of his dreams and his work. His three mutinous partners were abandoning the journey, taking most of the team's equipment and supplies with them.

"Get away from me, Halsey," warned Charlie Bratz, the apparent instigator of the dissension. "We're poorly equipped and on a ridiculous route. We all know we'll never make it to Quebec."

Dave tried to counter with spirited reminders of the exploits of their brethren in adventure, the historic importance of their own endeavor, and any arguments he could scrape up for them to continue. He paced in circles, head lowered and arms flailing. But the three weren't buying it. Lifting his pack to depart, Bratz, the erstwhile expedition photographer, delivered the coup de grace: "Quit trying to con us, Dave. You've conned the newspapers, the magazines, even a publisher. You can sure talk a good story, but you can't con us." The three walked off toward the road, never looking back.

Stunned by the abruptness of their desertion and the harsh personal attacks, Dave could not at first come to grips with the grim choice he faced: to continue on alone, ill-equipped and admittedly underexperienced for such a venture, or to pack it in—go home to his parents' house in Virginia, apologize to the National Geographic Society and others who had invested in his hopes, and acknowledge the wisdom of those who dismissed him as a dreamer and disparaged his prospects.

If the choice was far from clear to Dave at that moment, at least one person had no doubts. Maurice Halsey, a lobbyist for northern Illinois' natural gas industry and a dedicated fisherman, had whetted Dave's appetite for the Canadian backwoods by taking his sons on frequent fishing trips to the northern forests and lakes. On realizing that his oldest son's plan for dropping out of college to hike and paddle across Canada was no frivolous whim but a deeply rooted goal, he had done all in his power to help make the expedition a reality. A former naval flight officer and navigator, Maurice worked closely with Dave on route planning; the basement of their home in McLean, Virginia, became the repository for hundreds of detailed topographic maps and charts. As the expedition's supply coordinator, Maurice would keep in close touch with Dave and track his progress mile by mile across the continent.

When Dave called home that rock-bottom night for comfort and counsel, the elder Halsey commiserated angrily about the deserters and, as always, left it to his son to decide finally on his own course. But he made his opinion plain: that Dave ought to press on, at least for the present, and see what might develop in terms of reconstituting the expedition. The trip was brand new; there remained hundreds of miles of backpacking through British Columbia, which Dave could accomplish alone, before he would need a canoeing partner to paddle the rivers of Alberta.

Maurice Halsey knew, perhaps better than Dave himself at that point, how deep ran his son's desire to accomplish this journey, and how much he would regret abandoning it. Dave's mother, Jean, also supported his plan to continue solo and kept private her fear and worry over the possibility of her son lying injured and alone on the bank of some Canadian rapid. Both parents had some insight, too, into the dramatic disintegration of the four-member team before it had scarcely gotten under way.

Dave's original vision of the Trans-Canada Expedition did not include other expedition members. Although his explorer heroes were gifted team leaders as well as inspired adventurers, Dave's imagination was fired chiefly by solo exploits: single-handed ocean crossings and one-man mountaineering feats. And among his psychological paradoxes was that, while strikingly personable, intelligent, and persuasive, he doubted his ability to lead and he doubted whether the force of his dream could sustain teammates over the long haul the trip was sure to be.

At the start, Dave had conceived the essence of the expedition as a private struggle with all the obstacles geography and distance could put in his way. However, this vision was abruptly dissipated at Dave's first meeting with *National Geographic* senior editor Bill Graves. Graves told him bluntly that for his plan to have any chance of winning the Society's seal of approval, it would have to include at least one other team member: a qualified photographer. (Dave's camera skills then were of the Instamatic variety.) He and his colleagues were also concerned for Dave's safety: Old hands at the expedition game, they had a thorough understanding of the hazards this novice explorer faced.

For Dave to be sitting in Bill Graves's office arguing his case at all was an impressive measure of his persistence, aided by a stroke of luck. He had, naturally enough, written to the National Geographic Society — the prospective explorer's Mount Olympus — outlining his plans and soliciting its aid. His proposal languished unnoted for a time. (Jean Halsey recalls Bill Graves remarking that the Society receives up to three hundred "off-the-street" requests for support *each week*.) Meanwhile, Dave had been talking to local press about the trip, and one article about him, in the *Washington Post*, caught the eye of none other than *Geographic*'s boss, Gilbert M. Grosvenor. He suggested to his editors that they check Dave out. They did.

Despite his youth and inexperience, Dave's passion and careful planning for the journey led Bill Graves to take him and his goal seriously. "Dave was brash, sometimes prickly, and in many ways insensitive to others' needs and feelings," Graves would recall years later. "But he was born with that essential drive that all great explorers and trekkers have, a form of tunnel vision that excludes everything finally but the goal."

Thrilled and gratified by the *Geographic*'s support, Dave eagerly jumped through the hoops they customarily set up before endorsing any project. He drafted a seventy-eight-page proposal complete with annotated charts detailing the journey almost down to the step. And he began at once to recruit team members, running ads in metropolitan Washington, D.C., newspapers and poring over the resumes he received in response. He also contacted friends and acquaintances like Mark Jusko.

The Halseys had only recently moved to the Washington area; Dave had grown up mostly in the suburbs of Chicago, where he and Jusko had attended Downers Grove North High School. He'd gotten to know Jusko during a summer canoe trip in northern Minnesota and Ontario. After graduating, Jusko spent some time as a canoe guide for an outfitter called Voyageur Trails, and when he signed on, Dave designated him as the expedition's canoeing authority.

In fact, the qualifications of all four eventual team members to undertake a two-year expedition under extreme conditions were skimpy. Charles Bratz, twenty-four, was a photographer—the one essential component, according to *National Geographic*. Neil Kogan, also twenty-four, was a theater major when Dave met him at the University of Iowa. The team member with the best wilderness credentials was a forty-four-year-old assistant geography professor named Lyman Echola, whom Dave met at the Colorado Outward Bound school in 1974. Dave emphasized Echola's background in first aid and botany in his proposal—but Echola dropped out before the starting date.

Dave's own wilderness experience was limited to vacation canoe and fishing trips, winter camping with the Boy Scouts, and the Outward Bound course, a high school graduation gift from his parents. As it turned out, the critical factor on the expedition was not Dave's experience or lack of same, but his amazing affinity—even hunger—for wilderness hardship. This drive to test the limits of endurance may be a defining characteristic of explorers, and there are early hints of it in Dave's life. As a teenager, he had loved winter camping—the colder the better—and he was actually disappointed that his Outward Bound adventure wasn't more rigorous. He had wanted to learn where his "panic threshold" was, but was "never in a dangerous enough situation to find out."

So the Trans-Canada Expedition would be Dave's great chance to test his mettle as an explorer. Germinating as a fantasy, it quickly took root and flourished, crowding out virtually all else in his life. By the time he was a sophomore at Iowa State, he was spending nearly all his time in the library researching the history and geography of the route. By March 1976, he had dropped out of school to work full time on expedition planning and fund-raising. By mid-April 1977, he was on a plane to Seattle with twenty-five hundred dollars in seed money from *National Geographic*, headed for a rendezvous with his three partners at the home of some relatives. Equipment and supplies had been sent on ahead; from this staging point, they would proceed to Vancouver and the real kickoff of the expedition.

And by this time Dave was feeling totally overcome with doubt and dread—for his partners' safety and his own sanity. As the aircraft began its descent, he was thinking, "God, it was supposed to stop a long time ago! Somewhere, months back, someone was supposed to have convinced me that this trip was crazy, that I had nowhere near the experience for it. Life just doesn't work this way. Why didn't it stop? Why did I have to go so far?"

Hints of discord within the team began to surface in Seattle almost immediately, but Dave was too preoccupied with playing the optimist and appearing cheerfully in control of the situation to confess any of his own fears and uncertainties. His idea of being a leader meant never to admit to weakness or lack of faith; paradoxically, if he could have let down his guard a bit, he might have averted the bitter break that followed. As it was, his partners likely felt patronized and left out of the decision-making. Dave had chosen them hastily and solicited little participation from them during the previous months of planning. He may unintentionally have alienated them further when—partly on the *Geographic*'s advice—he asked that they sign contracts specifying the split of any profits from the expedition and releasing him from any liability.

Charlie Bratz, who had held out against signing the contracts, voiced the group's growing unease during the drive to Vancouver, proclaiming: "I don't think I'm ever going to see my family again." Dave held his tongue but privately condemned the remark as a selfishly theatrical gesture. Maybe that's what it was—but it might have relieved some tension if Dave had been able to appear similarly vulnerable, less unassailable in his conviction that the expedition *must* succeed.

The original team probably would have come apart sooner or later. The other members were not dedicated expeditioneers who had invested much of themselves in the endeavor. They had signed on for a lark, wooed by Dave's eloquent description of his scheme, but when confronted in Seattle by mounds of expedition gear and Dave's air of do-or-die determination, they seem to have contracted a mass case of cold feet. Dave, struggling with his own demons, hadn't the energy or the psychological acumen to deal with the problem. In a sense, he had set the team up for a fall—and so now he stood in the rain, watching his partners' receding backs and looking ahead to a solo journey without even a tent to shelter him.

As it developed, however, lack of equipment was never a make-or-break issue for the Trans-Canada Expedition: One of its salient features was how successfully Dave learned to live off the land, his own resources and ingenuity, and the kindness of strangers. At this critical moment in the journey, what he had was more important than what he lacked. He had the unwavering support of his family, the backing of an influential organization, and, most of all, a quality within himself not only to endure the sternest challenges but to rise to them with relish.

The following chapters detail what happened after Fort Langley and over the next two-plus years: Dave's summer of solo backpacking in the high desert and mountain forests of British Columbia; his gradual acquisition of bushcraft and, in Alberta, of a new team that endured for the remainder of the expedition—a Chicago photographer named Peter Souchuk and the coyote-dog, Ki, who wandered into their camp one day and stayed. The months of snowshoeing and dogsledding across frozen Saskatchewan and Manitoba; of paddling canoes through Athabasca whitewater, windswept James Bay, the sloughs of Ontario, and the rivers and lakes of Quebec. The countless adventures, disasters, friends found and left behind, triumphs small and large—until, on August 17, 1979, they beached their canoe at Tadoussac, where the Saguenay enters the St. Lawrence and the Atlantic whales venture upriver: 4,700 miles from the Pacific Coast and Vancouver.

These chapters were written mostly by Dave Halsey and finished with my help as a cowriter. Dave was a gifted enough writer to tell his own story vividly and well; he had an eye for close observation, a flair for timing and drama, and the discipline to keep prodigious records of the expedition. The reader and I are particularly fortunate in the last of these, because about two-thirds of the way through completing his manuscript, Dave's luck ran out. He died as a probable suicide at age twenty-six, about six months after being diagnosed as manic-depressive and starting treatment.

Dave's parents had begun to notice a change in him during his high school years—a common time for manic-depression to emerge—and more noticeably after the expedition, doubtless exacerbated by subsequent disappointments and postachievement malaise. Those who know something about moodswing and related conditions may recognize symptoms of the disease in aspects of Dave's behavior during the journey—although it seems that the wilderness environment had a stabilizing and healing effect on him. Leaders of wilderness outings for emotionally or mentally troubled young people report that the clear-cut, objective challenges of outdoor survival have therapeutic value. Apparently that was so for Dave.

The present writer is not tasked, nor qualified, to investigate at length Dave Halsey's tragic illness. Doing so would be beside the point in any case—the point being that while he was living, he accomplished something extraordinary. After his death, his family, his literary agent, his publishers, and all who knew him agreed that the story of this achievement should be told.

To finish telling Dave's story as successfully as possible in his absence has been my rewarding task. As Dave's editor at Sierra Club

Books, I was captured by his tale on first reading sample chapters, then doubly saddened by his death and the possibility that the book he had put so much of himself into might vanish into limbo. So the opportunity to help him tie up the loose ends has been deeply satisfying.

The primary sources for completing this book have been Dave's draft manuscript; earlier handwritten drafts; his rough notes, journals, and eloquent letters home; a few published articles; the pretrip prospectus he assembled for *National Geographic*; and a trove of painstakingly annotated topographic maps. Even all this would have been insufficient without the immeasurable aid of Jean and Maurice Halsey and Peter Souchuk. Most of the middle part of the story existed in some form, but for the beginning and the end, especially, we relied heavily on their vivid memories, firsthand and vicarious, of events.

The question of whether to tell the story in Dave's voice or in the third person was discussed at length and more or less resolved itself. Since the extensive existing manuscript was already in the first person, new narrative created from his drafts and notes to bridge the gaps was left in his voice as well. Here and there, the manuscript called for sections of exposition to chronicle background events, breaks in the trip, or lulls in between the high points—times when not much went on except for logging daily mileage. Such transitional sections, as well as an occasional editorial comment, are written in the third person and set off from Dave's narrative typographically. Direct quotations and excerpts from Dave's journals and letters are identified in standard fashion.

When an author is not present to review a manuscript and respond to queries and requests for clarification, an editor's interpretations are vulnerable to misreadings, lack of firsthand knowledge, unfounded assumptions, and other pitfalls. As part of the effort to make this book conform as closely as possible to the story Dave would have told himself, the Halseys and Pete Souchuk read the final manuscript carefully, and Bill Graves of the National Geographic Society reviewed material pertaining to that institution. Any faulty interpretations that remain are the cowriter's responsibility, but we hope and believe that this has turned out to be a book Dave Halsey would have been proud to have his name on.

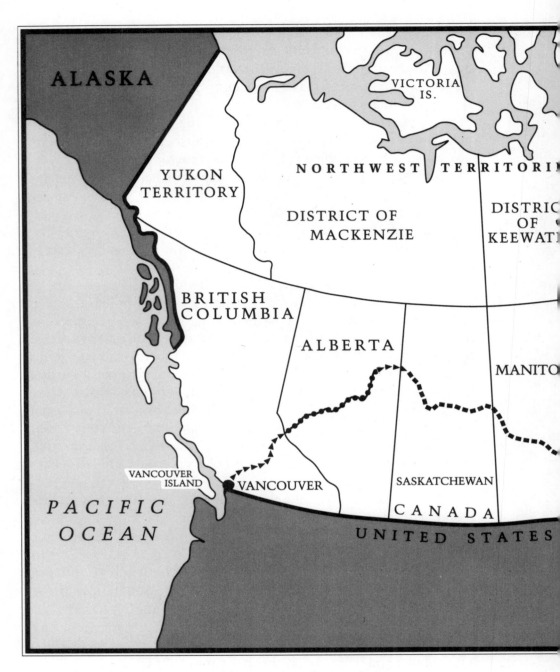

Route of the 1977–79 Trans-Canada Expedition

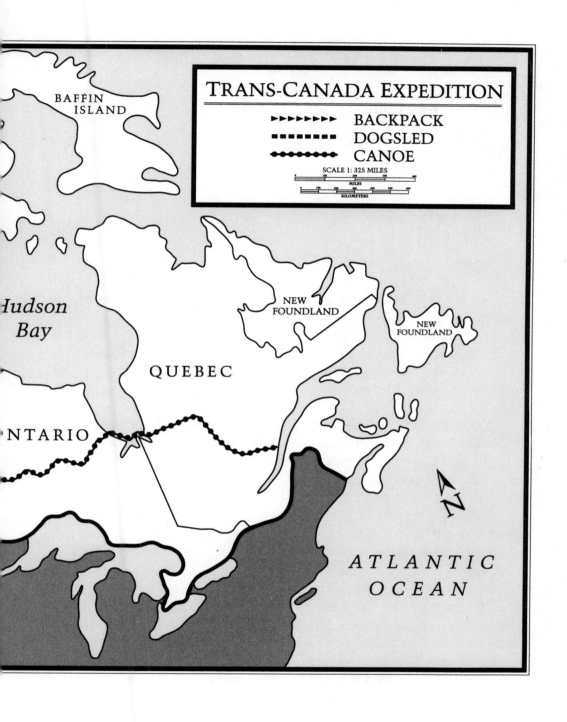

1 | Starting Over
Fort Langley to
Merritt, British Columbia

May 6, 1977. The night after my partners split from the expedition, I was holding down a bar stool in a Fort Langley pub, staring into my beer glass and feeling pretty sorry for myself. When the man on the next stool tried to strike up a conversation about backpacking—my monstrous pack would have been hard to miss—I answered in monosyllables. The last thing I wanted to talk about was backpacking.

Yet when he got around to asking where I was headed, the dam broke. Obviously I needed to carry on to someone about my smashed dreams, and Gary Richardson was just the right man at the right time. The beer loosened my tongue, and half an hour into the story, Gary was practically falling off his stool in excitement.

"Quit!" he protested. "You must be out of your mind! You talk about Canada like it was your backyard. . . . You sound like you know every lake, river, and town between here and Quebec. You can't quit." He shook his bearded head vehemently. "Canada's a great country, and you're going to have a great story to tell."

His eyes on fire, he proceeded to bend my ear with tales of explorers: Scott, Amundsen, Mackenzie. I could swear he spoke the same phrases I had used to exhort my ex-teammates in my vain attempt to rekindle their spirits the day before. What was it about this journey that tapped into the vicarious longings of so many people? I had heard the same wishful note over the phone again and

12

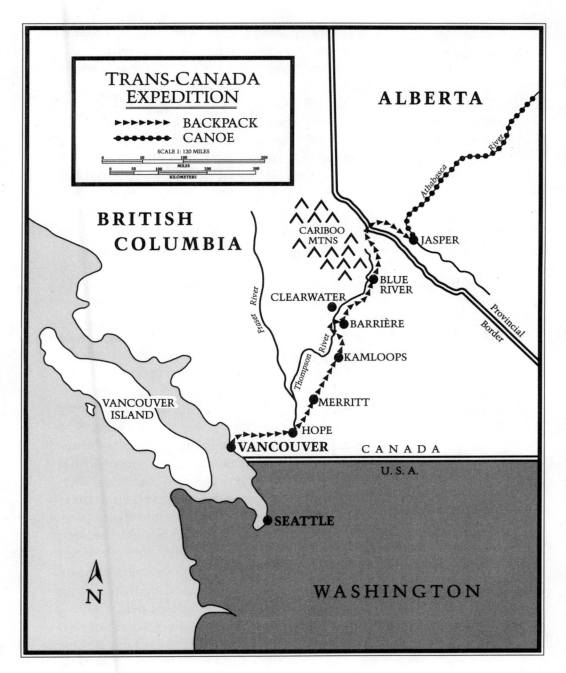

Vancouver, B.C., to Jasper, Alberta, May–September 1977

again, while hunting down information or supplies or support money.

Pouring me a last beer, Gary concluded, "To hell with those guys. You saw where depending on others got you. Now depend on yourself and go for it alone."

Two weeks later I would toss my pack on my back and start hiking toward Quebec. Gary's encouragement had turned the tide for me, and I spent the intervening time resupplying, reorganizing, replanning the route, and being treated to some wonderful hospitality in and around Fort Langley. That first night, Gary and I stumbled off to the home of a friend of his, a middle-aged woman named Dorothy Gilroy who was happy to lend me a piece of her floor. I never saw Gary again, but he left me with a book and the admonition to "read this" when I got discouraged or low. It was *The Venturesome Voyages of Captain Voss,* the harrowing tale of a man who circumnavigated the world, even weathering North Sea gales, in a dugout canoe. So who was I to worry about a few freshwater lakes?

A little sight-seeing seemed in order during the stopover. In my first four days of hiking with the others, we'd seen little but Vancouver suburbs, save for the beautifully wild Stanley and Lynn Canyon parks on the edge of that city. But Fort Langley had some interesting history. Now a rural town of a few thousand, in the nineteenth century it had been British Columbia's capital. Back then, the mighty Fraser River—one of North America's largest—could accommodate oceangoing vessels as far upriver as Fort Langley. The big ships hauled imported and industrial goods as far as the port, from which these items would continue east into the interior on barges and then finally on mule teams. Making the return trip would be wilderness riches, mainly furs. The fort was a major rendezvous and trading site.

Eventually the river silted in, and when Fort Langley became inaccessible to the larger vessels, the capital moved west to the coast and the fort became another has-been boomtown. Nowadays the old fort, realistically restored down to period-costumed characters demonstrating chores and crafts, is a lively reminder of past glories.

Early in my stay in Fort Langley my base camp was the town park—not especially private but a good place to meet people. One day I was sitting around frustratedly examining the one camera remaining from *National Geographic*'s donation, wishing I knew the first thing about f-stops, apertures, and ASAs. An elderly Asian gentleman happened by and seemed amused by my predicament. "You play with camera, very funny! Take pictures easy. Come to my store, I show."

Thus with another stroke of luck, one of my chief worries was on its way to being eased. When I showed up at Fung's grocery store, he contemptuously waved at his surroundings and explained that the grocery business was merely an occupation. Then he led me to the back storage room, which contained a fully equipped darkroom and shelves neatly burdened with a huge array of photographic equipment. The walls were covered with dazzling color blowups of Hong Kong—Fung's hometown—as well as certificates and plaques from photo contests he had won there and in Canada.

In the course of a few visits to his store, I learned from Fung the basics of 35-mm photography. I happily clicked off roll after roll of film, and was even presumptuous enough to send the results to *National Geographic*. (Later, after receiving their opinion of my efforts and acquiring a new teammate who was a real shooter, I went back to being the humble camera toter.)

My last temporary home in Fort Langley was a commune on a farm just outside of town. I was invited to stay there by two of its female residents I'd met while walking in the park. Catherine's prospector husband had died in the northern bush several years earlier, and she supported their four children by making candles. The teenage kids were streetwise peddlers. Kathleen's husband, a German immigrant named Wolf, was unemployed except for crafting exquisite stained-glass windows and reading philosophy. The colorful company was rounded out by Wendy, a nurse, and Mike, an unemployed hard-rock miner, who lived with their two young boys in a converted Canadian Air Force bus, luxuriously appointed inside with even a solar-powered shower. I became fishing buddies with three-year-old Eli and spent many pleasant hours on the banks of the local trout stream.

But the May days were growing longer, and I had to get back on the trail if I were to have any hope of reaching Flin Flon by winter. The morning after a convivial send-off dinner at the commune, I again shouldered my pack and became an "expedition."

Dave's original route called for a lengthy segment of canoe travel in late 1977, between Hinton, Alberta, and Flin Flon, Manitoba, via the Athabasca, Clearwater, and Churchill rivers. At Flin Flon, the plan was to switch to cross-country skis, snowshoes, and pack toboggans for the demanding winter travel. Making Flin Flon before the rivers froze up, therefore, was the chief motivator urging Dave forward through the summer and fall months.

May 20, 1977. 6:00 P.M. Four hours of daylight remaining. I walked past the campfire site where my companions and I had parted ways two weeks ago, took the ferry across the Fraser, and hiked on along the gravel road shoulder paralleling the river. The fading light and my indulgences over the past weeks prompted a brisk pace. Ten miles down the road, I pitched a hasty camp in the dark and, with coffee and oatmeal on the fire, settled down to some overdue letters.

The next morning I hung around to watch the annual Fraser River Raft Race: twenty-odd miles of madness with categories ranging from historic replicas to "anything goes" craft, some made entirely from beer kegs and cans (sponsored by breweries, of course). Also featured were some crazy skydivers, trailing smoke plumes, who landed among the spectators. Fleeing the chaotic traffic jam in the aftermath of the race, I made good time on the trail, covering thirteen miles of the flat riverbed by late afternoon.

My map showed a logging road bearing north into Douglas Provincial Forest, and with trout on my mind, I turned up it into the surrounding mountains, headed for a campsite at a stream called Norrish Creek. The trail was steeper and rougher than it had looked at the start. About three miles in, it was still climbing; I hadn't seen a level campsite anywhere, and already I was 500 feet above where I was supposed to intersect the elusive Norrish Creek.

I had just given up the logging road as a bad job when I came to a break in the thick brush: the path of an old avalanche. From the top I could see that the scree slide led straight down to the creek, so I decided to take the express route. Running steep scree (loose rocks and gravel) isn't for novice hikers, but I'd done it many times before. I handled the slide all right, running in the traditional pedaling manner to keep from being buried in the wave of rock. (Scree ski-

ing, as it's also called, is not unlike a combination of slow snow skiing and surfing.) I was thinking I ought to slow down a bit when
I saw that after dropping about 500 feet, the scree abruptly ended
in a 100-foot sheer cliff. Instantly I was down on my back, letting
my pack take the punishment while I aimed for something big
enough to stop me.

My aim was good, landing me feet first on a solidly planted
boulder not twenty feet from the verge. Below, a pool boiled fiercely
as the shower of rock continued over the edge and into the water.
When my heart slowed I looked north and south for a route around
the cliff, but in vain. I didn't even have a rope—my former companions, grumbling about "excess baggage," had talked me out of bringing one.

After bushwhacking about half a mile upriver, I finally found
a place where the cliff ended, in a steep slope solid with thistles
and wild roses. I'd have to hang on to the rose stems for balance,
but it looked like the only way down—so, pulling on spare socks
for gloves and cursing my cutoff shorts, I grabbed the first plant and
stepped into the unseen void beneath the leaves. Around 8:00 P.M.,
scratched from head to foot, I reached the water.

Heavy clouds were building in the west, and without a tent it
looked like a fairly miserable night ahead. I thought longingly of
the beautiful mountain tents that had been donated, along with considerable other gear, by a store in Washington, D.C. Except for my
sleeping bag, all of it was gone. Luck was with me, though; the night
stayed dry after all, and fifty yards upriver I found an ideal campsite—a beautiful natural cave arching into the rock, about twenty
feet long, six feet deep, and eight feet high. The ceiling, already black
with soot, took on another coating with my blaze.

Now for that trout. The only productive-looking pool seemed
inaccessible from my side of the stream. But then in the fading light
I spotted a cable stretched thirty feet across the stream between two
trees; on my side a large wooden box was suspended from it by two
pulleys, like a crude cable car. This must be a reasonably well-used
spot for some hardy locals. Well, trout or no trout, I wasn't going
to miss the ride, and in a flash I was up the tree and in the swinging
box. With a flick of the anchor rope we were off, gravity taking me

three-quarters of the way across and hand-over-hand hauling the rest.

The pool was productive all right—full of four-inch rainbows that hit my favorite flies with nearly every cast. But nothing more substantial obliged, and I eventually gave up on the juveniles. In light drizzle and gathering dusk I headed back toward the cable car, empty creel in hand. A stiff breeze ran down the canyon, making an eerie, low-pitched whistle, and odd shapes seemed to emerge from clefts in the narrow, vertical walls. The gloomy hour, the claustrophobic canyon, and the knowledge that I was in "Sasquatch country" all made me hurry along, glancing over my shoulder now and then.

Rounding a rocky outcrop, I saw my cable car . . . swinging lazily in the middle of the stream! Now I really felt spooked: I distinctly remembered tying off the car with a sturdy clove hitch, even giving the knot a good tug before leaving. Peering through the dimness, I saw the loop I had secured around an anchor post now dangling from the box with the knot intact. That left two possibilities: I chose to think only that some animal might have tripped the loop in passing.

In another ten minutes, with the heavy cloud cover, it would be quite dark. Unlike an open plain, where there is always some ambient light, an overcast night in a deep canyon is black as a cave. The most logical way across the creek, in hindsight, would have been to lash my rod and tackle around my waist, climb to the cable, and crawl hand-over-hand to the box. Pressed for time and not thinking logically, what I did instead was try to ford the creek at the widest, shallowest point I could find.

Tying my wool pants around my neck, holding my tackle in one hand and a balancing stick in the other, I plunged into the icy stream, probing for unseen holes. The current was stronger than I'd expected. Half a dozen times I was halted by the onrushing waters and had to lean upriver to stay on one leg, the other fighting the current as it tried to rejoin its partner. Two-thirds of the way across— about fifty feet—I was stopped short of the inviting far shore by a chute, a river within a river. With my probe I found that it wasn't more than a foot deeper than where I was standing, but the current was half again as fast. There didn't seem to be much choice, though, and after thirty seconds of hesitation, I took the first step. Okay. Then the second. Whoosh!

It is next to impossible to regain one's footing after losing it in swift water. A chute's suction prevents its passenger from reaching the slower water on either side; you just keep surging down the river, legs running as they vainly seek the bottom. All you can do is try to keep your head above water, avoid oncoming rocks, and search for your ticket out—usually a pool.

I recalled having seen a pool just above my camp, and I was headed in that direction. With luck, the chute would run into the pool and deposit me not ten yards from my camp. My luck held, and as I staggered from the pool I vowed never again to leave solid ground. Not more than thirty seconds had elapsed since I had begun the 100-yard trip down the chute, but in that time the curtain of night was drawn, the blackness total. My campfire embers still glowed faintly, a welcoming beacon. I thought briefly that I'd escaped the mishap without loss—pants still around neck, fishing tackle clutched tightly—until I emptied my sodden pockets and found that my beloved pocket watch was no more.

I spent the next day huddled in my sleeping bag, waiting out the rain. By the following morning it let up some, and I set off downstream at a brisk pace, hoping to reach the road before the next cloudburst. I had given up on dry clothes; after a heavy rain in the bush you get quite thoroughly soaked just from brushing against water-laden branches. Actually, the constant sprinkle was refreshing after two nights in a smoke-filled cave.

By midmorning on May 23 I was headed east on the Canadian Pacific Railroad tracks. For the next three days I alternated between railroad and highway, depending on the traffic. In the more remote parts of lower British Columbia, the bush is extremely dense, with few passageways except the gravel path of the tracks. This is the more scenic route, but track walking is tiring. Measuring each step between the ties, you can catch the scenery only in quick glances, as a poorly calculated step can easily result in a twisted ankle. Except in tunnels and on bridges, trains can be avoided just by stepping over to the alternate track. The danger, though, is that the noise of a passing train may mask the approach of another train from behind you. Most of the time I took the easier route via the highway. If traffic became too heavy for me to enjoy the hike (about thirty cars per hour was my criterion), I returned to the tracks.

On May 26 I reached beautiful Lake of the Woods, two miles north of the town of Hope, eighty miles and a week past Fort Langley. The lake is surrounded by inviting snow-covered ridges, and the atmosphere of the region holds a taste of homesteading and gold rush days. There is a lively jade industry here, as elsewhere in the Fraser Valley: the legacy of Chinese railroad workers who were the first to recognize the local mineral's value.

I spent three days at Lake of the Woods, logging many hours of successful trout fishing and cleaning myself and my clothes. The cool nights I spent catching up on my notes by candlelight and battling the slugs that seemed to find my tarp a dry haven. After a few nauseating encounters, I learned to sprinkle a fine film of salt on my ground cloth every night in wet country.

I had planned to hike the 170 miles from Hope to Kamloops via the Fraser Canyon highway, but five miles along I heard of an alternate route—a little-known logging road up the Coquihalla River that would cut off nearly forty miles of hiking and get me off the tourist route besides.

As I turned up the Coquihalla, I briefly regretted leaving the Fraser, which I had followed for 130 miles from Vancouver. Near the coast, the Fraser had been an old graybeard of a river, lethargic with its burden of silt. But it had regressed in age as I traveled upriver; at Hope it was middle-aged: narrower, swifter. It seemed a shame that I would never see Old Man Fraser in his torrential youth.

But the grandeur of the Coquihalla Valley proved a worthwhile trade. The dirt-and-gravel road, infrequently traversed by logging trucks, provided a nice change of pace from trains and traffic. In the first ten miles—the "urban" stretch of the Coquihalla—I counted no more than three cabins and half a dozen trucks.

At about the ten-mile point I stopped to observe one of those cabins; a horse grazing in the adjacent clearing and smoke wisping from the chimney contradicted my first impression that it was uninhabited. Hoping for a cup of coffee and maybe some conversation, I rapped on the hand-hewn door. A rough-edged voice responded, "Door's always open."

Randy Davis and his girlfriend, Donna, welcomed me warmly and fed me an enormous meal of ham, potato, and corn stew sopped up with bannock (pan-fried bread), the whole washed down with tea and molasses. After dinner we smoked and talked by the coal-oil lamp. My host and hostess were both from Ontario but had met in the wilds of Yellowknife in the Northwest Territories. Randy was the son of a country-western singer and looked the part, with his Johnny Cash haircut and weather-beaten face; he was clad in fur mukluks, jeans, gun belt, and skin-out vest. Donna's background was in high-society oil, yet she too preferred the simple life of their Coquihalla cabin.

Randy was rightfully proud of the cabin, three soundly built rooms under a moss-covered roof, plus smokehouse and outhouse. There were two stoves, and running water was piped down directly from a nearby waterfall.

The next morning Randy woke me early to go grouse hunting "for tonight's stew." We never found the elusive thumpers but did come across a patch of young elderberries. The boiled shoots were delicious, Randy explained, "tender as asparagus." During the hike back, he described his own off-and-on career as a singer in bars and his greater ambition to be a mountain man, like his neighbor Clayton Morris. Randy insisted that I couldn't leave the area without meeting this remarkable character, but warned that my chances of finding him receptive to a visit were minimal.

A Red Rose tea sign decorated the door of the ten-by-fourteen-foot tar-paper cabin. Clayton Morris beckoned me inside with barely a nod. As I looked around the interior, what caught my eye amid the woodpile, spruce-log bed, and walls adorned with magazine pictures and flattened corned-beef tins was a drying screen covered with roots, greens, and bark. Skipping introductions, Clayton handed me a mug of steaming "coffee"—actually a home brew of dandelion greens and birchbark.

Without being asked, he then launched into a detailed explanation of his profession: prospecting. With two hundred dollars in gold dust in a jar, he was still scrounging around the cabin for cigarette butts; he might or might not get around to cashing in the dust. Later that afternoon, in a light drizzle, I followed him on a nature hike, growing more and more impressed by his knowledge of plant and bush lore. I madly scribbled notes for future reference: on food sources (boiled thistle root, nettle and curlydock leaves, flour ground from the inner bark of poplars or late-summer yellow bullrush tips); on medicines (burdock leaves "for the blood," willow bark in coffee for a stomachache, and as an anesthetic, a teaspoon of puffball powder heated in a sardine tin, the vapors inhaled); and on and on.

I'd been invited back to Randy and Donna's for a last dinner, and at 7:00 P.M., weighed down by another tremendous feast, I shouldered my pack to continue north up the valley. The incessant rain had let up, foiling my excuse to stay another night. Renewed by a few days of the pioneer lifestyle, I stepped gingerly among the puddles, bathed by rays of sun slicing through the cloud cover.

Two days and thirty miles later, I collapsed at the Coquihalla Lakes, near Merritt. (After hiking some 170 miles I still felt out of shape.) These lakes mark the boundary where an amazing climatic change occurs: Here the coastal rainforest ends and the country changes to semiarid over a one-day, fifteen-mile stretch. I was looking forward to the dry country after weeks of daily showers and cool weather. But first I was looking forward to a climb up the beautiful snowy ridge 4,000 feet above the lakes.

Von and Shirley Randall, the proprietors of a little-used resort on the north shore of the main lake, treated me to another double helping of Canadian hospitality, putting me up overnight in one of their cabins, complete with stove and bed. The next morning Von drove me up a side road to the base of the ridge and left me with a parting gift of lunch. From the logging road the climb looked simple enough. Above the timber by noon, on the summit by midafternoon, back to the lakes by dark, I thought, setting off in high spirits.

The timber, of course, was heavier than I'd expected, and I first hit snow after about 500 vertical feet. The brush thickened and the islands of bare ground disappeared as I climbed higher, plunging into knee-deep crustless snow with each step. Common sense suggested turning back. Needless to say, it was ignored, and I emerged from the timber and rotten snow about two hours behind schedule.

Before me lay a glorious sight: a highway of hard-packed snow stretching unbroken 2,000 feet up to the ridge. The ridgetop itself was hidden behind an awesome, 500-foot wave crest of snow. Reaching it in another hour, I stopped to take in the view. To avoid setting off an avalanche, I ventured no farther on the crest than what I guessed to be the cliff edge, buried dozens of feet below.

The south face, which had been hidden from my view during the climb, was an impassable sea of rock and ice surrounded by three barren, windswept peaks. Eight miles to the northwest the Coquihalla Lakes lay tucked in their valley like sparkling sapphires. To the north and east, densely timbered peaks stretched to the horizon. I had been warned to keep clear of that northeastern timber, in which hikers had been known to vanish.

I had planned to hike west along the ridgeline about two miles as it gradually descended, but bad weather was coming and that argued for an earlier descent. I had raced weather before and lost. A light breeze could develop into a full-fledged whiteout in a matter of minutes, and a snow-covered ridge at 7,000 feet is no place to camp.

The new route I chose—cutting a mile and a half off the ridge walk—didn't look too encouraging either. An initial descent down a defunct avalanche path brought me to the tricky part: To reach the bowl below, I would have to traverse a steep slope for about 100 yards, directly under the crest, which was definitely avalanche material. At least it would be out of the wind, sheltered by the crest from the southerly gale.

Lacking ice axe, rope, or any other climbing gear, I held my camera tripod as a makeshift ice axe and started across the slope. I wanted desperately to scamper to the safety of a ridge descending north from the main divide, but progress was painfully slow. Without crampons, each step kicked out with my boots had to be perfect.

The crest held, and soon I stood on the north ridge, breathing easier. The fledgling gale had turned out to be a false alarm. As I glissaded the remaining 100 feet to the bowl, a spectacular afternoon sun cracked the cloud cover. Enough sight-seeing—with about three hours of light remaining, I would have to hustle to make the lakes by dark. I would have to navigate the remainder of the descent by sight alone, as I was half a dozen miles off my topographic map and not carrying a compass.

Dave here attempts to explain his mystifying failure to have a compass along, noting that wherever possible he preferred to rely on his senses for direction. He points to the example of old-time backwoodsmen, who by dint of vast experience of terrain, vegetation, and weather seem to plot their courses by "instinct." Developing this instinct was his motive for scorning a compass. On this night descent, however, he would have been happy to swallow his pride and take a compass bearing.

The best descent route available from here seemed to be a modest ridge north of my ascent path. (The ascent path itself would have been preferable, but I was determined not to retrace my steps.) A glissade across the open bowl took me into the timber on the ridge. I'd hoped for enough wind even here to keep the snow packed, but it eroded quickly. After thirty steps on pack snow, I plunged to my knees, and from then on the gap between plunges grew steadily less. With sixty pounds on my back, pulling out of deep snow was no fun at all. Very soon my despised ascent route began to look more attractive, and I headed back toward it across the snow-filled valley.

I never did find the ascent route and couldn't reclimb the slope I'd just come down, so I was condemned to the valley. The snow here, many times deeper than on the ridge, was capped by a crust that might support a hundred pounds, but not me and my pack. At that point I would have traded a six-month food supply for a pair of snowshoes. It had been two hours since I'd left the bowl, and I was probably about halfway back to the logging road. With heavy cloud cover returning, I estimated that the sun had just set, or was about to, and that meant an hour of light left, on the outside. It began to look like the mountain was winning.

Before I had covered 300 yards, nervousness started to slide toward panic. To advance ten feet I had to walk thirty, zigzagging back and forth while hunting for pack snow. Occasionally I found fifty feet or so of pack, but mainly I used the step-plunge routine. I carefully assessed each step, circling around the slightest variation in the snow surface. Bent saplings created hazardous air pockets; the trick was to spot twigs protruding from the surface, or small drifts and depressions. Twice I missed the signs and plunged over my head into a tangle of fir boughs and snow. When I tried to move faster, I invariably ended sprawled on my face.

I knew that panic in the bush could bring the strongest and ablest men to their knees. I had never been close enough to know whether I would succumb to it, even in the Outward Bound course I'd taken. Now, though, perched on an island of firm crust, the realization that I was in panic range washed over me like a freezing wave. The urge to dump my pack and run blindly was almost overwhelming, but I made myself sit still, light a smoke, and consider my options.

If I gave up and bivouacked here overnight, I would probably be picked up by the local search-and-rescue team within forty-eight hours. On the other hand, British Columbia was supposed to be the easiest leg of the whole journey. For most of the 4,500 miles ahead there would be no search-and-rescue teams handy. If I gave in here, what could I expect when I didn't have a choice?

A good self-thrashing calmed me down. Now it was time for yet another route. I was stuck with the valley, but a creek bisected it; emptying my pipe, I got up and headed toward it. The creek banks were impossibly steep and crusted, but the flowing water was only a foot deep, though swift. If there were rocks in the right places, I might even stay above water half the time. I had been forced to wear shorts all day to keep snow from packing inside my pant legs, and had no idea what effect the near-freezing water would have on my bruised and abused shins. I didn't even worry about my feet; snow had been packed solidly between my socks and ankles for so many hours that I had long since quit feeling them.

I made good time through the water, though rock hopping proved too slow and precarious. Tossing away my broken and bent tripod, I replaced it with a stout stick and sloshed along until eventually the terrain leveled out and the snow disappeared. The darkness was complete by now, though a half moon shone through the broken cloud cover to light my way.

The boggy muskeg I now stumbled through seemed to be continuing much too long. Could I have overshot the logging road and ended up in the dreaded northeast timber? I didn't recognize my surroundings. It was certainly time to camp, but I wanted to fix my location first. I tried to compensate for a possible error by exaggerating a southwesterly course. It worked: I hit the logging road fifteen minutes later.

Collapsing on the road, I lit a candle and peeled off my socks to assess the damage. The skin on my feet was white, puffy, and lifeless; the bruises on my ankles and lower shins had broken into open sores. Pain was returning to my feet—a good sign.

It must have been close to 11:00 P.M., and with six miles of downhill travel to the lakes, I might make it in two hours. I don't remember much of those six miles. Walking in a daze, I sang and talked to myself to keep moving. I could have camped anywhere along the road, but my heart was set on reaching the lakes.

I never did, though. I must have missed the turnoff in the darkness. As I dropped my pack, defeated, I knew I could not start again. It was Saturday night; I could hear campers singing around their fire not more than a quarter-mile down the steep grade as I crawled into my sleeping bag with a cup of uncooked oatmeal.

Hadn't I fought that damn mountain long enough? Hadn't I served my sentence for taking on more than I could handle? Evidently not. My legs cramped into a bent position, forcing me to sleep that way. Two days elapsed before I could walk normally again.

2 | Comings and Goings
Merritt, British Columbia, to Athabasca, Alberta

Journal entry, July 25, 1977. The heat burns my nostrils while the sweat burns my eyes. Christ, I never knew there was a desert in the middle of British Columbia. I can't carry this pack any further. The others were right; I should have just quit when they did.

This note from my journal tells the tale of central B.C. Tired of rain and chill, I had looked forward to the terrain and climate changing from coastal rainforest to interior plateau. After a few days of hiking in near-100-degree heat, however, I would gladly have gone back to the rain.

I left the Coquihalla behind in early June, and with thawed feet and refreshed spirits bore north toward the town of Merritt. The first day, my still-healing legs held me to a mere five miles, but with the aid of a hard-packed road and improving weather, my daily mileage increased. I had estimated covering the 140 miles between Hope and Merritt in eight to nine days; the side trip on the snow ridge stretched that to thirteen.

Despite its heat and dust, Merritt was a welcome sight, as my supplies were running low; for the last three days I had lived on oat flakes, rice, and a bit of bouillon.

Dave's stopover in Merritt was typical of his resupply points. Often his parents would wire a small amount of money ahead to the post office, just as he was down to his last dime. Never much of a money manager, he resisted temptation "only by being eternally broke."

After setting up camp in the town park or handiest open space, Dave would bathe in the river and luxuriate in the local laundromat with newspapers and junk food while his trail-weary clothing ran through several wash cycles. Generally at some point he would make his way to a likely looking tavern and regale an ever-available audience over a number of beers.

Depending on how long this went on, his remaining budget for food supplies might be generous or lean—but never more than twenty dollars a week. Later in the journey he would supplement his store-bought rations by hunting and fishing, but during this period he lived on an unexciting diet of staples (rice, squashed bread, flour, and oatmeal); instant foods (milk, potatoes, macaroni and cheese, sauces, and drinks); high-energy snacks (peanuts, raisins, and honey); and a few luxuries (tobacco, tea, garlic sausage or canned corned beef, and occasional fresh fruits).

Town layovers also gave Dave a chance to catch up on letters home—to his parents and younger siblings, Sara and Steve. From Merritt he wrote to Steve, who had just graduated from high school in Virginia as a state champion in cross-country running. Dave's big-brotherly advice to the college-bound Steve might as well have been a pep talk to himself:

> I hear you had a tough time these last few months of running. . . . There's something I hope you'll remember in running and in college. That is, the world is full of the average, people who talk a big story and then settle back to mediocrity. Shoot for the stars, to be the best there is. Don't let average people around you make you believe your goals are too great. . . . that philosophy is what got me out of Ft. Langley and has kept me going when I wanted to quit. There's nothing worse than a dreamer who never tries.

In the same letter, Dave mentioned a prospective new partner for the upcoming canoeing leg of the expedition:

> By the way, I talked to C. W. [Hughey, a friend from Virginia] and have decided for him to join me at Jasper after all. He's flying there to meet me end of July.

In another letter, written from Nicola Lake around June 11, Dave mentioned his efforts—futile thus far—to recover some of the equipment lost to the mutineers. He also expressed some ambivalent feelings about acquiring a new companion:

> In a way I regret having C. W. join me, as I much prefer traveling alone. I wish I could do the canoeing alone, but . . . I'd only be fooling myself. . . . I learned a lot the other day on that snow ridge.

Near Merritt, Dave had another run of luck in meeting interesting and hospitable residents: a Texas-born rancher; a friendly female forester who lent him her geodesic dome home for a few days while she was off on a surveying trip; and another retired prospector, Fred McCoy. Dave made several visits to McCoy's home on Nicola Lake, twenty miles north of Merritt, and was impressed by this man's gift for living well on his own terms:

Fred never made it past the eighth grade, but one night when I was there he took out a nearly completed book on prospecting that he'd compiled. It would have rivaled any college text. He turned the pages slowly and lovingly, pointing to pasted-in pictures of minerals. From there we moved on to his garden, with its intricate irrigation system, and then to the unblemished beach formed from sand accumulating behind the breakwater he'd built out into the lake. Trout and squawfish lay in the sun just beneath the surface of the lagoon. Fred liked to live with a flair!

After dinner with Fred that evening, I rounded the northern edge of the lake and continued north toward Kamloops. I hoped to make the thirty-five miles by morning in a forced march; I had used up my supplies during the dome stay, and the ghastly 100-degree-plus daytime temperatures made night hiking all the more practical.

A short evening shower cooled the first five miles to a comfortable 60 degrees Fahrenheit. Then the clouds broke with perfect timing to reveal a double rainbow *and* a fiery sunset, brilliantly painting the sage-covered hills. The rain-cooled road was good to my soles, and by midnight the temperature had dropped another 5 degrees—ideal for hiking in cutoffs and T-shirt. Rather than slackening, my pace actually picked up and my strides lengthened as the night wore on. This was a hiker's rare and magical moment: when muscles and mind are in balance, the body performing like a precision machine. With two miles to go and half an hour till sunrise I gazed down the valley of Kamloops to its lights below.

Kamloops, at the junction of the North and South Thompson rivers, is a good-sized town of fifty-three thousand. Though it boasts a hundred-year heritage of being a gateway for homesteaders and has the prestige of being British Columbia's largest inland city, I didn't appreciate its urban charms and felt eager to press on. Again low on funds, I wangled some "handshake credit" from local merchants. Time and again throughout Canada, this tradition of trust saved me from having to abandon the trek.

The highlight of this stopover was an evening shared over pizza and beer with Martin, an ex-sociology professor from the University of California now making his way to Toronto via boxcar on a budget of seventeen dollars. Since I bought the rounds, he graciously invited me back to his rolling bachelor suite for the night. When I saw that he slept on the wood floor without so much as a blanket, I passed him my wool clothes and guiltily slipped into my mummy bag. There is something wondrous about waking to sunshine slanting through a boxcar door. The air is enticingly heavy with the smell of travel, and I might have traded places with Martin had he asked.

Back on the road, hiking due north along the west bank of the North Thompson, the heat was staggering. Average temperatures pushed 80 degrees by noon and topped 100 by midafternoon. My progress plummeted, with hiking time restricted to early mornings and evenings. Though jack pine became more common as I moved northward, the sage-dotted sand hills gave no indication of ending soon.

Since I had followed mostly a route on road and rail so far to avoid the impenetrable bush, I decided to take advantage of this open landscape by heading cross-country through the hills for a few days. Though I still had no compass, clouds were scarce over the central plateau and the North Thompson rarely veered from its northerly course. All I had to do was parallel its path a few miles to the west.

Before setting out I made sure my quart water bottle was full. The topo map showed a watering hole four miles to the northwest, and I felt sure a quart would get me that far. It didn't; less than halfway there, the remaining pint drenched a shriveling weed as I reached clumsily for some raisins. Siesta time came and went with water yet to be found. When the water hole, or rather quagmire, finally did appear, I played hopscotch through the cow patties for a reward of brown liquid that tasted suspiciously like beef bouillon.

The water situation improved steadily over the next forty-eight hours, but I'd had my fill of British Columbia's plateau and gratefully returned to the river valley. At the McClure Ferry, thirty miles north of Kamloops, the desertlike terrain began to ease. Crossing to the east bank on the ferry, I made the remaining eleven miles to Barriere by midnight. Two more days of dust brought me to a crossroads town called Little Fort.

At this point I decided that the only way to survive the heat, which I found intolerable, was simply to hike at night and sleep by day. For the next seventy-five miles, my day was split into an evening stroll from 8:00 P.M. till midnight or one, and a morning hike from 8:00 A.M. to noon. The same road that during midday was a blacktop griddle at night became a silent river gently accepting my steps.

On reaching Clearwater, a growing town of about three thousand, the depression that had weighed on me since leaving the Coquihalla began to lift. For the first time in nearly 200 miles the flora was more conifers than sage. The end of the dreaded hot country couldn't be far away. I had been hiking scared through the plateau — afraid to stay long in one place, afraid of the feelings that had been welling up inside me. The heat I so detested brought me nearly to the point of quitting.

About fifty miles past Clearwater, the first snow-covered peaks made the sand and sweat seem to drain from my veins. The Cariboo Mountains rising above the central plateau felt stronger, more virile than the Coast Range I'd left at the Coquihalla. These peaks loomed closer, more sharply and vividly defined than those farther west; I felt nearly overwhelmed by their arrogance. Likewise, the North Thompson River flexed its muscles for the first time, shed-

ding its turbid southern cloak. Another four and a half days at a conscientious pace took me seventy miles above Clearwater to Blue
River, where at last I was truly free of the heat, sage, and sand. Blue
River's "welcome billboard," an explosion of snow and rock, spread
out around me in a fantastic mountain panorama.

*From Blue River, Dave hitched a ride with a trucker 130 miles to Jasper,
across the Alberta border. He had to return and cover the same miles
on foot, of course, but by leapfrogging he was able to scout out ac-
commodations for his family, who planned to rendezvous with him
in Jasper for a week's visit in late July. He also had notions of finding
one or more of his late partners, who had talked about trying to get
summer jobs in the heavily touristed town. A letter to Bill Graves of*
National Geographic *reports the dubious results:*

> Surprise, surprise. I tracked down Neil Kogan . . . here in
> Jasper (washing dishes!). After two hours of mediation by
> Canadian police I recovered one tent, one pack, and one bag.
> After six weeks of no tent . . . the added five pounds on my
> back is certainly welcome.

*Backtracking from Jasper, Dave hitched all the way to Clearwater to
take part in a raft race. But that wasn't the highlight of Clearwater
redux, as it turned out. On the afternoon of July 3, a twenty-three-
year-old photographer from Chicago named Peter Souchuk also arrived
in Clearwater. A few weeks earlier, Peter had read in* Quest *magazine
that one David Halsey was hiking alone across Canada. (The* Quest
*coverage was only one element in a modest media blitz surrounding the
early part of the expedition. Canada's CBC radio and television carried
regular interviews with Dave from Vancouver through Jasper, and occasionally after that; in fact, the media's focus on Dave as the trip's spokes-
man contributed to the hard feelings among his original teammates.)*
*The description of Dave's adventure had struck a powerful note
in Peter, who was restless in his job as a public relations photographer.
The opportunity to get experience photographing in the Canadian
wilderness and the possibility of breaking into* National Geographic
or other major publications were also strong incentives. Peter contacted

Dave's parents in the Washington, D.C., suburb of McLean, Virginia, and discovered that, coincidentally, he and Dave had grown up in adjoining Chicago suburbs (though the Halseys had since moved east). After getting a reasonably good fix on Dave's expected whereabouts, he loaded his car with camping and photographic gear and spent several days roaming around central B.C. in Dave's tracks. Peter recalls:

> I got into Clearwater and saw this huge red backpack leaning against the porch of the only hotel in town. I figured it had to be Dave's. He was pretty surprised to see me, but he always liked to have company. After spending an evening talking, we agreed to try a "test hike" of about a week. . . .
> God, it almost killed me. It was incredibly hot and pretty boring hiking, mostly highway. But Dave set a tough pace; he was in a hurry to get through that part and I think trying to impress me. It *was* a test.

By the end of the trial run Dave had a new partner. At that point, however, Peter had to return to the States for a class he was committed to attending, so they made plans to meet again in mid-September and continue as a threesome with C. W. Hughey. Meanwhile, Peter would process his film and send it to National Geographic *in the hope of getting the publication's official blessing as the expedition photographer.*

One evening when Dave and Peter were cooking dinner, an exceptionally bold coyote strolled into camp looking for a handout. Pete dove for his camera, thinking "Canadian wildlife!"—but when the scruffy-looking beast continued to show no fear of the hikers, they began to wonder. Dave eventually figured that it was a semidomesticated Indian dog, probably a coydog, and wanted no part of it. It continued to hang around for several days—not surprisingly, since Pete began feeding it behind Dave's back.

It soon became clear that Dave, against his better judgment, had acquired yet another teammate. If his earlier choice of companions had been unfortunate, the entirely unplanned company of both Peter and Ki (pronounced "Kye") proved incredibly fortuitous; their steadfast friendship and faith throughout the journey would more than compensate for Dave's bad luck at the start.

———————

Hinton, Alberta
August 4, 1977

Dear Mom, Dad, Steve & Sara,
Well, another delay. We got into Hinton Tues. morning.
. . . C. W. and I are getting along fine. Whereas the other
three were on my back about my doing all the talking on
CBC, C. W. asked that he not be any part of it. . . . By the
way, he's quite a bean chef. . . .

I can't tell you how much I appreciated your coming to
Jasper. It meant a lot to me. . . . And all those gifts! I practiced with the rod & reel; the two are very compatible.

We took Ki to the vet yesterday. They call him (possibly)
a husky-coyote cross . . . said he was in good shape and
about 5 years old. The only problem is that his left eye is
scratched. . . . I'm supposed to put 2 different kinds of
medication in it 3 times a day for 10 days. If that doesn't
work, the only thing that will save his eye is a $300 opera-
tion! I'll make the decision at Ft. McMurray, whether to put
him to sleep or not. . . . I'd rather that than have him go
with one eye. Keep your fingers crossed! By the way, he
rides the canoe beautifully. The other day I put him ashore
to take a leak. When we drifted out a bit, he swam to us,
thinking we were leaving him!

We've had 3 days of torrential rain and . . . now I've got
a rip-roaring, full-fledged cold. C. W.'s been playing nurse
(I call him Mom!). Love, Dave

*In early August, after resting and re-outfitting in Jasper, Dave and his
Virginia buddy C. W. Hughey set out in their new eighteen-foot freighter
canoe on the next leg of the expedition: a 600-mile plunge down the
Athabasca River, northeast through Alberta to Fort McMurray, near
the Saskatchewan border. The journey took on a different character
with the move from land to water, less "urban" than Dave's town-to-
town trek through British Columbia. The earliest stretch was not yet
remote wilderness; the gateway to the true bush was the village of
Athabasca, about 400 miles downriver. Along this first part, settlements and farms dotted the riverbanks, and Dave and C. W. found
open doors, hot meals, and curious company in many places. Dave*

describes a typical idyllic evening "guzzling apple cider with the farmers, talking of politics and crop failures while the wives plucked chickens for supper and set coffee pots on the stove."

Occasionally someone would offer the use of a vacant hunting cabin, a preferred option to an often rain-soaked camp-out. Dave clearly enjoyed the increased opportunities to hunt and fish, which he loved, during these "carefree, lazy days paddling down the Athabasca. . . . Grouse sizzles in the skillet while C. W. talks about days back on the Missouri farms [where he was raised]." Unassuming and clearly willing to play a supporting role, C. W. Hughey was a satisfactory interim companion while Dave waited for Pete to rejoin the team. But C. W.'s future with the expedition was uncertain, as he had left a wife and young child back home.

The town of Vega had been designated as the point where Pete would rendezvous with the others, and Dave and C. W. took up residence in a cabin there for a few weeks while they waited for him.

Vega, Alberta
August 23, 1977
Dear Folks,
Well, we're pretty well settled in to cabin life. . . . It now looks like we'll only be able to make it to La Ronge, Sask. (about 300 miles from Flin Flon) before freeze-up. The farmers are predicting an early hard winter . . . (Ki's fur is thickening, too).

[The owner of the cabin] seems delighted to have someone living here. . . . Besides lending us the cabin he's letting us do all the hunting and trapping we want. C. W. and I are re-chinking the cabin, puttying the windows, etc., for him. . . . Between woodcutting, cooking, and cleaning during the day and writing at night, I'm pretty busy.

I am so full right now. We had a 2-lb. goldeneye apiece for breakfast. . . . [This morning] I got 3 grouse and 2 squirrels with 6 shots. . . . Ki ate one of the squirrels, but we fried up the rest. Remember those little ground squirrels at Tekarra [near Jasper]? Well, they're good eating. Ki trees 'em and we shoot them out. [*Though Dave never reported on it, Ki's earlier eye problem apparently cleared up.*] . . . With hunting

season a week and a half away, we're getting ready. Bears
are all over the place and every day we see fresh deer & elk
tracks. We're going to take one yearling bear and one yearling
deer. We want to tan the hides and jerk the hindquarters,
which should be all the meat we can handle. The rest we'll
give away. . . . I'm pretty excited about getting them.

*Toward the end of their stay in Vega, Dave's ardent wish to bag a bear
was finally fulfilled:*

> *Journal entry, September 5, 1977.* It suddenly occurs to me
> that I have never shot anything larger than a pheasant
> before, as I stare down my shotgun barrel at a raiding
> bear. . . . For three days we salted and jerked bear meat, and
> rendered bear fat into milk-white lard. For three more days
> we bloated ourselves on bear-fat doughnuts.

I stirred the last helping of bear's heart and liver in the skillet and
turned a toasted slab of freshly baked bannock on the stove. A fine
sprinkling of salt between the hot metal and bread kept the toast
from sticking. Strips of bear meat hung from the rafters to dry, casting
waving shadows before our bear-grease lanterns. Freshly rendered
lard cooled in tubs along the windowsill, and still-warm bannocks
were packed in discarded flour sacks. Twenty-pound parcels of meat
were salted, then sewn into saltwater-soaked canvas. We reduced
a fifty-pound crate of last season's apples to quarts of amber-tinted
apple butter, saving enough fruit to make a pulpy but potent batch
of hard cider. Pete ought to be surprised by the bounty of our grub
box.

*Unfortunately, in taking advantage of this particular bear's proximity,
Dave was guilty of hunting without a permit. Word got back to the
local game warden, who promptly confiscated the bulk of the carcass,
infuriating Dave. He complained to Alberta's minister of wildlife, who
arranged for the "loan" of the dead bear for a CBC television report,
as well as unrestricted permission for the expedition to take big game
in the future. Rather than deal with the paperwork necessary to keep
"his" bear, however, Dave gave it back to the officials, figuring there
would be plenty more. The incident strained relations with* National

Geographic *slightly, as the* Edmonton Journal *reported that a Society-sponsored expedition was killing bears out of season. Bill Graves fired off a succinct note on the subject to Dave.*

On September 7, Pete Souchuk rejoined the Trans-Canada Expedition for good, and exactly a week later C. W. Hughey left to return to his family in Virginia, where he was needed. Now the final team of Dave, Pete, and Ki was poised to embark on the first truly hazardous portion of the journey. The last several hundred miles down the Athabasca to Fort McMurray would be replete with treacherous rapids, and no longer would there be handy cabins to retreat to when things got tough. Dave and Pete got a few lessons in advanced paddling from a local expert but nonetheless felt considerable anxiety about the whitewater looming ahead.

As always, finances were tight. A few days before Dave's twenty-first birthday, he and Pete collected beer bottles behind a tavern in Smith (near Athabasca) to redeem for a birthday celebration.

Athabasca, Alberta
1:00 A.M., September 19, 1977 [*Dave's birthday*]

Dearest Sara [*Dave's sister's birthday was just two days after his; this letter was his gift*], Happy seventeenth! I had planned to make Athabasca (town) a few days ago so I could get your card out in time. But these last 160 miles have been constant rain, 40 degrees, and gusting head winds, turning a two-day stretch into a week.

. . . Since the damn game warden stole our bear after we had eaten only 20 lbs., we again are low on meat. . . . Now that bird season has opened we rarely are able to get closer than 200 yds. to ducks & geese. . . . A storekeeper in Smith gave us an old (30 yrs.) "Coony" 22-cal. single shot and a box of shells. It looks like it's ready for the garbage but is "dead on" and should improve meat prospects. . . . just one of the many examples of Canadians' generosity.

Since the CBC-TV show [from Smith] was just aired last week, many people have recognized us. Athabasca had a big sign on the hillside welcoming us. . . . It really gave me a warm feeling.

A lot of people have tried to talk us out of canoeing the last 260 mi. to Fort Mac. There's about a 100-mile stretch of bad rapids there that have claimed more lives than victors. . . . I've been told that only a few dozen have made it in the last 50 yrs. . . . Believe me, we intend to portage and track around 90% of the dozen or so sets. [Apparently] Nat. Geo sent their own expedition down the Athabasca in 1963 and ended up losing all film and equipment in a dump (rapid swamp). [*Dave got this wrong, as the earlier expedition came back with enough material to produce an article for the Geographic.*]

C. W. is gone and I feel pretty lonely without him . . . he was kind of a big brother to lean on. . . .

The leaves have all fallen off the trees; combined with these persistent headwinds and unusually low temps, it's put me in a rather depressed mood. It's so damned hard to get out of the sleeping bag on mornings like these. But don't get me wrong—that's what I came here for. . . . [Even though] the initial thrill is over and it has become a job, I wouldn't trade this trip for anything. . . .

After 4½ months here I've noticed a dramatic change in myself. . . . I now feel very accepting [of] whatever nature wants to dish out. You're constantly cold, constantly wet. Yet you learn to live with it. . . . I guess what I'm trying to say is that you get to the point where you want to say, "Hell with you, nature, gimme all you've got."

Just a little farther down the Athabasca, Dave would find out what that meant.

3 | The River Strikes
Athabasca to
Fort McMurray, Alberta

September 24, 1977. We returned to the river on a Friday evening, leaving Athabasca Landing at 8:00 P.M. By ten that night a three-quarter moon with a glorious halo had risen to illuminate our path. The river experienced a total metamorphosis by moonlight: The current became serene and conversation rarely broke the silence.

Wildlife, highlighted by the moon's glow, was much easier to approach. We passed within twenty feet of a shoal crowded with geese and cranes, and with thoughts of a royal dinner I raised the Coony shotgun. But almost in the same motion I returned it to its place, ashamed to disturb the humbling silence. For nearly twenty miles we drifted, even dozing now and then, thanks to the send-off party at Athabasca. Normally we wouldn't touch alcohol while on the river, but we knew of no fast water just ahead.

After several hours cradled in comfort, we made shore to sleep at about 3:00 A.M. as the morning mist was gathering. Arising at noon to a perfect day, we found to our joy that the dreaded head-winds that had tormented us since Vega had subsided. We pushed off again, Ki proudly atop his perch on the food pack.

Three days of uneventful paddling put seventy miles between us and Athabasca. September's chill had finished off the last of the mosquitoes, but this advantage was offset by the heaviest river traffic we had yet encountered. Big-game season had opened, and rarely did an hour pass without sight of a jet boat laden with moose hunters bullying its way upriver. For some 400 river miles before Athabasca I had never seen a boat more than a mile from the nearest town.

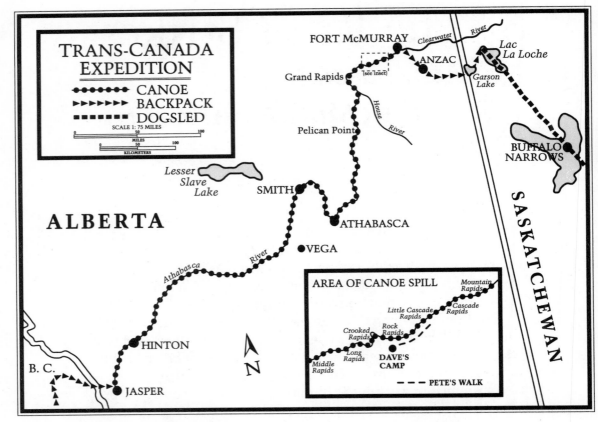

Within the map:

TRANS-CANADA
EXPEDITION
● ● ● ● ● CANOE
▶ ▶ ▶ ▶ ▶ BACKPACK
▬ ▬ ▬ ▬ ▬ DOGSLED
SCALE 1: 75 MILES

MILES
KILOMETERS

FORT McMURRAY   Clearwater River   Lac La Loche
ANZAC
Grand Rapids   [see inset]   Garson Lake
House River
Pelican Point
BUFFALO NARROWS
Lesser Slave Lake
SMITH
ALBERTA
ATHABASCA
●VEGA
Athabasca River
SASKATCHEWAN
N
HINTON
B. C.
JASPER

AREA OF CANOE SPILL
Mountain Rapids
Little Cascade Rapids   Cascade Rapids
Crooked Rapids   Rock Rapids
Long Rapids   DAVE'S CAMP
Middle Rapids
– – – PETE'S WALK

Jasper to Fort McMurray, Alberta, September–December 1977

Our first experience of Canada's hunting season left us dismayed. Most of these people were not unobtrusive local hunters who year after year culled a moose and packed the meat out for winter stores. Most were stereotypical city-bred hunters: bumbling, loud, and obnoxious. At the confluence of the Calling River, we interrupted a father-son shooting lesson, the boy of fourteen awkwardly peppering a tree-stump target not 100 feet from us. The pair, dressed in eye-grabbing scarlet, eyed our grimy flannels with disapproval.

"Better get out of here if you're not wearing red," the father warned, flicking his gun's safety off as if to emphasize his point. "Lots of inexperienced hunters around." We turned back to the canoe, abruptly terminating the visit. I wasn't anxious to have my rump mistaken for a moose's, or for the overeager boy to wonder why the coyote he'd just shot was wearing a collar.

Despite the mobs of hunters, game was thick. When the boats weren't growling nearby, shaking the leaves from the trees, we often spotted three or four moose daily. One evening we paddled to within fifty feet of a massive bull before he detected us, and another time I crawled close to a family of fidgety mule deer. Once, as an experiment, I cupped my hands and grunted the "uuagh . . . uuagh!" call of the bull moose, then slowly poured a pail of water into the river to imitate the sound of a moose urinating. Like a great grey ghost, a young bull stepped from behind the trees not thirty feet away, eager for a fight. On discovering a man rather than a rival bull, however, he merely studied me for a moment before melting back into the trees.

Tender young grouse accompanied nearly every dinner those first few days. Ki had made a science of the grouse hunt, rooting through the leaves in an ever-widening circle around camp as Peter and I sat by the fire sipping tea and discussing the day's events. Eventually we'd hear the unmistakable whir of grouse wings, and I would grab the shotgun and harvest birds from the surrounding trees. Though perhaps not the most sporting way to hunt, we considered it simple food procurement rather than sport. While the birds sizzled on roasting sticks, Ki savored his reward of grouse giblets.

At Iron Point, about eighty miles downriver, we stopped to explore an isolated, deserted cabin. As the story went, it had been built by a group of German canoeists who were waiting out an endless rain at Iron Point before continuing downriver. The cabin was constructed entirely by hand without a single nail. The hand-hewn door still swung easily on wooden hinges. Sunlight squeezed through a window covered with cotton rags, revealing roughly made furniture scattered around the dirt floor. There was a stone hearth in one corner for cooking, the smoke finding its own course through a hole in the roof.

Back on the river, the Germans hadn't fared so well. After mistaking a minor rapid for the deadly Grand Rapids yet to come some forty miles farther on, they paddled blithely onward under the impression that the waters ahead must be easily navigable. They realized their error on entering the true Grand Rapids, losing one life and most of their gear, and finally limped into Fort McMurray, where they seem to have disappeared. The silent cabin was a solemn reminder of the dangers lying in wait for us downriver.

Late on day four out of Athabasca, at about the 100-mile point, we spotted the bright glow of torches through the rain-laden dusk. This had to be Dick Naumann's place in Upper Wells—a well-known haven for weary canoeists and a welcome sight to us after paddling through the cold rain all day. Dick greeted us at the door, his hulking figure stooped from a lifetime's labor, and announced in a heavy German accent that we would be staying the night. "You are just in time to have dinner. The weather is too bad for you to go on tonight." Naturally we didn't argue.

The gas torches scattered throughout Dick's vegetable garden were fueled by a natural gas well that had once powered a sawmill (and given rise to the name Upper Wells). Dick had moved to the abandoned site a decade earlier and tapped into the shallow seam for all his energy needs. The gas heated his cabins, powered his stove and lights, even ran an old wringer-washer. Most amazing of all, it fueled dozens of torches in the huge garden so that here, less than 300 miles from the Northwest Territories, Dick Naumann was serving us fresh tomatoes with dinner though the first frost had been more than a month ago. He sometimes harvested canteloupes on Halloween!

The homestead was a comfortable island of self-sufficiency. We ate in the living room by flickering gaslight, the faint odor of natural gas in the air, shelves all around us sagging under the weight of mason jars filled with moose meat, venison, and vegetables. While we silently consumed many bowls of moose stew with gravy-sopped bread still warm from the oven, followed by nut cake and tea, Dick told us his history. Immigrating from Germany just after the war, he had lived through a difficult time when Germans were prohibited by law from owning any weapon larger than a .22-caliber rifle. "You have to be a pretty good shot," Dick affirmed, "to kill a moose with a .22." Clearly he had mastered the art, as it was the only gun he'd used to hunt moose and bear ever since.

Before moving to his present location, Dick had homesteaded half a dozen miles downriver, where he and his Cree Indian wife had raised two children. For a while he had made a good living in furs, but as trapping deteriorated, all the other settlers moved on and they were left alone. When his wife died, Dick packed his threadbare furnishings onto a scow and moved to Upper Wells.

After a food-drugged sleep, we spent most of the next day touring the homestead and hearing Dick's tales of river life. When we finally pushed off late in the afternoon, we carried his parting gift of fresh bread and tomatoes, and some badly needed ammunition. I thought of Dick Naumann, happily weeding his wonderful garden, many times afterward. [*While drafting this chapter, Dave learned that Naumann had died after a long spell of illness.*]

Several miles downriver we stopped for dinner at Dick's old home, the now-deserted settlement at Pelican Point (or Lower Wells). Gratefully taking shelter from the rain in the ten-room communal main cabin, we munched tomato sandwiches and explored the ruins. The rooms were littered with discarded books, tools, and clothing. In one, a pair of hobnailed boots lay beside the bed, as if their owner had forgotten to put them on before his final departure. A mouse had since appropriated one for its nest.

Outside the cabin, near a cache of oil drums maintained by hunting guides, lay the rotting skeleton of a thirty-foot scow. I imagined a youthful Dick Naumann navigating that scow upriver through the swift current, ferrying his beloved sofa to his new home. A movement nearby caught my eye, and I looked up toward a rusty Model T Ford mired in the bog. A ghostly glow shimmered behind the steering wheel, causing my pulse to race. When we crept closer, hearts pounding, we found the ghost not in the car but behind it: Natural gas bubbling from the pond had ignited, the eerie flames flickering through the wreck.

Beneath a rising full moon we reloaded the canoe and headed off into our first whitewater since Jasper. This was Pelican Rapid, the easy (Class III) stretch that the Germans of Iron Point had fatally mistaken for Grand Rapids. The canoe rode the modest roller coaster well, and we had grown so accustomed to night travel that we arrogantly decided to run the next rapid, Stony, as well. It, too, proved easily navigable by moonlight, and as we rounded the point below, we were rewarded by the welcoming beacon of a hunter's campfire a few miles ahead.

It was nearing midnight, and we bent to our paddles, eager for the warmth of the fire, which soon loomed huge. Within half an hour we were greeted by a dozen moose hunters on vacation from the States with their three guides from Edmonton. This group had hunted together for more than a decade, and their well-organized camp was a pleasure to visit compared with the slapdash, shoot-em-up style of other hunters we'd seen. Though the beer consumption was staggering, the atmosphere was experienced and professional: There were discussions of butchering techniques and of the relative advantages of different moose-calling techniques. We had barely beached the canoe before cold beers were passed to us and extra moose steaks thrown on the fire. Ki received an equally lavish welcome in the form of an awesome mound of raw moose liver. Odds were given as to whether his expanding belly would outlast the purple meat.

The festivities ran late; it seemed I had barely closed my eyes when the moose-call alarm sounded at 5:00 A.M. After cups of potent coffee, Peter and I packed and prepared to set off—probably our earliest start of the entire expedition. Then Gerry, one of the guides, pulled us aside for a parting word. "Take care downriver, boys. Those rapids you'll be running have caused too many obituaries. I want to hear from you, not read about you."

We had been hearing such warnings for the last 200 miles. In fact, the whitewater ahead had claimed at least one canoeist from Athabasca each year, and as we were the last to come through this season, the locals tried to convince us that our number was up. So far we had ignored the doomsayers, but the pleading in Gerry's voice couldn't be lightly dismissed. Autumn's low water added to the danger of the rapids now some forty miles north.

Gerry's final advice was to reconsider our route when we reached the House River. "That's your last bail-out point. None of us will travel downriver of the House, no matter how many moose might be down there. It's almost October; the eddies'll be icing soon, and you'll be running the rapids at their lowest stage. From the House you could work your way back up the Athabasca and catch a ride to town with a guide. But past there you'll find no help, and the current'll be too fast to turn around. Camp at the mouth of the House and think it over again, boys."

Sensing our determination to continue despite everything, Gerry made a last offer. "I'll make a run down to the House tonight. Wait there for me, and I'll give you a lift back to town." But even as he spoke, he knew it would be a wasted trip.

The thick fog that shrouded our departure began to clear as we approached the last minor rapid before the big sets. The Rapids du Jolli Fou (Jolly Fool Rapid) was a bucking thrill ride rather than a serious threat and dispelled much of the ominous feeling Gerry had left us with. But it wasn't entirely without danger, as an 1863 account by explorer J. B. Tyrell suggests. The rapid got its name when some "jolly fool" canoeist "lost his life by allowing his canoe to be smashed upon the most conspicuous rock in the rapid" (Comfort, *Ribbon of Water*).*

The remote cabin of trapper Earl Kay sits atop a bluff on the east bank, overlooking the Jolli Fou. Not finding him at home, we left a note, as is the bush custom, and paddled on. The note served a dual purpose: to exchange greetings in the wilderness and to mark our last-known stop should we run into bad luck and become the target of a search-and-rescue.

Our lunch stop was at the mouth of the House River—the point of no return. Sitting on the north bank of the House in the afternoon sun, we were practically giddy with the excitement of entering forbidden country. On the point of land where the rivers meet stands a cluster of Indian graves, but even that sight failed to dampen our adventurous mood. This spot we found so peaceful was shunned by the Indians, who considered it a place of evil. Riverboat captains told gruesome tales to their wide-eyed passengers as they rounded the point:

> These were the graves of an Indian and his wife and four children who pitched in from Lac La Biche to hunt, and

*For a complete list of references, see the Bibliography.

who all had died together of diphtheria in this lonely spot. But here, too, many years ago, a priest was murdered and eaten by a *weighteko*, an Iroquois from Caughnawaga. The lunatic afterwards took an Indian girl into the depths of the forest and, after cohabiting with her for some time, killed and devoured her. Upon the fact being known, and being pursued by her tribe, he fled to the scene of his horrible banquet and there took his own life. (Comfort, *Ribbon of Water*)

September 30. We heard the low roar of Grand Rapids a full three miles before reaching it late in the afternoon. The growing thunder is the only warning of this two-mile-long series of rapids and falls, which are nearly invisible until it is too late. As we approached, however, we could discern the halo of spray thrown up by the stair-case-steep falls. The rapids are Grade VI+, the highest assigned to whitewater. The vertical drop is a full sixty feet over three-quarters of a mile. As far as anyone knows, no one has ever navigated any kind of boat successfully through Grand Rapids, except by lining (guiding the craft along from shore with ropes tied to bow and stern).

Grand Rapids is split down the middle by Grand Island, a half-mile-long and very narrow slice of land with a noteworthy history. Between the founding of Fort McMurray in 1870 as a Hudson's Bay Company post and the recent construction of a road from the south, the town's only link to civilization was the Methy Portage, an arduous eighteen-mile trail from the east along the Clearwater River. The heavy wood scows of the day could navigate many of the Athabasca's lower rapids, but Grand Rapids remained an impenetrable obstacle. So in 1899 the Hudson's Bay Company built a tramway along the length of Grand Island, enabling steamers to ease up to the south end, unload their freight onto flatcars, and steam back upriver to Athabasca Landing. The cars were man-hauled to the north end of the island, where flat-bottomed scows waited to complete the journey to Fort Mac.

The island became quite a lively place by the turn of the century, with boat crews lingering to swap river yarns or listen to Sunday sermons. Even an occasional wedding was held on the island.

Because of Grand Rapids' formidable appearance and reputation, few fatalities occurred in the rapids, with the exception of a few Klondikers who were swept to their deaths through carelessness.

Landing on the island was too hazardous at the present low-water stage, so we planned to bypass Grand Rapids completely via the mile-and-a-half-long Free Traders Portage, which winds up and along the east bank. (The trail was so named when the Hudson's Bay Company, trying to discourage competitors, banned free traders from the tramway, forcing them to blaze the passage we intended to follow.) Our directions to the trail were hazy, merely saying to approach on the right to within a few hundred yards of the main cascades. The half-mile of water before the portage was treacherous enough in low water, with many more rocks exposed than usual. We careened off one unseen rock, narrowly avoiding a dump, and then made for shore to search for the elusive trail entrance.

After walking nearly half a mile up and down the shoreline without finding it, Peter and I split up and searched through the last hour of light. Pete checked the shore again while I climbed one of the 100-foot sandstone cliffs that flank the river here to hike along the east ridge. Out of sight of Pete, I was struck by our solitude: Fifty miles to the east was the lone road to Fort McMurray; to the west were hundreds of trackless miles of forest and marsh.

We never did find the trail that night and searched for an hour the next morning before finally spotting it, winding up a creek that cut straight into rock. We walked its length without the canoe first, to fix the landmarks. The first stretch was a steep grade of mud and rock that I could barely imagine scaling with a canoe. At the top it blurred into a grassy plateau, then dropped again into a boot-sucking muskeg. After successfully lining the canoe a quarter-mile downriver to the trailhead, we began the portage in late afternoon, Pete hauling the first pack load and I the canoe. Of hundreds of portage trails I've hiked before and since, Grand Rapids topped the list of dehumanizers; it was an exhausting battle with mud and canoe and brush and rubber boots that stayed behind as I lurched forward. In the end we left the canoe halfway along the trail while we camped for the night at the far end, leaving the last part of the slog till morning.

That night's camp was on a scenic gravel bar below the main rapids. Across the river, a wall of white plumes and spray boiled up in a deafening roar. We were exhilarated to have crossed the forbidding barrier of Grand Rapids, even if on foot; the next fifty miles were a stretch of river only a privileged few have seen from a canoe. The night was calm and clear, so we vetoed the tent and, in honor of our safe passage, built a monstrous blaze with driftwood from the logjam blocking one end of the gravel bar. The entire point was soon bathed in room-temperature warmth. While we baked bread on wood slabs and discussed what lay ahead, I thought of the contrast with my wet, pathetic, solitary campfires in British Columbia, where often I could barely nurse enough flame to cook with. Pete spent roll after roll of film on the moonlit cascade, and we retired full and content. I dreamed of brigades of nineteenth-century scows drifting past our camp, and woke around 3:00 A.M. to see a cow moose coaxing her calf across the river in the light of embers from our fire.

In the morning, after completing the canoe carry and reloading gear, we set off on our first big day of rapids. Ten stretches of Grade III+ whitewater lay between us and Fort McMurray, the first of which was Little Grand Rapids, less than a mile downstream. On his scout the day before, Pete had spotted a mammoth, peanut-shaped boulder near the head of the rapids, and he was determined to photograph it. Unfortunately, getting close enough for the shot meant that we had to enter the rapids from the wrong side and then swing back quickly to catch a narrow chute.

Twenty feet from the lip of the chute, I saw that we weren't going to make it. The first wave hit nearly broadside as I jammed hard to turn the bow into the assault. It seemed to me that we took the first two four-foot waves well; Pete's body in the bow acted as a break against the main volume of water rushing in. But as we were about to meet the third, he yelled back, "Dave, we can't take another!" (For the most part, the bowman's job in the rapids is to evaluate the situation and shout status reports to the stern, as well as to fend off rocks occasionally. The stern paddler supplies most of the steering.)

We entered the third wave straight on, and I watched in amazement as the front six feet of canoe were buried. The water we had shipped with the impact of the first two acted like a sloshing lead weight, and the heavy canoe dove into rather than over the third, sinking the gunwales to the waterline. Then we were through the rapid, the canoe still upright with us sitting silently in water up to our waists. After a stunned moment we came to life, Ki light-footing it to the highest pack while Pete and I lunged for sleeping bags, maps, anything that might float away.

By the time we dragged what we could to shore, we began to realize the true dimensions of the "adventure" we had so eagerly anticipated beside the House River. We hadn't even reached the really bad rapids yet and already we'd had a serious dunking. Pete shook his 300-mm lens and listened to the water sloshing within. I started to shiver; we would have to maintain a fire throughout the night to achieve any comfort. Only one sleeping bag remained, waterlogged like all our possessions. As Pete stumbled about gathering firewood, I hunted out a suitable campsite and struggled with shaking fingers to get a fire going. Long after dark a mound of kindling finally sputtered into flame in the corner of the semicircular rock shelter we'd constructed in the crumbling sandstone cliff. That night's first cup of tea was a memorable one.

We took turns sleeping and feeding the fire all night long. Around eleven, the sky burst into a brilliant display of northern lights, and for some reason I thought of a nightclub 3,000 miles away in Washington, D.C. I could see a waiter in black, surrounded by crystal, pouring champagne from a bottle wrapped in white linen, while I clutched our battered teapot with a greasy bandana.

When the long-awaited sun rose the next morning, we were finally able to tally the damages from the spill. Actual losses amounted to no more than one sleeping bag, one tripod, one glove, and one map—but the last happened to be the topographic map covering the entire series of rapids ahead. We would now have to run them entirely from memory. On the other hand, the pot of beans I had set to soak underneath the stern seat the day before had come through unscathed, every silly bean still in the pot.

Pete needed more sleep and our gear was nowhere near dry yet, so while he napped I scouted the channels downriver for about two miles along a beach strewn with boulders. Elaborately carved sandstone cliffs reared on either side of the turbulent river, which each year etched out another fraction of an inch in width. When we returned to the river that afternoon, Peter didn't speak of the apprehensions he must have been feeling. Neither did I, though I already felt I had betrayed his trust in me.

Three miles along, the current quieted and we enjoyed a few hours of peace amid wildness. This area was untouched by hunters; the yearling moose and deer had probably never seen humans. We counted half a dozen mule deer and as many moose by evening. A family of four whitetails watched us from a sandy point as we made camp, seeming curious and unafraid, nothing like their skittish farmland kin. A flight of geese, one of the last we would see, passed overhead. We had made twenty-two miles and decided to save the next set of rapids, Brule, until morning. Running whitewater in the evening was an invitation to weary, careless decision making, not to mention hypothermia.

That night's camp was no more comfortable than the last. The weather had turned foul, and though we bagged a young duck and a grouse for dinner, they couldn't roast properly in the falling sleet. Ki, at least, didn't seem to mind; he never tired of bird entrails. Pete and I slept poorly, scrunched together under the one sleeping bag with a poncho to shield us from the wet. The spongy, mossy ground wouldn't hold a tent stake in the wind. My sleeping shift would end when Pete would awaken, shivering, to reclaim his half of the sodden bag—that awfully warm piece beneath my stomach. And vice versa, and so on.

By morning the rain had matured to a steady drizzle. We packed in weary silence, stopping for a bite of cold grouse, and set out hoping to pass Brule, Boiler, and Middle rapids by nightfall. Lowered visibility would heighten the risk of these already formidable waters, and ideally we should have waited for better weather. But both food and time were running short, and our craving for a warm, dry bedroll in Fort McMurray may have unwisely influenced our decision to push on. Lack of sleep over the past two nights undoubtedly slowed our actions and clouded our thinking as well. We scouted Brule, then discussed for half hour: Should we portage? Line? Go for it? We chose the last, and I fought to keep the canoe in the only semblance of a channel as Pete shouted, "Left, left, *left!*"

We ended that battle as victors. Could we win at Russian roulette eight more times running? Progress declined throughout the day in proportion to our spirits. My body began shaking uncontrollably. When we couldn't properly hold our paddles, we broke for a rest and talked strategy for the upcoming rapid over a healing fire and leftover barley porridge. Originally called "Joe's Rapid," Boiler Rapid was renamed nearly one hundred years ago when a scow upturned in it, depositing in the river a steamboat boiler destined for Fort McMurray. Several lives were lost in that accident.

Three times during the approach we ran what we thought was Boiler Rapid, but all guessing ceased when Peter spotted the unbroken white line of the real thing a full mile ahead. Our lost notes had indicated that Boiler could be run only along the left bank, but our faulty memories chose the right instead. We realized our error 200 yards from the main cascade—much too late for a switchback. "Dig, dig, dig, *hard right!*" I screamed, while the canoe surged toward a wall of white. As the shoreline loomed, I jammed, whiplashing the bow upstream to avoid a collision. We grounded safely, and after securing the canoe, walked down for a look at the cascade.

"No way in an open canoe," Pete announced with finality, after scouting the crisscross of slop spilling over a series of limestone ledges. Nor was there any portage trail; round, wet, slippery boulders sloped into the foaming water. Lining, then, was our only resource. The Alumacraft responded well as I jumped from rock to rock, alternately playing out and taking in the steering ropes. But at one point the bow slipped too far to the left, and the current took advantage of the opportunity. Water began to pile up heavily on the stern, and Pete grabbed one rope as I strained to maintain control. Together we tried to inch the canoe from its precarious position, but the current's power was relentless. In one awesomely smooth gesture, it sucked the canoe's stern under.

I immediately released the rope, knowing we had no chance against the thousands of pounds of pull created by a foundering canoe. Pete, though, didn't let go in time and was hurled into the river by its force. Recovering quickly, he floundered out of the shallow water and we both sprinted downstream after the rolling tumbling vessel. I slipped and bruised my leg on a rock and fell behind limping; when I caught up to Pete a quarter-mile farther down, he was back in the water. With an amazing effort he had managed in chest-deep water midstream to reach the canoe and pin it against a rock in the swift current. Now he strained at one of the ropes, trying to keep the craft from pivoting off its perch.

I inched toward him, an ill-placed step tossing my legs behind me as I fought to stay upright in the surge. Finally I reached him and, while he still held the canoe, fumbled to release the shock cords that held our packs. For the next half an hour, one of us held the canoe and tried to keep loose items from floating away while the other struggled to relay equipment to shore. The water-soaked packs now weighed more than one hundred pounds each. Finally we managed to manhandle the canoe off the rock and angle it through the current to a landing downstream.

Shivering, not speaking, we stood on shore amidst the remains of our gear. Both the rifle and the shotgun now lay on the river bottom, along with all our food, maps, and cooking equipment. One paddle had miraculously been saved. Pete had been in the water much longer than I, and his body was shaking spastically, his speech slurred through clenched teeth. Though he needed immediate attention, the only wood in the area was cottonwood, useless for a fire, and with only minutes of daylight left we had to move on to find a decent campsite. By the time we reached a stunted stand of dripping spruce a few miles downriver, near Middle Rapids, Peter had been reduced to speechless, shuffling movements.

Once the tent was erected and some water wrung from the sleeping bag, I installed Pete inside. Then I nursed and cursed a single gasping flame for an hour before giving up on the idea of a fire. During my vain search for dry wood, I had discovered one jar of food that had washed up onto the sand, and we shared its contents for dinner: a bowl of uncooked cornmeal and water. We slept tangled in one mass to optimize shared body heat, using Ki for a pillow.

Morning brought the first sun we had seen in two days, but also a thick blanket of frost. We walked around camp prying frozen pieces of clothing and gear from where we had dropped them the night before. Later, Pete hiked downstream and I in the opposite direction, in search of anything salvageable that might have washed ashore, especially Pete's lost paddle. When we rejoined, he had a flat piece of wood that only a vivid imagination might construe as a canoe paddle, and I proudly displayed one jar of rice and the map covering the last rapid before Fort McMurray. With luck, our next night's camp would be on that map.

We were too weak to load the canoe properly, or to care. Dripping, half-thawed clothing and odds and ends were tossed in haphazardly. Exposure and lack of food had taken their toll. Yet our treatment of each other was remarkable. When under normal circumstances some minor personality trait might provoke an irritated response, now that we were in serious trouble we babied and soothed each other. ("I'm sorry to bother you, Dave, but could you hand me the axe?") We took comfort in false confidence, too. Peter's faith kept me from breaking down, and I suppose the idea of my leadership, however much an illusion, gave him strength. By this time I was haunted by self-doubt. It was Peter who saved the canoe from the rapids, and I had even failed at my task of providing life-giving fire.

But it was time to face facts. Before shoving off, I made a kind of speech to Pete. "We won't survive another dump. We get up each morning with half the strength of the day before. We're already too weak to lift a full pack, much less portage it. There's hardly any food, and with no gun we're not gonna get any more." I went on to explain pedantically that each move we made now was eating into our bodies. Every calorie we burned with a paddle stroke was one less calorie to get us through the night. I figured our bodies could take just one more night's camp. Ki watched me as I spoke. He hadn't eaten in two days, yet he never left us to search for game. He seemed to understand the severity of the situation and chose companionship over a full belly.

"We're going to have to keep our movements to a minimum by drifting with the current when we can and running every rapid on blind faith." If we flipped in another rapid, we were done. But if we went slowly and cautiously, wasting energy and time lining around rapids, we'd probably be done anyway. We might as well go with the roll of the dice.

Somehow the act of stating our chances baldly seemed to brighten the dreary outlook. Four rapids down, seven to go: Middle, Long, Crooked, Rock, Little Cascade, Cascade, and Mountain. The last was navigable by powerboat, I'd heard, so if we made it that far, we might be rescued by morning.

The first 200 yards of Middle Rapids were a constant zigzag between rocks, and we slammed hard into one with an agonizing grate of aluminum on stone. We spent several minutes helplessly hung up there before gathering enough courage to step gingerly out of the canoe and haul it to shore. We shipped plenty of water in the process and lost our only remaining paddle as well.

Even in our semidazed state we recognized that paddling the last forty miles to Fort McMurray with a board was out of the question. It was almost with relief that we decided the only chance was to hike out, so after filling an overnight pack and stowing what was left of our gear under the canoe, we started walking northeast at around noon. Before we'd covered two miles, however, a moose grunt caught my attention, and when I looked back upriver, there lay the missing canoe paddle. We had walked right by it. Strangely grateful for another chance at the river, we retraced our steps in half the time.

As if reflecting our waning strength, the current now eased to a lethargic pace, and the miles dragged on to the monotonous dip of the canoe paddle. A light drizzle began, and it seemed we would never reach the next set of rapids. At this point we had passed beyond the sensations of cold and hunger. Even the desire to complain about such inconveniences seemed like a luxury. When one has no means of obtaining heat or nourishment, the mind eventually forgets their pleasures. With no environment other than coldness available, the body seems to accept that environment. Bodily functions slow to minimize output while mental capacity is reduced to one simple thought at a time. The subconscious mind still recalls toasty toes before roaring flames, but the conscious mind forgets that heat ever existed. It seemed that we no longer desired to reach Fort McMurray to find warmth, but only to claim victory over the environment that had made us forget the very sensation of warmth.

As we rounded the point just before Long Rapids, the familiar dull roar returned, seeming to come from all directions. We went through the procedure like robots: stopping, scouting, discussing the good and the bad of the channel in forced-casual tones. We spoke mechanically of last-ditch emergency measures and survival tactics. In our weakened state, the chances were good that another dump would separate us: Would Pete have the strength to continue if I didn't make it to shore? How would I react if it happened in reverse?

We didn't have to find out just yet. We passed Long Rapids, tearing through the standing waves with apparently divine luck. There was a two-mile breather before the next test, Crooked Rapids. An impassable point of sheer rock prevented us from studying the bulk of these rapids; we would have to run them blind.

We were riding the waves well as we arced around the blind, hairpin turn between the limestone cliffs. But the hidden stretch that now lay before us wasn't the tail of the rapids, as we had hoped. What was left of the channel crisscrossed four-foot walls of water separated by narrow, deep troughs. Worst of all, the channel angled to midstream, eliminating any chance of a quick beaching should we dump.

There was no dramatic canoe-flip; we simply sank beneath the battering of the standing waves. Our proud canoe turned keel up, and we clung to the rolling and pitching hull. After a few minutes of this, Ki's faith reached its limit; he leaped free of the canoe, gained the left bank, then ran along the shore trying to keep us in sight. We were tempted to follow him, but it would be suicide to lose the canoe now. Neither of us spoke as we kicked in a futile effort to swim the canoe to shore. We had both lost our rubber "Czech" boots, the current literally sucking them off our feet, and soon dead legs merely swayed in the current. Each time we neared the riverbank a crosscurrent swept us back to the middle.

Eventually Crooked Rapids spat us out and deposited us without pause into the new onslaught of Rock Rapids. True to its name, boulders beneath the surface battered our legs. There was no pain on impact, just the sensation of a leg being shoved unnaturally aside. About twenty minutes had passed since we first grasped the upturned canoe; violent cramps gripped my legs and dead arms lay across the hull. I could hear Pete's voice clearly, saying we had to leave the canoe and make shore, yet I found it difficult to speak at all. My thoughts were unstructured, and my last clear picture is of the canoe slipping from beneath my unfeeling hands. I heard Pete shout in the distance but did not even recognize the sound as human. Then I remember a fleeting glimpse of a stone ledge, and something in my hand as I climbed the embankment: a rock, a tree root. I fell forward headfirst onto level ground above the ledge. My last sensation for a while was of damp earth on my cheek.

Peter didn't know whether Dave had made it to shore or not and scarcely had time to worry about it. Though his stocky frame conserved heat better than Dave's lanky one, after nearly half an hour in the freezing water he realized that he too would soon lose control of his body and sink from sight. He continued slowly working his way toward shore; Ki's howl from the opposite bank seemed to give him new strength. A hundred yards below where he had last seen Dave, Pete felt the river bottom under his feet. Over and over he collapsed in the shallows, lunging forward to retrieve the escaping canoe. In a feat of strength drawn solely from willpower, he dragged the canoe and what remained of its contents onto a sandy spit of land.

Pete's numb feet shuffled over the rocks as he stumbled upriver in search of his partner. Snow flurries melted on his face; Ki still wailed from the opposite shore. Then another animal lay on the ground before him. Its paws were clawing earth and leaves and throwing them over its back. Pete rolled Dave over. A slight depression beside him showed where Dave had tried half consciously to dig a nest and cover himself with debris to keep from freezing. To his horror, Pete saw that his friend was no longer shivering; his eyes were open but not focusing. Forgetting his own condition, he massaged Dave's arms and legs, praying that the eyes would flicker into recognition.

The massage didn't seem to be working, and Peter recognized the signs of hypothermic shock. He doubted Dave would survive and couldn't think of anything he could do to improve his friend's chances— except possibly to get help. They were a full thirty miles from Fort McMurray. It was 6:30 P.M., the temperature below freezing, and the occasional snow flurry had grown into big, wet flakes. But he didn't think about the ridiculous odds of a starving, barefoot man, already in the early stages of hypothermia himself, reaching a town that far away. He saw only another man, sprawled on the riverbank, who would not survive the night.

The object that had been crouching over me suddenly rose up and began moving away. Its touch against my skin had felt good. I wanted it to stay but did not know how to communicate this desire; nor did I recognize the sounds it made while moving away over the rocks. I rolled over to continue digging my nest. Nothing in the world mattered but that.

I must have lost consciousness again, but not for long, as it was only now becoming full dark. For the first time I realized that the object hovering above me had been Pete, and the shock of recognition struck a solid blow. It seemed like days ago that we had been in the water. I looked around through swirling wet snow that melted upon everything it struck. I was on a ledge twenty feet above the river, covered with dirt and leaves. Bare footprints in the sand led away from me, and a vague memory returned of Pete shouting something to me. He must be trying to walk out.

I grew conscious of having difficulty breathing and thought, my God, my lungs are stopping. I began choking and snorting, unable to get enough air. Was this the final stage of hypothermia—the lungs contracting? The terrible cold was gone and my thoughts were clear, yet my body was going wild. I flopped around like a fish on land, in terror of suffocation. Finally the spasms slowed to a steady, hard breathing; I wanted to burst my lungs with the beautiful air.

It was dark now and the biting cold returned with a vengeance. From across the river I could hear Ki howling. Get out of the wind, I thought. I had to get out of the wind if I was to survive the night. I'd been wearing my poncho when we swamped; now I drew my knees to my chin and wadded the poncho hood into the head hole to block any heat loss. Every spare corner of the plastic drape was religiously tucked beneath my feet and rear against the wind that seemed to purposefully seek gaps in my sodden clothing.

To my surprise I stayed relatively warm as long as I kept even the slightest breeze from reaching me. Periodically I would lapse into fits of shaking and rock my hips back and forth for a minute to restore circulation. Even so, after an hour or so my muscles would cramp in this tortuous crouched position, and I had to risk stretching them and letting the wind in. Still, after a few hours it seemed that I would, in fact, live through the night. With that established, my thoughts turned to Pete. I wondered if he was fighting the same battle.

Early in his trek, Pete sat down in the gathering dusk to rest. He glanced upriver and noticed smeared streaks of blood on the rocks he had just crossed. It hadn't occurred to him until then that the unfeeling append-ages he walked on might not last through the night. He tore his rain pants in half and wrapped one pant leg around each foot.

The snow didn't bother him too much, but the clouds that blocked the light of the moon did. He groped his way along the riverbank, crashing into trees and falling off rock ledges. When the black expanse of the river made a wide turn, he cut inland to save distance, only to find himself lost in the timbered hills. Somehow he found his way back to the river.

When he sat down once more to rest, the cold gripped him like iron and he stood up, determined not to stop again. Thinking of the joyous warmth of sunrise carried him through the rest of the night, his movements mechanical but unceasing. Now certain that his part-ner was no longer alive, he still refused to rest, believing that if he did, he would surely suffer Dave's fate. He did not even notice that the dawn brought no sun, only a blanket of steel grey cloud. He kept walking.

October 3. It wasn't my imagination; it *was* getting light. I continued my vigil under the poncho, though the temptation to throw it off was nearly overwhelming. Finally, when I believed there was more light and heat than the wind could overcome, I raised the poncho from my head, hoping to see the sun climbing over the jagged black line of trees on the horizon. Instead, I saw a grey, sunless world. While the wind chuckled, I wondered beneath which patch of dull sky Peter's body lay.

I groped my way down the limestone face to the river, still barefoot but no longer feeling the sharp stones beneath my feet. For the rest of the morning I sat unmoving in a small cave about five feet high and running a dozen feet into the cliff. I was loathe to leave its protection, but the thought that Pete might still be alive some-where downriver finally drove me back out into the wind. My idea was born of simple desperation: If I could find the canoe, I would simply shove off into the river. With three rapids ahead and no paddle, my chances of drifting the thirty miles to town were nearly nonexistent. Yet I was sure I wouldn't last another night.

I found the canoe sometime that afternoon, lying on its side half in, half out of the water. The packs were still strapped to the thwarts, all twisted in a heap and much of their contents spilled, the frames a mass of gnarled metal. Too weak to carry the packs, I made repeated trips into the water to remove gear one piece at a time. I yanked the sleeping bag and tent free, along with a jar of rice, a few bouillon cubes, and a bit of writing paper. But when it came time to invert the canoe to drain it, I couldn't even lift the bow. So much for getting back on the river.

At least I could now make a semblance of a camp. I reluctantly passed up a sheltered spot in the spruces in favor of the rocky, wind-blown spit where I'd found the canoe; the chances of being spotted from there were better. The tent wobbled, threatening to collapse with each gust; inside I piled everything that might be of some use to me. The rest I scattered around the sandbar to make myself as visible as possible from the air.

Crawling under the still-soaked sleeping bag, I propped up on an elbow and chewed a handful of raw rice, then washed a bouillon cube down with icy river water. It was hard to swallow, but the calories might get me through another night. Just in case, I then made myself write a letter to my family, explaining the accident. Though the letter, barely legible on soggy paper, expressed guilt for their loss and Pete's death, I felt surprisingly calm and remorseless as I wrote. The act of writing left me encouraged; it was an attempt at communication, a reminder of the civilized world beyond this desolate river.

Tuesday, October 4 [*The letter was actually written on October 3, but Dave had lost track.*]
To: Maurice E. Halsey Family
Dear Mom, Dad, Steve, and Sara,
Sorry, cold, hard to write. Fri. night Pete and I dumped the canoe below Grand Rapids. Then we lost her while lining

Boiler. Dumped her again last night. Spent ½ hour in water. I passed out when we reached shore and Pete said he was walking. [*Dave must have inferred this; Pete recalls no conversation before he set off.*] Both of us are barefoot. I didn't think I had a chance last night but made it through O.K. Since it dropped below freezing & snowed last night I fear he didn't make it. Please tell Mr. & Mrs. Souchuk how sorry I am that I ruined their fine son's life. . . . I love you all so much. You're all I've been thinking of these last few days. I'd like nothing more than to sit in the family room & eat crackers and drink milk. So weak. Guess I've finally found my limit. We lost Ki too. I get sick to my stomach when I think of Pete. If I can hold out through tonight. Found the canoe and gear today—things looking up. Love you so much, Dave.

I longed to sleep but needed to urinate first. I couldn't bring myself to open the tent flap and let precious warmth escape, so I simply rolled over. Then I went into deep hibernation and didn't waken until the next afternoon. Depression set in immediately as I lay there, nearly warm, thinking of Pete's cold corpse resting on some shore. Gazing at the tent ceiling and listening to the rainfly flap in the wind, I felt a powerful desire to trade places with him.

Around noon on October 4, the jet boat of an aquatic research team studying fish populations churned up the Athabasca. Peter Souchuk heard, then saw it as if in a dream. He screamed and threw rocks into the river, but the boat raced by without its occupants seeing him. As he sank to his knees in despair, he heard a second boat.

Derek Tripp and Gary Hughes's boat slammed into the whitewater as they sped to catch up with their partners, Mike Jones and Rita Ford. A flash of color on the riverbank caught Gary's eye, and as they slowed, it turned into a dazed man standing beside the river, waving his arms in a trancelike motion. They quickly extracted the information from Peter about his missing partner, and after conveying it to the other boat, turned around and headed back to Fort McMurray and its hospital with their passenger.

A little while later that afternoon I awoke again, this time to the sound of an engine growling somewhere in the distance. I dismissed it, rolling over to go back to sleep. The flight pattern to Fort McMurray paralleled the river, and I'd already heard three airplanes. Since I couldn't see them, they obviously couldn't see me either.

But the sound was getting louder, not fading away. Finally, I couldn't stand it and tore open the tent flap. Not 200 yards downriver was a powerboat headed toward me. I don't recall the mad screaming and arm waving I must have performed, only repeating a dozen times "God . . . it's over!" as the tears streamed down my face. The boat's occupants, a man and a woman, looked shaken as they debarked and cautiously approached me. The woman led me down to the boat as her partner began storing my gear under the canoe for salvage later. I was soothed and comforted by her soft face and gentle arms; I had forgotten such simple joys during these last days.

Both Mike and Rita were strangely silent as they went about their tasks. Not until I was safely bundled into the boat did they begin to answer my babbled questions. The first was about Pete, and I dreaded the answer, but Mike replied calmly that he was fine and probably at the hospital by now. "The helicopter is on its way out for your body. Pete said you were dead. That's why we were so surprised when we found you."

Then I remembered Ki and tried to insist that we go back and look for him. Though I hadn't heard his cries since the night before, I believed that he was still patiently waiting for us on the other side of the river. But Mike and Rita gently refused, assuring me that we could search for Ki later. During the remaining half-hour or so of the trip to Fort McMurray, they filled me in on what they knew of Pete's ordeal. But I hardly heard them, or noticed the town as it grew from behind the river bend. Part of me was still back on the limestone cliffs of the Athabasca, with Ki.

4 | Walking into Winter

Fort McMurray, Alberta, to the Saskatchewan Border

The bathwater seemed to scald my buttocks as I lowered myself into the tub. Though the nurse said the water was only tepid, after four days of inescapable cold it was almost too warm for comfort. But temperature adjustment be damned; with no care for the conse-quences, I dropped into the tub and was blanketed by glorious heat. Not the isolated handful of warmth from a last matchstick, or the faint insulation of half a sodden sleeping bag, or the fleeting warmth of one's own urine—but unlimited, magical heat from the simple act of turning on a faucet. I rolled and played in it, while outside tree branches thrashed against the window.

A few minutes earlier, as Mike and Rita had helped me into the hospital, I had caught my first glimpse of Peter. Clad in hospital pajamas and leaning heavily on a nurse, he crossed the corridor in front of me, looking more like a stooped, frail old man than my heroic partner. I tried to call out to him, but he didn't hear me, and they wouldn't let us talk yet. Still, just the sight of him helped ease my burden of guilt as I lay in the tub. The world seemed back on course.

I can still recall little of the first few days in Fort McMurray, but I know Pete and I talked that night when I was escorted into our double room. Neither of us could relax until reunited, even though we'd been told repeatedly that the other was safe. We spoke in excited spurts, then grew weak and slept for short stretches, waking to begin again. Our thoughts were garbled and our words slurred, but we passionately wanted to re-create the accident before sleep fogged our memories. Nurses came in and out to push more vitamins and fluid into us, and to scold us for talking instead of resting.

The second day we felt stronger but still forgetful and disoriented. I phoned my parents again, not remembering I had already done so the night before. It was hard to stand without swaying like a tethered balloon, and we sometimes forgot where we were.

An added misery for me was anxiety over the future of the team. All that day I waited for Peter to announce that he was leaving the expedition. I had failed our first true test, and had Pete not found the courage to try to walk out, the chances of either of us being rescued were minimal. When it came time to regroup and replan, I was sure Pete would say he'd had enough. Finally he rolled over in bed and introduced the subject himself, as I grimaced in anticipation.

"You know, Dave, it's a damn shame we don't have our maps with us. We could be planning our winter travel right now." This from a man whose shredded feet could barely carry him from bed to the toilet, much less across a continent. I was to recall those words many times and many hundreds of miles later.

Now my only remaining worry was Ki. I couldn't stop thinking about him, fearing that he might starve waiting on the riverbank for us to come back. Or that he had been injured and couldn't hunt, maybe falling prey to wolves. Or, believing we had abandoned him, had simply wandered off in search of new companions. I truly thought we wouldn't find him, and though the idea was upsetting, I was somehow almost resigned to it. After the trauma of giving Pete up for dead, the loss of Ki seemed less terrible. Both of us had been aged by recent events.

That same afternoon, a hearty, cigar-puffing man who was a dead ringer for Los Angeles Dodgers manager Tommy Lasorda burst into our room with a furious nurse on his heels. After grinding out his stogie with an apologetic "Jeez, sorry!" he introduced himself as

Joe Camp, vice-president of Great Canadian Oil Sands Company, the local boom industry. He was, in fact, our savior.

After the Halseys received Dave's phone call, ending several days of acute worry, Maurice Halsey got busy trying to arrange some local help for Dave and Peter. Through his work as an energy lobbyist, he had met some executives of Sun Oil Company (of which Great Canadian Oil Sands was a subsidiary) and knew of their Fort McMurray operation. A few phone calls led him to Joe Camp, and although the two men had never met, Camp immediately assured the elder Halsey that his son would be well cared for.

He was as good as his word, taking Dave home from the hospital on day three, with a stop on the way to replace his hopelessly filthy and mangled clothing and footwear. Peter's damaged feet required a few more days of hospitalization, after which he joined Dave at the comfortable suburban home of Joe and Carolina Camp.

Thus began two weeks of unlimited hospitality. Carolina's Italian heritage translated into fussy mothering of both Peter and me. She was not content unless certain that the pillow behind my head was perfectly positioned, and for the first two days after Pete arrived she didn't allow him to walk without her supporting arm. Her culinary specialty was pasta, and she was convinced that our frail bodies needed mounds of it. When our shrunken stomachs could hold no more, she would scold, "How are you going to go back to your expedition if you don't eat more? Come to think of it, I don't know why I'm trying to help you get better. You'll just go and freeze yourselves again. Your mothers must be grey!" With that, she'd plop another steaming heap of lasagna on our plates.

Joe, meanwhile, made it his mission to educate us about the lively past and prosperous present of Fort McMurray. As our strength increased we explored more of the town. Like other parts of Alberta, it had been transformed by newfound energy wealth, its population leaping from five thousand to nearly thirty thousand in less than a decade. Joe Camp's company pioneered a process to extract oil from the sticky, foul-smelling deposits of tar sands lining the Athabasca. Twenty-story buildings stand not far from the spot where, in 1870,

William McMurray built his fort at the junction of the Clearwater and Athabasca rivers.

McMurray, chief agent for the Hudson's Bay Company, founded his town on furs. The valley of the Mackenzie River, to the north, was a fur trader's paradise, but at that time the steamboat ferry between Athabasca Landing and Grand Island had not yet been established (see chapter 3), and the valley was inaccessible except from the east, via the arduous Methy Portage on the Clearwater. McMurray recognized this spot on the river junction as a prime trading site, where trappers from the north could sell their furs to Hudson's Bay Company in exchange for products from the east.

A robust, adventuresome man, McMurray had traveled in much of western Canada before choosing this site for his company town. The explorer J. H. Lefroy, an occasional companion of McMurray's, recounts this incident from one of their journeys together; it reminded me hauntingly of our own frozen camps along the Athabasca:

> It was intensely cold and nearly full moon . . . and we lay
> down to sleep side by side. I slept at that time in a bag
> made of one blanket, and with a second blanket over me.
> Again and again, I woke half frozen to find that McMurray,
> in his sleep, by persistent wriggling, had got all my blanket
> from me and wrapped around himself. Then came a tug and
> a struggle until I repossessed myself of it, only to repeat the
> same process after an hour or two. (Wallace, *Sir Henry
> Lefroy's Journal*, quoted in Comfort)

McMurray and his men had little use for the extensive deposits of tar, or oil, sands found throughout the region. A few used them to waterproof their cabin roofs or seal the seams of birchbark canoes, but most considered the noxious mires as merely a further inconvenience of living at a wilderness outpost. Today two-ton shovels scoop the goop onto conveyor belts bound for refineries, which produce in excess of 150,000 barrels of oil daily. There is no longer a market for birchbark seam sealer, and asphalt shingles cover the roofs of surburban homes where the cabins once stood.

Joe was a good storyteller and really warmed up when describing his hunting and fishing adventures. His tales of trophy fish and pickerel stringers too heavy to lift had me squinting with skepticism, until he produced his photo albums to back them up. While his own comfortable lifestyle was tied to development, he remained sensitive to the contradictions of living in a fast-growing city in the remote Canadian bush. Gesturing toward the backyard one evening after dinner, he described the occasional visits of bears, who were having some difficulty adjusting to aluminum siding, swing sets, and barbecue grills.

The Camps, originally from Texas, had three daughters. The two eldest, in their twenties, were living back in their home state: "A good thing," Carolina bragged to us, "or you two would probably never finish your expedition." That left seven-year-old Valeri Jo, for whom Pete and I represented new Monopoly victims. The Camp clan was rounded out by an eternal optimist of a German shepherd named Sunshine. Every time she wagged her tail, my thoughts returned to Ki.

Ten days had now elapsed since we had swum to the right bank of the Athabasca and Ki to the left. Fort McMurray's newspapers had repeatedly described him in the hope he might be spotted by a passing moose hunter, but there had been no sign. No longer did I envision him patiently waiting for us on the riverbank; I was sure hunters would have found him if so. His hunting ability could easily sustain him, and if he had moved off, there was small chance of finding him. At one point I planned to hitch a ride upriver on a jet boat and backpack the thirty miles back, on the chance he might be somewhere along the way. But that plan died early; I couldn't even lift the pack to my shoulder without stumbling.

When the knock on the Camps' door came on October 15, we were completely unprepared. Mike Jones and Derek Tripp, our original rescuers, smiled through the window; between them stood an emaciated animal in a serious state of shock. Its eyes divulged no recognition or emotion, and it chose its steps with great care, as if it might fall at any moment.

We pieced together the story from what Derek and Mike knew about Ki's rescue. He had watched and waited near my campsite for the last nine days, refusing to believe that we had deserted him.

Hunters passed by, but Ki was waiting for the humans he knew and did not reveal his presence to passing strangers. Then two moose hunters spotted our cached canoe and gear and recognized it as the fateful camp they'd heard about on the radio. They loaded our canoe and tied it behind their boat, planning to tow it back to Fort McMurray.

Ki spotted men at my old camp, packing his master's gear. Whether in the blurred vision of starvation he mistook them for Peter and me, or whether he simply intended to protect our gear from supposed intruders, he leaped into the river and swam toward their departing boat. When the astonished hunters pulled him from the river, they were surprised at how weak he was. It was obvious he hadn't eaten for many days, yet they had found the remains of another hunter's moose kill only a quarter-mile downriver—well within Ki's range of scent. Yet he had chosen not to leave his sentry post, even to search for food, in case we might return during his absence.

Ki seemed close to death. I was afraid to touch him, for fear the slightest pressure would cause him to collapse. In two more days, I doubt he would have had the strength to whine, much less swim toward his rescuers. But I no longer doubted that he would have continued to wait. Peter and I cried that night.

Thanks mainly to Carolina, Ki made an amazingly fast recovery. At first he accepted no more than a mouthful of food at a time, but by the third day he was eating full and hearty meals. By the fourth day, he showed some of his old pep and vigor, though several weeks passed before his eyes lost their distant stare. We never learned the names of the hunters who had saved him, but we thanked them over and over in the months ahead, when his backbone and faith were all that held the expedition together.

Though we were all regaining strength, the temperature was dropping fast. Nearly three weeks after we had been plucked from the river, Peter and I still could not walk more than a mile through Fort McMurray without sitting down to rest. Peter walked with a pronounced limp, which wasn't surprising—but our lingering weakness was. Meanwhile, I noted with growing alarm the changes in the river and countryside as winter closed in at the end of October. The wet snow flurries we had seen on the rapids multiplied, and now only a strong afternoon sun could defeat them. Instead of a slight skim of ice, the Athabasca's eddies were trapped under a thin but solid sheet. The last deciduous leaves had fallen in September, and the mammals were well furred by the time we entered the hospital. The locals' predictions of an early, hard winter seemed alarmingly accurate.

We had hoped to push far into Saskatchewan by canoe before freeze-up gripped the rivers, but now winter's ice would force us onto a land route from Fort McMurray. It was difficult for me to accept; I had been committed to canoeing through Saskatchewan via the Clearwater and Churchill rivers, making the transition to showshoes at Flin Flon, Manitoba—800 miles east of Fort Mac. My pride had already been bruised by the initial mutiny, the delay at Vega, and the rapids disaster; my ex-partners' advice to give up seemed all the more valid now. I had judged the first 1,200 miles to be the easiest of the journey, yet those "easy" miles had dispatched four partners and nearly killed a fifth. What would we encounter during the 3,500 "tough" miles that lay ahead?

Though I questioned my judgment, there was no questioning my desire—or Peter's—to continue. However, the change in route necessitated first returning to the States to make an equipment switch. We spent our last week before leaving town with new hosts: ex-Montrealers Roger and Danielle Leger. Roger and Pete had met at the hospital therapy center, and the French-Canadian construction worker had become intensely interested in our trek. Joe and Carolina had been perfect hosts, but we didn't want to overstay our welcome, and the Legers likewise entertained us royally. Both couples promised to look after Ki until our return.

Dave and Peter flew back to Washington, D.C., on October 28 and spent a month resting and resupplying for the overland leg ahead. Some outdoor equipment manufacturers had been hesitant about donating gear at the start but now changed their tune—no doubt influenced by extensive press coverage of the trek so far, as well as by Dave's vividly persuasive firsthand report. National Geographic had delayed additional funding for a time but now came through with a grant that would help offset expenses—particularly the hefty phone bills racked

up from Fort McMurray. Dave was passionately convinced of the ex-
pedition's potential to make money, yet concerned about relying too
heavily on his parents' support in the meantime. The break also allowed
Dave to catch up on his written chronicle of the expedition, having
lost more than half his earlier drafts in the rapids accident. "That's
okay, though," he admitted in an October 21 letter. "I wasn't pleased
with the stuff anyway."

We returned to Fort McMurray on November 25 to find the Athabasca jammed with gnarled blocks of ice. A foot of snow blanketed
the town, providing a clear warning of what lay ahead. The reception was warm, however, with the Camps and the Legers treating
us to back-to-back welcome dinners. Both Joe Camp and Roger Leger
questioned us closely on the details of our travel plans, and we
managed to convince them that we at least half knew what we were
doing.

Roger's experienced advice was especially helpful. "No, no, no,"
he interrupted, studying our maps. "You have planned to travel too
far at first. You are out of shape and not used to these temperatures.
Better to plan on no more than ten miles per day."

The next two days passed in a blur of packing and organizing,
again with Roger's valuable input. Meanwhile, I had some ground
to make up: The thirty-mile boat ride from the accident site to Fort
McMurray represented a break in my journey. Besides, a two-day
hike would give me a chance to test our winter gear. Though I
couldn't travel on foot the route we would have canoed, I felt that
a thirty-mile round-trip along the nearby Horse River would sym-
bolically balance the books. Peter had already paid his mileage dues
and more with his all-night walk.

I set out with Ki and a light pack, following a snowmobile trail
up the north bank of the Horse. The city noises quickly fell away
in the muffled stillness of the winter woods; Ki bounded ahead in
search of squirrels. There was no wind and the temperature remained
a pleasant few degrees above zero Fahrenheit—it was all a winter
walk should be.

At dusk I came upon a sheltering stand of spruce where the
Horse divides into two main channels—a good campsite. Relying

on a weather forecast for continuing moderate temperatures, I'd left the tent behind and laid my sleeping bag on a snow-free bed of spruce needles under a sheltering canopy of boughs. After a simple supper I lay watching the swaying boughs in the gathering dark, Ki curled into a ball at my feet. It was a good way to begin the winter.

I chose a slightly different return route the next morning, angling farther south to explore a picturesque valley. Trudging through unbroken snow soon left me a sweating, dripping mess, but Ki loved it. At each rabbit den he buried his head, sniffing for occupants, then shoved his muzzle forward and up in a shower of snow. A sneeze to clear his nostrils, and he was ready for the next hunt. As we topped the last hill above Fort McMurray, there was Peter, the ever-present camera dangling from his neck, waving at us from the street.

It was 1:30 P.M. on departure day (December 2) before we finished shaking hands with local friends and posing for newspaper photos. Roger walked to the railroad tracks with us, where we parted, Peter and I heading east along the Northern Alberta Railway toward the small community of Anzac twenty-seven miles away. The snow wasn't deep enough to call for our five-foot-long Alaskan-type snowshoes, chosen for fast travel through open country. Still, our progress was far from swift; Alberta's railroads were no more comfortable to walk along than British Columbia's. The ties were set too close together for us to step on each one, yet too far apart to take two in a stride.

The temperature — in the minus-20s — was not impossibly cold nor particularly comfortable, just cold enough to keep us moving. Our route snaked through stands of spruce along the meandering Clearwater River. Occasionally we flushed grouse from the trees, though always out of range of my .22 rifle. We spoke little during that first day's hike, each experiencing his own blend of exhilaration and apprehension, neither wanting to intrude on the other's thoughts.

That night we camped no more than seven miles from Fort McMurray. We were tired, sore, and out of shape, and it quickly became clear that this camp was a far cry from my balmy evening on the Horse River. The temperature soon hit 30 below, and our only source of heat was a single-burner gas stove. (In our ignorance of winter camping, we didn't yet know how easy it is to maintain a bonfire against a reflective snowbank.) We munched half-cooked cheese sandwiches and jogged around camp to stay warm, wondering whether we had taken our trial-and-error methods too far. The next morning we awoke inside an ice castle of hoarfrost. Our numbed minds had failed to consider that condensed breath is trapped in a tent and will blanket everything from boots to eyebrows in a thick, milky rime.

The second day was even more disappointing, advancing us a mere six miles. Hiking with a full pack through unbroken snow was vastly different than carrying a light load over a well-packed trail. It became painfully obvious that we were simply packing too much weight to make adequate progress in these conditions. At least we didn't have to pitch a camp that night, luckily stumbling on the small cabin of a trapper named Julian Powder. Julian, a jovial métis (French/Indian mixed-blood) welcomed the diversion; we smoked and swapped tales around his tin stove, on which a peppery pork stew bubbled and a bannock tanned. He suggested several tricks to speed our adjustment to winter travel, and applied a salve to Ki's bleeding, swollen pads.

Julian shook his head over our footwear—the finest Sorel pac-boots money could buy. "No wonder you're so damn tired. Those things are okay for skidooing, but they'll kill you just walking." (Most people in northern Canada refer to snowmobiles as skidoos, regardless of brand.) When we protested that everyone in the city had recommended these boots, he retorted, "Forget all that crap you heard in the city. Those people don't know the bush past their skidoo's windshield. Caribou moccasins—that's what you need. You should be able to have some made for you in the next Indian town."

He was similarly critical of our heavy packs, advising that we could do without much of the gear as we learned more. "You should travel light the first few weeks. Make short trips between settlements until you've gotten rid of your city-softness; then you can pack heavier loads." When Julian said that some friends of his were traveling to Fort McMurray in the morning, we had an idea: Could they take our packs to Roger Leger? That would let us hike bareback to Anzac, and Roger could ship our packs there by rail.

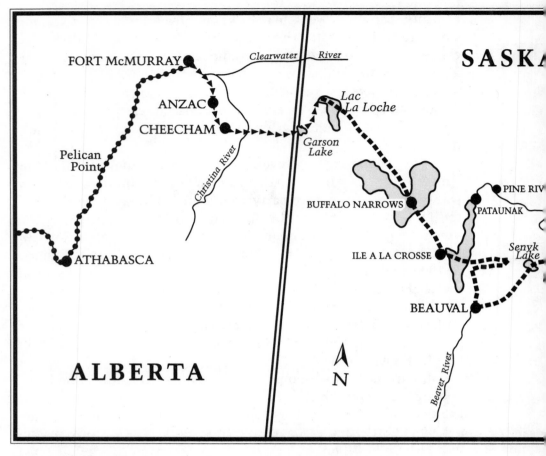

Fort McMurray, Alberta, to Flin Flon, Manitoba, December 1977–April 1978

Julian agreed, and the next morning after a pancake breakfast we left him our packs and a box of .22 shells that he needed, then returned to the cursed railroad tracks. We carried only our standard lunch: a fist-sized piece of bannock, four inches of garlic sausage, and a candy bar apiece, along with a quart of orange drink. Each morning we mixed orange crystals with boiling water and then wrapped the plastic jar in the sleeve of a spare sweater. Even so, the penetrating cold froze the drink to a thick slush by lunchtime.

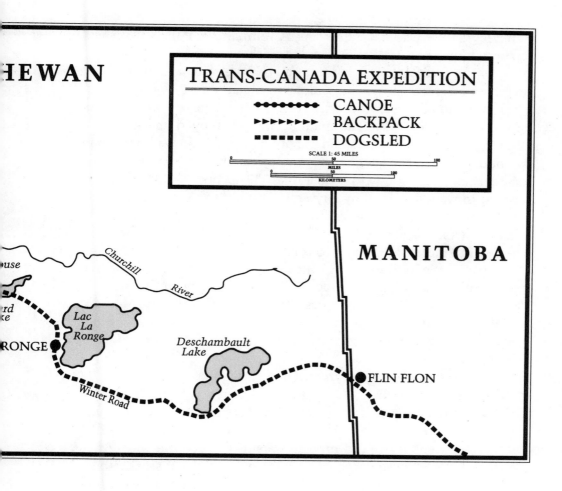

TRANS-CANADA EXPEDITION

●●●●●●●● CANOE
▶▶▶▶▶▶▶ BACKPACK
■■■■■■ DOGSLED

SCALE 1: 45 MILES

0   50   100
MILES
0   50   100
KILOMETERS

HEWAN

MANITOBA

Churchill

River

Lac
La
Ronge

Deschambault
Lake

RONGE

●FLIN FLON

Winter Road

Fourteen miles without packs hardly constitutes a strenuous day, but two more inches of snow had fallen, increasing the ground cover to fourteen inches. We walked through a strong headwind all afternoon, intensifying the minus-30-degree cold. I can't quote the day's windchill factor; the term is never used in the bush. Residents just say in a matter-of-fact drone, "It's 30 below and damn windy." By the time the sun set at a quarter past three both of us had frostbitten ears and cheeks. My right nostril was solidly plugged with ice and felt as hard as wood. A remnant of Peter's limp had returned, and Ki's trail was dappled with blood.

Despite our exhaustion, we began to develop a pattern of travel. Preferring a quick pace, I would barge ahead in a two-mile spurt, then rest and have a smoke while waiting for Pete to catch up. His steady, slow pace drove me mad; besides, I enjoyed and needed a short break every hour. Pete, on the other hand, could walk for hours without resting at his deliberate, energy-saving pace. This tortoise-and-hare combination worked just fine: Throughout the day I pushed him to move faster, and by day's end I was the first to begin spotting promising campsites. But the tortoise was never ready to camp and always managed to drag me two miles farther down the trail.

By full dark we still hadn't reached Anzac. Only the reflecting snow of the tracks' outline and the ties beneath our feet told us we were heading in the right direction. Just as we'd begun to wonder if we could somehow have missed it, a light flashed ahead and a familiar French voice shouted our names. Roger appeared through the gloom and led us to a government storage shed, where Danielle set before us a sirloin steak and a pot of potatoes. They had decided to deliver our packs in person and had taken a circuitous route by road, driving south, east, and finally north to reach Anzac before us.

We were barely able to appreciate their surprise. The combination of wind and extreme cold had left our faces scabbed with frostbite. Nausea shook us and muscle spasms gripped our legs. After gulping hot tea we managed to swallow a few bites of steak. Roger had gotten two beds in a forestry bunkhouse, and I remember climbing into one—but nothing more.

During the night the temperature dropped to minus-58 degrees Fahrenheit, and we awoke to find Anzac obscured by a shroud of ice fog. It would not rise above minus-35 that day. We were stiff and sore, and our faces burned at the slightest exposure to the cold; it was a good day to heed Julian Powder's suggestion that we ease into life in the winter bush. We spent it visiting some local residents, including Mennonite trapper Jim Mulawka and his Chipewyan wife, Lenora. Their trapping cabin was twenty-five miles southeast, along our route, and Jim offered to put us up if it was too cold to camp when we got there.

After loading our packs onto the train bound for Cheecham, the next stop on the line, we left Anzac around noon the next day (December 6) with only a camera, a rifle, and lunch. The temperature was minus-44 degrees. At four, just after dark, we lost the trail and found ourselves back on the tracks, thus stretching the day's walk from eighteen to twenty-one miles. By five we had refrozen our faces and felt the waves of shaking nausea. Poor Ki was now balancing his steps along one of the iron rails to avoid the burning snow that packed between his pads.

By six I was truly, unashamedly, afraid. I feared that we had walked farther than we realized, passed Cheecham, and were now following the tracks away from the settlement. The next cabin was twenty miles beyond Cheecham. We had found a railroad switch-man's hut, maybe four by six feet, and huddled there having our first argument of the winter through lips that refused to obey and slurred our words. I argued that we should spend the night in the hut and build a fire in the doorway. Pete thought we should keep moving, that Cheecham had to be still ahead. I wasn't convinced we were past it, but if so, we would be too weak and cold to maintain a fire by the time we discovered our error. This was an odd reversal of roles, since normally I was the risk taker and Pete the cautious one.

Finally I agreed to keep going, and we shuffled onward—toward Cheecham or away from it. At 7:30 P.M., four hours after sunset, we rounded a bend and spotted the lights of Baxter Gillingham's cabin. Baxter flung open the door and introduced himself. He had to repeat his name much later, since we were then oblivious to words. I saw only a scruffy salt-and-pepper beard below watery blue eyes as he escorted us into the cabin and helped us into chairs. Ki followed and dropped beneath the table.

Baxter had been expecting us. When the biweekly train had stopped near his cabin that afternoon, the baggage man had tossed our packs and snowshoes to Baxter's trapping partner, Johnny Lemaige (Jim Mulawka's brother-in-law), along with the news that two Americans were hoofing it down from Anzac. Johnny in turn had told Baxter when he brought our gear to the cabin. Baxter, who had spent most of his sixty-odd years in the bush, had planned to trap that day but decided to straighten up his cabin instead when he saw the temperature nudging 50 below. He knew that two unseasoned Americans would be in trouble after walking twenty-one miles on such a day, and considered going out to look for us. But he remembered his younger days as an arrogant first-year trapper, when in similar circumstances he would rather have dropped in his tracks than be rescued. Then, too, there was his present comfort to consider. "I'll give 'em a few more hours," he had decided.

Having thawed out himself countless times, Baxter wasn't surprised that we couldn't talk or eat or so much as acknowledge his presence when we first arrived. He kept our mugs full of heavily sweetened tea but refrained from asking questions for the first half an hour or so, knowing he could expect only garbled, illogical replies. This thawing period, a return to normalcy, would become standard evening procedure for Peter and me. Our minds had been operating in a trancelike state from the energy drain of moving all day in extreme cold. Under such circumstances, small motor control is lost, and anything more complex than placing one foot before the other becomes inconceivable. It is a form of shock, the mind gearing down for self-preservation. Were the mind to continue functioning at normal capacity, the sensations of pain, hunger, and cold would overrule the need to maintain forward motion. So consciousness narrows to the primary drive: to keep walking. While still in this state, it's impossible to absorb the sudden collage of stimuli in a trapper's cabin.

Slowly our voices and appetites returned. We ate some bannock and got acquainted with our host, who shared his cabin with a young Chipewyan bride. Johnny Lemaige and his wife, also Chipewyans, lived there too. All had much to offer us in the way of bush lore, and we talked long into the night. Periodically Baxter would clear his throat, spit a wad of phlegm into the slop pail by the stove, then smear a fingerful of Vicks VapoRub on his tongue. He maintained that this habit kept him in perfect health.

Baxter frowned at our cumbersome boots but smiled in approval at our scabbed faces, assuring us that moderate frostbite would eventually toughen the skin and prevent further discomfort. We'd already discovered what all trappers know: that face masks are impractical, becoming hopelessly encrusted with ice from breath condensation within minutes in extreme conditions. On the coldest days, Baxter suggested, we should try smearing Vaseline or grease on our faces to provide some insulation.

Our most priceless lesson from Baxter came the next morning, when he showed us his string of rabbit snares in a nearby willow thicket and described how to make one. You begin by measuring a thirty-inch length of single-strand brass wire along an outstretched arm, from fingertip to shoulder, and cutting or snipping it, then folding it in half. Place a stick slightly smaller in diameter than a pencil in the fold and twist to form a loop in the wire. Holding down the loose ends with your foot, you then twirl the stick until the two strands become a single twisted one; then rub the wire back and forth across a pole or your thigh to smooth out any kinks. Draw the severed end through the loop from the stick (now removed) and coil the snare for easy transport in a pocket. (Single-strand snares will work but wear out and break after catching a few rabbits.)

Snares are set in willow thickets where the creatures congregate to feed on the bark. ("Rabbit" in this part of the world always means the large, white snowshoe hare.) A rabbit trail is selected and its sides blocked with small fences made of sticks. The snare's loose end is twisted around a three-foot, inch-diameter drag pole, which is set diagonally over the trail with one end anchored in the snow. Finally, the wire noose is expanded to a three- or four-inch circle whose bottom hangs no more than two inches above the trail. When the rabbit is funneled onto the trail it usually doesn't see the snare and pulls the wire loop tight trying to free itself.

Such snares cost only pennies apiece, and in productive country, setting out a dozen can yield three to four rabbits by morning. Occasionally none are caught, but one evening in northcentral Saskatchewan I set ten snares and retrieved seven snowshoe hares. Baxter's gift of bushcraft would literally provide us with hundreds of meals over the next 3,500 miles.

Baxter's cabin was overcrowded with the addition of us and our gear, but Jim Mulawka's trapping cabin was located four miles down the trail toward the Saskatchewan border, now just fifty miles east. Since our muscles were very sore and our faces burned the moment we stepped outside, we decided Jim's cabin was the logical place to wait out the cold spell. Following the directions Jim had given us back in Anzac, we had no trouble finding the place.

It was more luxurious than we'd anticipated: two large, well-furnished rooms lighted by double-pane windows. Opposite a wall lined with bookshelves was a huge cast-iron stove, not the usual cheap tin variety. An array of rifles and shotguns hung from pegs above the door, and a radio sat on the kitchen table. To our surprise and delight, the reception was excellent; Jim had strung an entire spool of snare wire through the trees and thence into the cabin. We tuned into a central Alberta station and caught up with world news while doing our evening chores. Pete serviced the camera equipment while I excitedly twisted length after length of snare wire—Baxter's farewell gift.

Taking a flashlight outside, I set eight snares along rabbit runs in the woods behind the cabin. The temperature was about 30 below and the damaged skin in my face stung in the frozen air. But I was in a fine mood, happily arranging my blocking sticks and cheered by the warm glow that radiated from the cabin. The temperature could drop as it pleased, the wind gust and swirl the sandlike granules of snow against the cabin door. We would be in a warm cocoon with a glowing cast-iron heart, watching nature's fury through double-pane glass.

Baxter's tutoring and my efforts were rewarded the next morning by three fat white hares. After skinning and cleaning them, we dropped them whole into boiling water and cooked them for an hour. Removing them from the pot, I took the meat off the bones in small chunks and returned it to the cooking broth, adding split peas, potatoes, onions, powdered soup mix and tomato sauce, and seasonings. This boiled slowly for another several hours, until the meat fell apart in tender shreds. Thus was born our version of rabbit stew, which became our staple winter meal. At the time we found it superb, and I congratulated myself on its creation. Months later, after eating it day after day, we had to force the stuff into our mouths, and I cursed the day I'd invented the recipe. Five years later I still find it hard to enter a kitchen where rabbits are cooking.

As we gulped bowl after bowl of stew that afternoon, a plane's engine droned steadily in the near distance. Eventually we stepped outside and scanned the sky, spotting a twin-engine Beechcraft above the treetops. The plane skirted a lake in front of the cabin, then turned and reversed direction as if searching for something. It turned again and flew straight toward the cabin, buzzing us low enough that we could see the hulking, slightly balding figure in the passenger window. It was Joe Camp, taking a detour to check on us on his way to Edmonton in the Great Canadian Oil Sands Company plane. As Joe made several passes, we leaped and waved and gave him thumbs-up; finally the plane dipped its wings in farewell and banked off to the south.

Our fourth night in the cabin was the end of our "vacation." I had caught a total of fourteen rabbits to supplement our food supply. The pain in Peter's feet, a remnant of his ordeal on the Athabasca, had vanished, and Ki's paws were rapidly healing. The damaged skin on our faces was greatly reduced, though the right side of my nose was still hidden beneath a shell of scabs. The weather, though, was our chief motivation to resume travel: On December 10 the temperature climbed to a remarkably comfortable minus-5 degrees.

Jim Mulawka showed up that night, a fortunate piece of timing. He had a small overnight cabin we could stay in seven miles east on Hay Creek, he told us, and without his directions we probably wouldn't have found it. That was the good news. The bad news, he said, was that, as yet this season, no one had traversed the *next* ten miles between Hay Creek and trapper Jean-Marie Janvier's cabin on the Christina River. We would have to break our own trail through two feet of snow.

This suited Jim just fine. He wanted to run a line of traps from Hay Creek to the Christina, but had put it off in the hope that someone like us would come along and break trail for him, thus cutting his travel time in half. This is traditional trapper cunning. They putter around with various camp projects, working traplines on previously broken trails because "there's no fur to be found down that line." "That line" is generally the unbroken trail. So they wait for the young fool, and if he doesn't show up, one or the other of them will eventually get around to breaking the trail himself.

Then suddenly everyone finds a reason to travel that trail: Fur is found where none was supposed to be, and excuses are made to visit old friends. In this case, everyone was satisfied. Jim had found his fools, and we were honored to be the first to reach the Christina River from the west.

The seven-mile hike to Jim's minicabin was quick and uneventful. The pleasant plus-10-degree weather didn't bother our healing faces, and the trail was well packed and easy to follow. Even Ki's paws were not a problem, though they weren't quite ready for steady travel. I imitated some leather dog moccasins I'd seen by fashioning booties out of a large wool sock and snare wire. When I put them on, Ki pranced around in distaste, shook his feet, and tried to chew off the strange objects, but eventually quit complaining and joined us on the trail. He lost three of the four by day's end, but they stayed in place long enough to prevent his wounds from reopening.

Sunrise on Hay Creek and Jim's unbroken trail. Pete and I eyed our snowshoes warily before donning them for the first time. Neither of us had ever used snowshoes; no one could say we tested the water before diving in. Perched innocently in a storefront window, they had symbolized to me all the romantic wildness of northern Canada. Now they were simply tools to aid our advance to the next destination.

"They look simple enough," Pete ventured.

"Yeah," I replied. "I guess your toes are supposed to rest on the front crossbar so the ball of your foot rests in the hole." It seemed to work; a few clumsy sidesteps put us on the snow-covered trail and off we went, grinning with pride at having become true northern bushmen.

"Jesus, I didn't know it was supposed to feel like this," Pete complained between strides. It did seem to be taking a lot of effort to lift the snowshoes, but we assumed it was just a matter of getting used to a new technique. Only after we had crippled our feet in this manner for some 200 miles did a trapper eventually remark, "You dumb bastards are wearing your snowshoes wrong!"

With our toes over the front crossbar, each step lifted the entire apparatus, making our toe joints ache terribly. The proper method is to harness the foot farther back on the snowshoe, so that the toes—not the ball of the foot—lie over the hole. This leaves the heel free to rise from the babiche (untanned hide) webbing, so lifting the shoe is much less strenuous. With this revelation the brave bushmen once again became two American tenderfeet trying to cross a continent.

We fell frequently until we began to master the simple snow-shoer's stride. Our incorrect foot position didn't hamper progress, it just increased our workload and strained our foot muscles. But there were plenty of other hazards. Branches hidden beneath the snow took particular pleasure in tripping us. Once I turned just in time to see Pete dive headlong into the snow, one showshoe pointed toward the sky, its nose impaled on a buried branch. A step farther on, another branch lay in wait for me. Pete zipped past as I rolled over and tried to regain my footing.

Jean-Marie's trapping cabin was more typical of the species. It had one small, soot-streaked window, and the secondhand stove was rusted nearly through. Strips of smoked, dried moose meat hung from the rafters, and two dried, prunelike castors (beaver testicles) hung above the door. Castors are sold to perfume manufacturers, and trappers use them as effective bait for their lynx traps. We unrolled our sleeping bags on the cleanest section of floor, where the brown snuff-spit stains and frozen rabbit blood and entrails seemed thinnest.

We spent the entire next day searching for the trail to Saskatchewan. Jean-Marie's traplines ran in a dozen directions; each trail had to be scouted the first mile or two to determine whether it was the right one. A day later we finally found it, then managed to advance thirteen miles before stopping to camp—not more than twelve miles from the border.

This was our first pleasant outdoor camp of the winter, as the temperature was quite moderate. No longer would we make the mistake of using our tent in wintertime; since just past Fort McMurray it had been dead weight in our packs. Instead we snowshoed back and forth to level a sleeping platform, then gathered armloads of spruce boughs to make a thick, insulating mattress for our sleeping bags. The arrangement was far more comfortable than the cramped, frosty tent. We fell asleep with the comforting knowledge that one more day's travel would bring us to a small Chipewyan village in

Saskatchewan called Garson Lake. There, we'd been told, we could purchase additional supplies from the resident fur trader. And none too soon—snaring had been bad the last few days and we had hiked for the past two on half-rations.

I had entered Alberta on a sunny midsummer's afternoon. It had taken five months—and what seemed like a lifetime's worth of hard lessons—to cross that single province.

5 | The White Boys from Little Time

Garson Lake and La Loche, Saskatchewan

December 15, 1977. Our last day in Alberta began windy and overcast. We huddled by the fire, trying to dodge the wind, and ate the last of our rice and bannock for breakfast. I'd hoped that my snares would provide lunch, but they yielded only one rabbit, which we'd promised to Ki. We hadn't been able to feed him for two days, but he never complained. Even after going days without food, he wouldn't touch my meal if I set it beside him and walked away. Although we often ate the same things, he somehow knew which food was for us and which was meant for him, and never crossed the line. He knew this rabbit was his, and watched in dignified anticipation as I skinned it.

It should have been possible to bag a grouse or two during our morning hike; I counted four easy shots in a parklike stand of spruce and tamarack just west of the provincial border. But I had dropped the .22 and broken its front sight, rendering the gun worthless. We might still have had food if we had practiced more strict rationing. But we followed the feast-or-famine approach: When we had it, we ate it. This often caused temporary food shortages, yet I believed the benefits outweighed our hunger. When the wind is blowing and the snow appears to be falling horizontally, it's too easy to roll over in your bag for more sleep with a full belly. Chronic hunger was the best motivation to hike a few more miles each day, aiming for that hot meal at the next supply point.

Shortly after noon we reached the west shore of Garson Lake, which straddles the two provinces, and an hour later, the Saskatchewan border. We didn't stop to celebrate, as we were in the middle of snowshoeing across the ten-mile-long lake and the wind had increased substantially. At each point of land extending into the lake, we encountered eight-foot-tall pressure ridges—chaotic hummocks of upheaved ice. They weren't diffiicult to cross but they broke our trancelike state and reminded us of our growing cold, hunger, and exhaustion. The temperature was only 20 below, but the wind made it feel like 60. Darkness fell quickly, and we squinted toward the horizon trying to spot a welcoming flicker of light from the Garson Lake settlement. Finally, it appeared, and we adjusted our course ten degrees south to head straight for it.

Soon we could hear snowmobiles and children yelling and laughing. Headlights darted up and down a hill in front of the settlement as they raced one another down the slope. We were spotted while still half a mile away, and the headlights raced toward us. Four boys aged about twelve to sixteen pulled up and stared at us with bewildered expressions. "You're white!" the oldest announced. "Where did you crash?"

We explained that we had walked from Fort McMurray, 100 miles northwest, but apparently they didn't believe us. They weren't accustomed to anyone but the occasional Chipewyan trapper arriving from the west, and the only explanation that made sense to them was that we'd walked out from a plane crash. It confused them still more when we declined their offer of a ride into town. "Just haul our packs for us," I requested.

Garson Lake consisted of about a dozen cabins, occupied by six Chipewyan families, clustered around a wide skidoo trail. By the time we topped the hill and entered the village our entourage had grown to tèn Chip kids, giggling and pushing each other out of the way for the privilege of being our closest escort. Ki was not so warmly welcomed, challenging every Indian dog he met in the process of establishing "his" territory. The ensuing fights were fairly evenly matched, until the local dogs decided to defend their turf collectively.

When Ki found himself beneath three sets of snapping jaws, with more on the way, he wisely chose to delay his land-grabbing tactics.

The kids left our packs at the trading post, which turned out to be an unlit cabin with a cold, smokeless stovepipe. The trader had packed up and left the week before, one boy explained, adding that the nearest stores were in La Loche, thirty miles northeast. This was devastating news, since we were totally out of food. Moreover, from Garson Lake we'd planned to hike forty miles southeast through the Grizzly Bear Hills, then cross Peter Pond Lake to reach the Cree village of Buffalo Narrows. Detouring through La Loche would add fifty miles to our route.

For the moment we would have to depend on handouts, and set up housekeeping in the trader's cabin before beginning our hunt for food. By now the news had spread to every cabin that two whites had walked out from a plane crash. As we unpacked, villagers began appearing at our door to meet "the white boys from little time."

The name, we later learned, derived from the rare occurrence of a white reaching Garson Lake from the west; the occasional teacher, trader, or doctor always arrived from the east. When we had crossed into Saskatchewan, we left the Mountain Time Zone ("little time" to the Chipewyans) and entered the Central Time Zone—an hour ahead and thus "big time." The description stayed with us during our Garson Lake visit and even preceded us to La Loche.

Regardless of whether the villagers believed our tale of walking from Fort McMurray, they knew we had no food. None could spare enough supplies to take us across the Grizzly Bear Hills or even as far as La Loche, but everyone brought a small contribution to our evening meal. Eventually we had enough tea, sugar, rice, and bannock for an ample supper and breakfast. Even Ki wasn't forgotten: A shy eight-year-old boy who had been horrified at Ki's mauling by the village dogs (not realizing Ki deserved whatever he got) stole a large moose bone from his father's dogs and appeared in our doorway with his gift, smiling pensively. Aware that attention was focused on him, Ki feigned chagrin and began licking his imagined wounds.

Quite a crowd gathered in the trader's cabin, and the adults, through their bilingual children, plied us with questions about life in the United States. Some of the children had never even heard of our country. They knew of cities to the south, but weren't aware of another nation "down there." In fact, the whole concept of separate countries was foreign to them. The parents, smiling at this, offered as an example of another country the province of Alberta, with its different time zone and laws. A few teenagers had attended boarding school in the city of Prince Albert, thus becoming instant authorities in the community. When I drew pictures of skyscrapers, one boy shouted, "New York! Rod Stewart!" Rock-and-roll: the universal language.

After our hosts dispersed, Peter and I studied the map and debated our dilemma. No one seemed to know of any trails through the Grizzly Bear Hills, but the thirty-mile trail to La Loche was evidently well packed and frequently traveled. This offered an exit from Garson Lake but didn't solve our food shortage.

The next day a solution appeared out of the sky with the arrival of one of the rare flights from La Loche. The single-engine Beaver aligned itself between two rows of young spruces anchored in the lake ice to indicate a two-hundred-yard runway. Its skis skipped along the snow-packed ice; then the plane settled and dropped its speed. The pilot was to fly a family to La Loche, with a return planned for the same afternoon. I could hitch a ride and bring back the food we needed for the hike, while Pete stayed behind to take advantage of Garson Lake's photo opportunities.

La Loche was a good-sized village of about 1,200 Chipewyans and a dozen or so white teachers, nurses, government employees, and Hudson's Bay Company staff. On landing at the terminal—a mobile home next to a bulldozed runway—I didn't stop to sight-see but hustled to the HBC post to purchase enough garlic sausage, macaroni, flour, tea, tobacco, sugar, and candy bars for a two-day hike. I was back at the terminal in an hour, only to learn that ice fog had canceled any further flights that day. "Come back tomorrow," the pilot advised, "and we'll see if we can't get in the air."

With nothing else to do, I ambled over to George LaPrize's cafe. George, a big Indian, serves up the best (and only) burgers in town. The buns drip with grease and the fries likewise are limp and translucent. But fat is what the body craves in 30-below climates; an American fast-food burger would taste as dry as sawdust. As I happily scarfed down the meal, a barrel-chested man introduced himself as Ron McCormick, the local parole officer. On hearing of my plight, he invited me to spend the night in his trailer, and drove me back to the terminal in the morning.

There was still too much ice fog to risk flying, the pilot said: Come back in the afternoon. Ron, doubtful of my having any luck that day, offered his trailer for another night. But when he saw how determined I was to get back, he suggested an alternate plan. A trapper from Garson Lake was in La Loche picking up a fifty-gallon drum of gasoline for the settlement. The drum was already lashed to a toboggan, hitched to his snowmobile. All was ready for departure — except the trapper, who Ron suspected was by now too drunk to drive back to Garson Lake.

Ron directed me to a tar-paper–covered two-room cabin in the center of town. A single string of Christmas lights dangled from the door, all but three bulbs burned out. Frozen laundry hung on a clothesline above two ancient dog kennels. Inside, an obese Chippewayan woman stopped skinning rabbits long enough to point out the trapper, who was indeed past the point of navigating a skidoo anywhere. He was delighted to have me finish his errand so he could proceed with his binge.

I had never ridden a snowmobile before, much less driven one, and had only a vague idea of the trail back to Garson Lake. Since I'd planned to fly back, I was without map or compass. It was past 3:00 P.M., so I would make the thirty-mile trip — twelve miles across the lake and eighteen through the bush — in the dark through an area crisscrossed with traplines. But I was impatient and anxious about Peter, so I bid Ron farewell and yanked the starter cord. Ron pulled off his finely crafted caribou mittens and offered them to me, saying, "They're Eskimo; I got them when I was in the Territories. Take them; I want you to have them." He grinned. "How are you gonna write about me if you freeze your hands?"

My problems began no more than four miles out onto the lake, when a large patch of snow-free glare ice appeared ahead. Anticipating that the toboggan would fishtail, I throttled down to half-speed — exactly what I should not have done. Without speed to maintain momentum, the heavily burdened skidoo lost traction on the slick ice. I revved the engine again and again, succeeding only in adding tread wear to the helplessly slipping rubber tracks. There was nothing to do but unhitch the toboggan and drive back to town for help. With three skidoos hooked to the load, the toboggan inched across the ice to the solid traction of packed snow. I thanked my helpers and went on through the darkness across the remaining miles of lake ice.

On the far shore, near a three-cabin minisettlement called La Loche West, I encountered problem two: The lake bank was so steep I couldn't top it with my load. Six times I raced toward it from different locations, getting three-quarters of the way up only to stall and slide back down. Finally an elderly Indian, hearing the commotion, walked to the bank from his cabin and wordlessly pointed downshore. A few hundred yards farther on was another trail, where I topped the crest on the first attempt.

Four miles down this narrow, crooked trail, the toboggan swung wide on a tight turn and rolled. Fortunately the drum didn't break its lashings and tumble down the embankment, but there was no way I could right the load alone. Angry and embarrassed, I again unhitched the snowmobile and went for help. Back at La Loche West I met Narsis Janvier, whose father, Joe, had directed me earlier. The father and son quickly agreed to follow me to the stranded toboggan, which we soon righted.

The three of us stood there in the moonlight, awkwardly smiling at each other. I wanted to compensate them for the gas their skidoo had burned but thought they might be offended by an offer of money. This is often the case in the northern bush; if an Indian offers help for a cash payment, the help is probably not worth receiving. More often the white man's giving cash as thanks will be resented. (This doesn't apply farther south, where tourism has corrupted age-old customs, or in areas frequented by fly-in sportsmen with fat wallets.) If I'd had my pack, I could have offered a handful of ammunition, a standard expression of thanks.

Tea! That's what they wanted. They certainly had plenty in their cabin and would be far more comfortable enjoying a mug next to the stove than by a campfire in the snow. But you never meet someone on the trail, much less accept their help, without offering a boil-up of tea. I kicked myself for being so shortsighted as not to have a pot and searched my mind frantically for an acceptable substitute. Finally I remembered the Snickers bars in my grocery bag and passed two to each of them. Narsis broke the ice: "Snickers is the best!" he pronounced while munching the frozen bar.

We shook hands and parted friends. Before going on I filled the gas tank by siphoning fuel from the drum. My hands were drenched with gas and burned in the night air; once I fumbled and dropped the funnel in the snow. Retrieving it, I finished the siphoning, started up, and continued down the trail. I was driving blindly now, arbitrarily choosing a trail whenever I came to a fork. I thought I was still traveling southwest, but without a map and compass I couldn't be sure. I regretted skipping the merit badge for star identification in my Boy Scout days.

Ten miles short of Garson Lake the engine missed a few strokes, then died. The sudden silence was profound, broken only by my unprintable cursing. I applied my lawn-mower mechanics to the skidoo, removing anything that would turn by the pressure of my fingers, working by the dim glow of a flashlight whose batteries I'd forgotten to replace. I had no idea what I was doing, but I couldn't tell the people at Garson Lake that I'd abandoned their skidoo without trying to fix it.

Scared to delay any longer, I finally gave up, grabbed the groceries, and jog-walked down the trail. After what I guessed was five miles, I became certain I'd taken a wrong turn somewhere and was now ambling off toward an obscure beaver pond. I decided to double back and try another trail—a totally illogical idea, but unless I did something soon, the fear gnawing my gut would become uncontrollable. One earlobe made a metallic pinging noise when I touched it, and the previously frozen side of my nose threatened to self-amputate. "I'll just top this hill, then turn around and try another trail," I thought aloud.

At the foot of the hill, a magnificent white tablecloth stretched to the horizon beneath the moon: Garson Lake. I ran down the slope and jogged along the lakeshore toward a single faint light about a mile away. It came from the trader's cabin, and some time after 2:00 A.M. I flung open the door to a rush of warmth. Pete, lying in bed in his long underwear reading a novel, looked shocked beyond words to see me.

"Don't even come looking for me; that's okay, you bastard," I chided.

"Dave! I thought you were in La Loche having a good time!" In fairness to Pete, he had hardly been enjoying himself. They were extremely short of supplies in Garson Lake, and he had eaten nothing but rice and bannock during my thirty-six-hour absence.

The residents were understanding about my problems with the skidoo when I explained things in the morning. Two young trappers from La Loche, Tobe "Tiger" Lemaige and Archie Janvier, offered to haul our packs as far as La Loche West while we hiked there on foot. On the way there, they would stop to repair the skidoo, which one of them could drive back to Garson Lake.

When we met them on the trail at noon, they had fixed the machine and had a roaring fire and a pot of hot tea waiting. In daylight the place seemed friendly; I could barely recognize topographical features from the night before. The whole experience seemed like a foggy dream. Over mugs of heavily sweetened brew Tobe explained the mechanical problem: Water had somehow gotten into the fuel line and frozen. I remembered dropping the funnel in the snow while siphoning and not bothering to make sure it was dry before using it again. I was too embarrassed to admit my mistake.

We caught up with our packs at Narsis and Joe's cabin around suppertime. Though I had no more Snickers to give them, we tried to repay their hospitality by helping them decipher some paperwork: government documents, bank statements, and so on. It turned out that Narsis was behind on his skidoo payments because he didn't understand interest. Try explaining that to a man who prides himself on his honesty. After consuming one of Joe's massive bannocks in the morning, we left for La Loche, where we planned to stop overnight, in a flurry of handshakes and thank-yous.

Though the hike across Lac La Loche was not difficult, we stopped for a midday boil-up on a long peninsula nearly bisecting the lake. Normally we wouldn't stop for lunch with town just a few miles away, but a couple of Chip teenagers had met us there and were in the mood to visit. It would have been rude not to build a fire. Pete reached for the teapail, but the elder boy shook his head and proffered a *mickey* (pint) of rye. I turned the cap to break the government seal and took a mouthful, then passed the bottle to Pete. In midswallow I realized the liquor was much too weak to be 80 proof; Peter's surprised eyes said the same. Though the seal had been unbroken, the rye had been watered by as much as half. The boys, for their part, both uttered the "aahhgh" that usually follows a stiff belt.

I asked where they had bought the bottle, how much they had paid, and if they had previously opened it. No, it hadn't been opened, they said. They had paid twenty dollars to a white man in La Loche for the bottle; liquor was illegal in this part of the country, so that's what "they" (the bootleggers) charged. After diluting the liquor and marking up the price, I figured, the dealers were making a profit of about eighteen dollars a pint. I looked at the stuff again; the color, a light tea tone, was right. Apparently a dye had been added with the water. A trace of glue from the seal was smeared to the side, hinting that it had been steamed off and reglued.

A quarter-mile from town we spotted Ron McCormick waving to us from the road. As we approached he shouted, "You boys sure take your time! I've been waiting for ya to join me for burgers since yesterday!" We proceeded directly to George LaPrize's cafe for another round of oozing burgers and vinegar-sopped fries. Nor was Ki forgotten, enjoying his own feast of meaty bones and table scraps the waitress sneaked to him outside.

Our plans to stop overnight in La Loche soon changed. Christmas was only a week away, and neither of us particularly wanted to spend it on the trail. Our brief layover turned into nine days, with plenty of opportunities to witness the good and bad of life in a Chipewyan town.

The Chipewyans are a small tribe living in settlements throughout northwestern Saskatchewan and northeastern Alberta. They are considered a subarctic tribe, like the related Eskimo, or Inuit, as opposed to woodland tribes such as the Cree. The Chipewyans dislike both these more numerous neighboring peoples, for good reason, and the feeling is mutual. The Eskimo pushed them south out of the bountiful tundra into the "land of little sticks," a thinly forested belt of muskeg where game and timber are poor. The Cree then drove the "Chips" north and still look down on them as uncivilized.

La Loche is the northernmost town in Saskatchewan that can be reached by road (gravel), but many more people drive snowmobiles and dogsleds than cars. As in most Indian bush towns, some people still make a living by traditional means—trapping, trading, ice-fishing—but most live on welfare, and alcoholism is a way of life. Ron McCormick told us in graphic detail about some of the cases he had to deal with in his joint role as parole officer and social worker. Several binge-related shootings and stabbings occurred while we were in town. These usually resulted from some understandable provocation; worse were the child abandonments, almost a nightly occurrence. We accompanied Ron on a few calls and were disgusted and outraged by what we saw.

One night we found a four-year-old in diapers and his seven- and nine-year-old siblings in a cold cabin. The fire was nearly out and they hadn't known where to find more wood. Their supper had been some leftover bannock and rabbit they'd scrounged. There was a smell of woodsmoke, but it didn't come from the fire: One child had placed a Coleman lamp beside a wall, and its heat had scorched the tinder-dry wood almost to combustion. In a few more minutes we might have confronted something more than simple abandonment. In reality these children had not been abandoned, just forgotten by normally conscientious parents out drinking. They had probably been able to purchase more liquor than expected, and one night out quickly became three—or however long it took to finish the last bottle.

Some could not afford twenty dollars for a pint of bootleg rye, or didn't get enough of a kick from the liquor. These turned to products off the shelf. Children began by drinking mouthwash, after-shave, or vanilla extract; later they advanced to sniffing gasoline and drinking Lysol. The really far-gone consumed antifreeze and shoe polish; one old-timer told me that the best high was achieved by drinking melted record albums. (He used only old 78-rpm records as "the new ones don't work.")

The Indians naturally resented the white bootleggers who exploited their weakness, and some accused the Hudson's Bay Company of cynically profiteering as well. They demanded that HBC stop selling certain items: "Everyone knows what people buy Lysol and antifreeze for," one person told me.

These problems were brought home to me in dramatic fashion. I've changed some names in the following story. John, a senior member of the Chipewyan band council, had honored Peter and me with an invitation to their Christmas party. The atmosphere was festive, and apparently the liquor ordinance was being ignored in honor of the holiday. As I sat playing cards and sharing a bottle of rye with John and some other older Indians, I grew bold enough to ask how a strong, proud man could destroy his life with alcohol.

It was probably foolish to expect an in-depth answer under the circumstances, but John did his best. He related his people's history of being kicked around by stronger tribes and told how plagues of smallpox and tuberculosis had devastated his father's generation. "The government builds us houses and gives us money because they say we can't make enough from a trapline to feed a family. We survived the wars and the disease, and now they say that we can't support ourselves. What else is there to do but drink?"

This brought up the subject of bootlegging. John explained that the bootleggers were too powerful to be stopped, and several old men at the table nodded agreement. I asked why the RCMP (the Royal Canadian Mounted Police) couldn't do something and was told that a fifty-dollar reward had been offered to anyone who would buy bootleg with marked money. "But fifty dollars is a good chunk of money," I protested. "Why doesn't someone do it?"

"You don't know the bootleggers. Anyone who helped the police would get his arms broken."

The state of my own wallet, no doubt abetted by the effects of rye, gave me the idea of volunteering for this mission. I felt that we would have enough police protection, staying at Ron's, and the reward money was attractive. We could time the buy to take place just before we left town. Besides, I was ready for some excitement.

We talked in low tones, John warning that the bootleggers paid children to eavesdrop. He described a little-known trail heading east out of La Loche, and it was agreed that I would make a purchase with marked money on the day of our departure. The card game was just about to resume when an Indian who had been standing by the door whispered an order for silence. A man knocked, then opened the door and entered; John casually shuffled cards and stepped on my foot under the table.

It was Steve Johnson, the biggest bootlegger in the area. He grinned and repeated "Merry Christmas" several times, as most of the card players left the room. "Greetings," Johnson announced to the three of us who were left. "I brought you a Christmas gift." He placed a mickey of rye on the table, his eyes not leaving John and me. "A lot of people around here don't like me," he went on almost apologetically. "I just wanted to show you that you can't believe everything you hear." With that, he gave a wave and left.

John and I stared at each other in disbelief, then shrugged. Maybe Johnson had some Christmas spirit after all. John poured each of us a drink from the bottle, and the card game proceeded.

I awoke the next day in Ron's trailer, my head pounding, my body doubling up with cramps every few minutes. Pete told me that after our first drink of Johnson's rye I collapsed on the floor, writhing in pain. I had vomited on everything, including the men who had carried me to the trailer, and eventually passed out. John had experienced the same symptoms. It seemed clear that one of Johnson's runners had overheard our plan, and we had been drugged as a warning to stay away.

Such malice, however, was not our dominant impression of La Loche—quite the opposite. People went out of their way for us, and we were the beneficiaries of all sorts of bush wisdom. Among the most memorable was the well-meant advice of an old fur trader named Vic. Shortly after our arrival, he welcomed us to town and commiserated on the lonely life we had endured in the bush, ending with this warning: "Half the women in town got VD and half got TB. Make sure you get the one that coughs!"

Through Ron McCormick we met Jim Perry and George Frederick, schoolteachers who spent much of their spare time training sled dogs and gill-netting through the four-foot lake ice. When Peter and I weren't running errands, mending our gear, or photographing local scenes, we sometimes helped Jim and George with their daily net checks. It was some of the coldest, most miserable work I'd ever experienced.

To reach the net lines, you had to chop through the foot of ice that formed overnight in established holes. Someone then had the unfortunate job of reaching into the water, perhaps to his shoulder, to catch the line with a hooked stick. He began to pull, walking backward across the ice to haul net and fish out, while a coiled rope attached to the far end of the net played out into a second hole. To reset the net, the process was reversed.

As the net spread out on the ice, two other people stood on either side to remove the fish, working quickly yet carefully so as not to tear the fragile netting. The most difficult part of the job was untangling, with frozen fingers, the sections of net snarled by fish flailing around in it. The prize was usually worth the effort, though. George and Jim often netted fifty to one hundred pounds of fish daily, saving the whitefish and pickerel for their own dinners and feeding the rough fish, such as pike and ling, whole to their dogs.

Our friendship with Jim and George, and their passion for training sled dogs, led to a major change in the nature of our expedition. When we first toured their kennels of purebred Siberian huskies, Jim remarked, "You know, you two are crazy to haul those packs when a team of dogs could do the work for you." We had talked about the possibility of acquiring a dog team—Peter had friends in Iowa with a professional racing team—but the whole thing seemed so complicated. We would need a sled, harnesses, dog food. And the animals themselves: even moderately successful racing Siberians cost a minimum of five hundred dollars.

But Siberians are bred to pull light loads at high speed. Jim convinced us that what we needed were freight dogs: wolf-husky crosses, thick-skulled, hundred-pound brutes that could pull tremendous weight over long distances. Indians had been using such dogs for generations, but the current economic reality of feeding a family on a trapper's income had replaced freight teams with noxious ski-doos. The working dog team was becoming a thing of the past.

Jim knew one old trapper, however, who refused to abandon tradition. Just now he was up north somewhere with his dogs, but he was expected back shortly. "I'll bet," Jim speculated, "that if you catch him in a good mood, that cranky old ass would sell you some dogs." The idea of having a dogsledding outfit ourselves was beginning to seem more feasible.

By the time the trapper did return, we only needed two more animals, for in the meantime Tiger Lemaige had given us a couple of year-old pups. They had never worked in harness, and their legs sometimes got tangled when they walked. But they were adventurous, and at a hundred pounds already, they showed potential for great strength. According to Tobe, their parents had been sled dogs, and he reasoned that they should catch on after a week in harness. For a while we called the caramel-colored pup Number One and the brown-and-white one Number Two; we later named them Scotch and Wheels.

While I was recovering from my brush with bush law enforcement, Pete managed to purchase two more dogs from the old trapper for a bargain price of thirty-five dollars, including chains and harness. These dogs were half the size of the pups, about fifty pounds each, with more mongrel and less husky blood. Their personalities were even more strikingly different: These were seasoned trail dogs, survivors who had learned that might is right and would fight their teammates to the death for scraps of food. They had lived by the whip, never knowing affection.

Silver was the foulest-tempered mongrel we had ever seen. He seemed mad at the world, like a moose in rut, and might at any time take a bite out of his owner's leg or lunge for the neck of a nearby dog. Whiskey was a one-eyed lead dog who walked a little crookedly in harness. Unlike Silver, who only became meaner with each lashing, Whiskey's spirit had been broken, and he cowered when he saw the whip. Given a chance, though, his urge to kill was equal to Silver's.

Scotch and Wheels, in contrast, acted as if they were still teething; had it been spring, they would have passed the time chasing butterflies. Putting these two Bambis together with seasoned killers seemed a terrible mismatch, like two New York thugs taking a couple of Nebraska farm boys to the fights. Then there was Ki: How would he view this infringement on his territory? And how would he, with his bonehead love for fighting, fare against practiced killer dogs?

The Catholic priest of La Loche donated an eighth member to our party: a whip. We weren't sure we wanted it, but the priest had traveled thousands of miles by dogsled in his younger days and assured us we would need it. I ran my hand over the braided moosehide—it was long, thin, and greasy-black, a veteran of many freight teams—and wondered if I'd ever be able to use it to lash the back of a dog.

We scrounged the remaining harnesses and chains here and there. Though chains may sound sinister, they were used merely to confine the dogs when they were unharnessed, so they wouldn't run off or attack each other. The harness we used was a true freight design, a yoke collar of rigid leather with a double trace—that is, reins running along each side of the single file of dogs. More modern racing harnesses use only a single trace of nylon webbing.

Jim provided an old handmade six-foot birchwood toboggan that he said he'd been waiting for an excuse to get rid of. With his help and Tobe's we spent an afternoon sanding its bottom and rerigging its sides, or "walls," with fresh hemp. Like the ribs of a canoe, this rope framework was the supporting structure for the cariole, the elongated open canvas sack that would hold our food and gear. Jim added a touch of new technology to this venerable vehicle, gluing strips of Teflon to the underside to decrease its drag against the snow.

Our last evening in town was frantic with packing, preparation, and nervous apprehension. Peter organized 250 pounds of food and equipment—half the weight being frozen fish for dog food—while I sewed canvas bags and cut babiche for snowshoe and harness repairs and general lashing-down. Making babiche involves soaking untanned moosehide in water until pliable, then cutting it in a long spiral from outside edge to center until the sheet is reduced to a twenty-yard strand. Rolled into a softball-sized sphere, it is dried and stored for future use.

Our personal gear, too, had devolved from modern to traditional materials. The rubber and cowhide pac-boots were gone; we had given them to Tobe and Archie for skidooing. Our feet were cradled in moosehide moccasins, made to order by a Chipewyan woman from heavy hides she had tanned herself. After cutting the hide to a pattern traced from our feet, she had stitched it together in the traditional wraparound design, bound with a moosehide thong. The upper had a canvas top that reached to midcalf and acted like a gaiter to prevent snow from packing beneath the pant legs. The moccasins were extremely light and conformed to the shape of our feet; insulated with felt insoles and liners, duffel socks, and three pairs of wool socks, they were much more comfortable than the bulky boots. Also left behind were the goosedown-and-nylon mitts; our hands now flexed caribou skin, moosehide, and beaver. Ron had inherited our conspicuous nylon packs and tent, along with the useless gas stove. I had even trimmed my parka hood with strips of black bear fur.

December 29. Our first day as dogsled masters. At least we looked the part, in our new/old bush garb. The toboggan was loaded, if somewhat awkwardly; the dogs were in harness, though in no particular order as yet. A small crowd had gathered to witness our departure. Since we hadn't found reliable directions through the hills, we'd decided to take the more direct route, 100 miles south by road to Île-à-la-Crosse. It would be an easy breaking-in for the green team.

With Pete out ahead of the team and me behind, I yelled *"Marsh!"* (sometimes corrupted to "mush!" from the French *marcher:* to walk) and slapped the whip against the cariole. Ki yawned. Our mismatched team lurched forward, barely missing the skidoo ahead of us but neatly colliding with the tobaggan it was pulling. Within the first twenty yards it was apparent that the dogs would not respond to our feeble commands of *"Gee!"* (right) and *"Haw!"* (left), though we'd been told Whiskey knew them. Over the next half-mile through town we managed to create three dogfights (thus getting on-the-job experience untangling dog harnesses while dodging snapping jaws), overturn the toboggan twice, collide with another toboggan, get stuck in a snowdrift, and probably cause more than one terrified child to wet his pants.

The Chipewyans obviously found the show great fun. We, on the other hand, were never more eager to get out of town. It was just as well that we were on an easy route — or so I thought at the time.

6 | Strong Medicine
La Loche to
La Ronge, Saskatchewan

For sheer emotional trauma, those first days of dogsled travel, from La Loche to Île-à-la-Crosse, were among the expedition's worst. The dogs fought far more than they pulled, and we tried everything we could think of to stop them. Finally—and it didn't take long—we resorted to the whip.

We had them harnessed in what seemed like the logical pulling order, but it caused problems from the start. One-eyed Whiskey was in the lead, the position he was supposedly trained to, with Scotch second, Silver third, and Wheels in the "wheel" spot, closest to the toboggan. By alternating the veterans and pups, we had hoped to minimize fighting between the old dogs and goofing-off from the youngsters. Most important, we hoped that if the pups had nothing to do but watch a master sledder just ahead, they might get the hang of their job.

It was a good idea in theory, a disaster in practice. Each dog had his own complaint. Since Wheels hadn't yet caught on to pulling, his reins were usually slack, so that every time the toboggan lurched forward he got smacked on the rump. This prompted his logical reaction to run forward, thereby butting Silver squarely in the ass. The first time this happened, Silver dove for the throat of Wheels, who screamed and tried to climb onto the toboggan, naturally jerking the two foremost dogs back in their harnesses.

To Scotch, the more naive of the pups, this signal meant playtime or rest time. Letting his baby fat sag over his eyes, he rolled onto his back, lolled his tongue, and curled his paws as if anticipating

having his belly scratched. It might also have been a posture of sub-
mission, but in either case, the lead dog, Whiskey, was having none
of it and proceeded to give Scotch a harsh lesson in sledding etiquette.

This chain reaction occurred throughout the first day. On film
it might have seemed comical, but in reality the fights were brutal
and scary, each threatening the lives of our dogs and the future of
our journey. Neither Peter nor I had ever struck an animal with
anything but a folded newspaper; now, mere hours into our first sledding day, we began beating the dogs with the whip until we feared
their hides might split, and kicked their sides until it seemed their
ribs or our toes must break.

Eventually they would collapse, not from defeat in battle but
simply from exhaustion and pain from the beatings. The veterans'
jaws fell slack beside the pups' throats, the pups shoved their muzzles
into the shoulders of their would-be killers, and another fight was
over. Peter and I would stare at each other in shock, horrified at the
violence we had just witnessed and inflicted. If we had not intervened,
ignoring our pet-loving past, we would sooner or later have had dead
dogs. Yet the experience always left us with sour mouths and nagging guilt.

Between brawls we did manage to advance a few miles, though
our progress wasn't impressive: twelve miles the first day, fifteen the
second. Rather than following a pristine trapper's trail or an expanse
of lake ice, we were traveling on the unromantic shoulder of a gravel
road. Paradoxically, this actually hampered our mileage, first because
the gravel-strewn snow dragged like sandpaper against the bottom
of the toboggan, and second because the dogs were constantly tempted
to stop and sniff the multitude of road scents. Moreover, we became
a tourist attraction. With dog teams a rare sight these days, every
non-Indian motorist wanted us to model for a snapshot. The attention
was flattering at first but eventually wearing—and time-consuming.

But this was the only practical route at present. The part of northcentral Saskatchewan we were traversing on the way to Flin Flon,
on the Manitoba border, is lowland, often marshy (*muskeg* is the
northern term), heavily laced with lakes and rivers along the water-
sheds of the Churchill and Beaver rivers. We had originally hoped
to follow a more northerly, wilderness route along the meandering

Churchill River, passing through the settlement of Patuanak and beautiful Knee Lake. But we'd heard that there were too many open leads (places where currents or tides keep ice from forming) on the Churchill, and no winter route could take us from Knee Lake south to La Ronge. So we were stuck with the road as far south as Île-à-la-Crosse, where we would pick up a network of trails east to Pinehouse Lake and thence to La Ronge.

We spent our first night out of La Loche in an empty cabin at Post Creek, home to half a dozen families who make fence posts for Saskatoon. Both Peter and I felt ill, maybe in reaction to too much celebrating prior to our departure—or maybe it was just the year-end blues. The dogs acted up nearly as badly the second day, but we made it as far as Bear Creek settlement, where we visited for several hours with two old Chipewyan men. The one who spoke a little English told us an amazing tale, which went something like this:

> Be careful crossing ice. Giant green frog monsters live in some of the lakes. They make traps by thawing the ice and covering the hole with snow. If you fall through, they'll eat you.

The next day, New Year's Eve, we made only nine miles, and both of us felt sick enough to lay over on January 1. That night, while setting out snares, I got caught in an overflow on lake ice and soaked my moccasins. (Water lying on top of ice—often concealed by snow—is a hazard, especially near the shore.) Though we were still feverish the next day, we decided to travel. The third was a better day: With the dogs performing well, we covered twenty miles, reaching Buffalo Narrows by late afternoon. This was the largest settlement in the area, so we stocked up on supplies at the Hudson's Bay Company post and reloaded the toboggan with sixty pounds of fish for the dogs.

We had the odd experience of being minor media celebrities in Buffalo Narrows, due to a CBC television program we had taped in La Loche a few days earlier. Apparently it had aired nationwide, as we would get the same treatment in La Ronge later. While Pete got a ride in a small plane for some aerial shots, I visited the forestry office for information about the trails to Pinehouse via Île-à-la-Crosse. I was still disappointed about not seeing the Churchill River country, but the foresters confirmed that doing so would be impossible — it would require an extra three weeks of trail breaking to avoid the open water.

We made minimal progress the two days after leaving Buffalo Narrows, as the dogs went on strike, probably from overfeeding. On the seventh, however, a *métis* trapper named George Malbuth hauled one hundred pounds of our load the rest of the way to Île-à-la-Crosse and broke trail for us over the ice to town. We set a hard pace, making twenty-one miles — our record to date — and pulling into Île-à-la-Crosse (population 1,500) around 10:00 P.M. After setting us up for the night at the Canada Manpower trailer (the ubiquitous social service agency), George dragged us off to his house for a party, which ended in the traditional gift exchange.

George had had great luck that winter and was in a generous mood; he offered us lynx and wolverine pelts (which we refused) and insisted we take a bear hide, two lynx traps, a 12-gauge shotgun, and ten pounds of moose meat for the dogs. All we had given him was my .22 rifle with the broken sight; I added four hundred rounds of ammunition to even things up a bit.

George, like most of the locals, was mostly Cree; we had passed out of Chipewyan country on leaving La Loche. The Cree, tribally related to the Navajo, think of themselves as far more civilized than the despised "Chips," having lived with whites much longer. They hold fast to many old customs, though, and George flattered me by choosing to share one. At the end of the trading session, he placed in my hand a tiny caribou-skin pouch no bigger than a man's thumb: an Indian lynx lure. It would bring good fortune to his *kiskwa kistimugiman tutum* (crazy American friends), he explained:

The bush holds many secrets, too many secrets even for the Cree. You are not like other *emsiguso* [white men]. White man thinks his books know all and his money protects him. These men are fools. You are white but you have no money. . . . Keep this medicine with you always, and you will not be harmed. Your dogs will run well and your snares will be full.

Like most Indian medicines, the lynx lure is supposed to be forbidden to white men. I didn't know what was inside the tiny bag (George said its powers would be lost if it was opened), but from the smell and feel I guessed some kind of roots. Its faint odor of decaying plants and soil took me deep into the boreal forest, as if I were sleeping on the ground with my face buried in rich humus. That smell is the source of its practical magic: You simply rub it on some sticks near a trap, and the sticks act as a lure. George's recent success seemed proof of its effectiveness. I was exceedingly proud of this gift and showed it off to several people in Île-à-la-Crosse.

We spent January 8 repairing gear, baking bannock, making snares, reading, writing, and photographing—the usual layover chores. We looked forward to starting out for Pinehouse the next day; some trappers had just told us about a shortcut that trimmed the distance to sixty miles, almost due east. We planned to make it a three-day run: eighteen miles the first day to a couple of Cree cabins on the Pine River, twenty-one miles the next to Senyk Lake, and another twenty-one miles by winter road to Pinehouse on the third. We could hook up with George here and there along the way, as he had traps to tend in the area. We didn't get out of town until the tenth, however. George was the culprit: Unbeknownst to us, he had fed the dogs all the moose meat they could hold, ruining them for a run on the ninth.

That was only a trivial setback, compared to what followed. The first day went well, though we didn't quite make it to the cabins. The dogs pulled like champions early in the day, even with our heaviest load yet (280 pounds). Around four in the afternoon they got balky, but we pushed on, crossing the trail north to Patuanak, then crossing three lakes. Earlier, I had stepped off the trail on the Beaver River and sunk into a foot of overflow; the trail on ice was an eighteen-inch-wide plateau flanked by three feet of powder, often hiding overflow. My feet were soaked to the skin but we had no time to stop and make a fire. I figured that when the moccasins froze they would provide some warmth. Around 10:30 P.M. we hit a large lake; it was clear the dogs could go no further, even though Pete had found the cabins by scouting a mile or so ahead.

We spent a comfortable night on a bed of pine boughs and passed a similar day on January 11. By now our winter camping routine was pretty well set, each of us seeing to our preferred chores. We'd travel until 7:00 or 8:00 P.M., perhaps as late as 10:00 if the dogs were running well. Cabin or camp, it took about two hours to gather enough wood for the night and morning. Our backpacker's stove had quickly gone the way of the tent, its meager output unjustified by the time spent fiddling with it. After we both unhitched and fed the dogs, Pete did most of the wood collecting, along with unloading the toboggan, while I cut wood, tended the fire, and cooked (about another two hours in all). Cleanup was mutual; I then set the snares and we retired, with perhaps a few minutes to read or chat. Breaking camp in the morning was time-consuming, too, with game to clean (if we were lucky) and breakfast to cook. Generally we didn't get on the trail until around 11:00 A.M., but we were constantly learning new tricks to speed our pace, especially as the dogs' performance improved.

Our mileage dropped to about ten that second day, and even less on the twelfth—by then it was snowing heavily and the trail was hard to follow. Late on the twelfth we crossed an unnamed lake with much overflow; when we found a trapper's tent at the edge of the windblown muskeg, our frozen moccasins convinced us to camp there. We later named it Turnaround Lake, since it was as far as we got by this route. On the morning of Friday the thirteenth, we found that the trail ended stone-cold half a mile south of the tent.

> *Journal entry, January 13, 1978.* I'm in a Cree tent, sitting on George's bearskin and drinking pea soup. We had planned to be in Pinehouse yesterday, but with no trail, up to 4' of snow (6" last night), and high winds, we won't make it for another 3–4 days. It's only 32–35 miles, but now it seems as far away as New York. Next to the Athabasca Rapids and my near-fatal peak ascent in the Coquihalla Valley, this is by far the worst situation we've been in. . . . Pete left early this morning heading north on snowshoes, trying to find a trail. . . . With all the snow we got last night, snaring will be nearly impossible, [yet] it is essential we snare at least 4 rabbits tonight as we have no dog food left. (Found a beaver carcass for the dogs.) Since Pete has never successfully

snared game and I hate snowshoeing (he likes it) we decided
I would stay behind, cut wood, and set 30 or so snares. . . .

Peter's trip north was unproductive, so we decided to head south
on the fourteenth to search for the winter road to Pinehouse—about
ten miles away, we'd been told. But after progressing only three, we
hit heavy bush and had to retreat to the tent. It would have taken
at least a week to cut a trail south with just our axe. George was
supposed to meet us at Senyk Lake with supplies, but we'd failed
to find a way east. Now not only the dogs were out of food. We gave
the last five pounds of flour to them and ate potatoes for dinner while
we contemplated our only remaining alternative: backtracking thirty
miles to the winter road from Île-à-la-Crosse. We could follow it
south to Beauval, then northeast to Pinehouse—an extra 100 miles
of travel in all.

But our punishment was far from over. On Sunday the fifteenth,
we got a late start, and the temperature dropped 50 degrees in the
late afternoon to almost 40 below. The dogs were already drunk
with weakness and hunger: At half past five, Whiskey collapsed in
convulsions. For the next hour I carried him while Pete harnessed
himself in the lead spot and helped pull. By half past six, Whiskey
was so bad that we shot him. At least we were spared the task of
feeding him to his fellow dogs, as we feared he might be diseased.

Around 10:00 P.M., halfway across another unnamed lake, the
dogs gave up. We unharnessed them and dragged the toboggan to
shore ourselves, leaving it and the dogs there while we walked to
the Pine River cabins, which we reached at 1:00 A.M. We left some
rabbits we'd snared earlier for the dogs—they were the first game
we'd gotten in days.

Late the next day Pete and I caught a ride into Beauval Forks
on the old logging road and gorged on a hot dinner at Rose's Cafe.
Again, we'd left the dogs and toboggan cached thirty miles up the
road; Leonard, the cafe owner, helped us retrieve them the following day with his truck and skidoo. We stayed in Beauval three more
days, both of us recovering from flu and Pete getting treated for blood
poisoning from a cut hand as well. We worked a bit in the cafe for
our keep, bought supplies, and gave the dogs a well-deserved rest.

One night in the cafe I was brooding about our run of bad luck since Île-à-la-Crosse. My lynx lure medicine bag didn't seem to be working; aside from the disastrous shortcut, I'd had far better results snaring before George gave it to me. I glanced up in surprise to see Vic, the old white trader from La Loche, and over coffee I quizzed him. "Say, Vic," I began, "you've been living with these people most of your life, eh?"

"Hell, yes," he replied. "Ain't a Chip or Cree in a hundred miles ain't sold me a fur."

"Well, then, tell me." I set the lure before him. "Ever seen one of these?"

"God damn Jesus! How the hell'd a kid like you get ahold a that? That stuff's powerful; don't go . . . " Vic's warning was cut off as a Cree woman yanked me from my seat and hustled me into the back room. Her eyes burned into mine as she whispered, "Fool! Stupid white fool. That medicine was made for you alone. Use it wisely and it will keep you safe. You show your medicine to that man like it was a joke. You have made the Maker angry. Wetigo [the Cree devil] will not leave your camp now."

She told me that the only way to make peace with the Maker was to take the medicine deep into the bush and bury it in a safe place, along with a gift. "Tell him you are sorry. Tell the Maker that you are white and do not know about these things. Tell him this with your heart. This is the only way to drive Wetigo from your camp. When you leave, do not look back. If you look back, you are unsure of your path. A man must know his path or he is not a man. The Maker will not help such a man."

The encounter impressed me, but I wasn't ready to let a crazy old woman scare me into tossing away my most prized gift. We set off for Pinehouse on the twentieth. Having sent one hundred pounds of our supplies ahead by truck, we sprinted twenty miles that day and still camped by 8:00 P.M. The next day we made eighteen miles to camp near Senyk Lake, the three remaining dogs pulling surprisingly well, and another uneventful twenty-one miles on the twenty-first brought us to Pinehouse.

We rested three days in a cabin at Pinehouse Lake, Bing Crosby's old fishing haunt. We had good company: a wealthy Cree fisherman named Alfred Hanson, and bush pilot Gord Wallace, who showed us a good route to La Ronge. Traveling again on the twenty-sixth, we made the last seventy-five miles to La Ronge in another five days. This leg was relatively without incident; we lost the trail briefly a few times but always managed to find it again.

The dogs were finally looking like a team, with Silver at least adequate in his new role as leader. The pups had lost most of their baby fat and were amazingly strong; Wheels was proving an exceptional wheel dog. They no longer fought, and now that they were used to us and their roles, we could at last show them affection. They went wild with delight when we played with them. Ki wasn't crazy about the new situation, though, and was on thin ice in his self-appointed job as team foreman. He sometimes tried to butt into the lead, huffing and snorting like a make-believe sled dog, but the real workers had grown wise to the fraud and ignored him. The dogs were our family; we took their training and nutrition seriously, and rejoiced at seeing them put in a hard, steady day without balking.

> *Journal entry, January 30, 1978.* A more-or-less typical day: Hung around until 1:00 P.M. to give Pete time for photography. A storm was coming up fast with heavy snow, strong winds, and −10 degrees F. . . . Crossed Hall Lake into the Morin Lake Reserve, one of the most destitute and backward reserves I have seen. Crossed Sanderson Lake as winds increased to the worst we have seen all winter. Stopped for a breather in a Cree cabin on Sikachu Lake, then continued north along a river out of the reserve and into Egg Lake. Camped at 8:00 P.M. in the lee of an island in West Egg Lake. Again, we had gathered enough wood to make an enjoyable evening around the fire, though on the lake the wind howled. Eggs and potatoes for dinner. I set snares about 11:00 P.M. while watching the most brilliant northern lights show of fluorescent green. (16-mile day)

It was a real culture shock to hit the paved road a few miles outside of La Ronge, a modestly booming resort town of five thousand. The dogs were so excited by the new scents that I had to ride the last three miles to keep them at a reasonable pace. Gord and Beckie

Wallace showed us the cabin where we were to stay, and then fed us a taco dinner. We hadn't been to a pub since the end of November, so we celebrated the halfway mark of our winter travel (December 1 to February 1) at a tavern with Gord and some of his pilot friends. Or at least they did: Pete and I dozed off rather soon.

La Ronge
February 2, 1978

Dear Mom, Dad, Steve & Sara,
Bad news. We spent all yesterday flying in a Cessna [to check our] proposed route to Flin Flon—over Lac La Ronge to Deschambault Lake via Wapawekka Lake—only to find that the trail ended after 40 miles. Most winters this route is as hard-packed as a highway, but it hasn't been used this year. We were lucky to have found out this way, or we'd have had another Pinehouse incident. So now we're con- demned to the drudgery of 170 miles to Flin Flon by road. We spent quite a while flying over the Churchill River, spotting moose and caribou; Pete got some of his best wildlife shots ever. . . . I didn't mean to complain about the winter [earlier in the letter]—it's by far my favorite part of the trip thus far. . . . I'm not tired of the bush travel—I'm tired of thinking, talking, and being "expedition" 7 damn days a week. Pete has mentioned several times that I always get in a bad mood the last day on the trail (coming into town), stay in a lousy mood in town, then am on top of the world upon leaving.

We were told that after the first twenty miles of pavement, the road to Flin Flon would be dirt, nicely covered with packed snow. After checking around in vain for some fresh sled dogs, we left La Ronge on the fourth, looking forward to a few days of easy travel. Instead, we got winds, the worst we had yet encountered, from a southern Saskatchewan blizzard. And the dirt road had just been scraped by snowplows, leaving mostly bare gravel to drag the toboggan over. The wind continued to blow steadily for two days, and game seemed to vanish; once again we were nearly out of dog food.

After covering a scant twenty-five miles in two days, we decided

Peter would have to hitchhike back to La Ronge to buy wheels for the toboggan. After he left, I set my snares in some promising-looking game runs and waited in a cabin a few miles away. The wind blew fiercely the next day (February 8), and my snares remained empty. When Pete got back that night, I tentatively raised the question of our miserable luck since receiving the lynx lure in Île-à-la-Crosse. He and I agreed that a person makes his own luck—but I was beginning to wonder.

I went out to check the snares again around midnight. I had set them carefully and was confident that the evening's bright moon would reveal half a dozen neatly strangled rabbits. The strong wind burned my cheeks as I followed my trail past one empty snare after another. Tension grew into near panic, and I squeezed the lynx lure for reassurance as I approached the last snare.

Empty! My mind raced and stopped; Wetigo *had* to be with me. The medicine must be real, and it was finally time to bury the damn thing. I thought guiltily of the dogs going hungry but comforted myself with the hope that our luck would change after I made the offering. Yet I had none of the traditional gifts—tobacco or ammunition—to leave with the pouch.

Just as I turned back to the cabin to get some, a particularly strong gust of wind blasted snow and willow branches into my face. As I stumbled and fell, I saw not three feet away a flash of white in the moonlight. After that gust, the fierce wind abruptly dropped, and in the sudden stillness I could hear the thrashing and screaming of a rabbit, caught in the snare I had checked not sixty seconds earlier. I jumped quickly, snapping the neck of our supper, and thanked the Maker for his miraculous gift. Then I realized that it truly was *his* gift: the gift to be buried with the medicine pouch.

Ki sat on the edge of the ravine where I dug through the snow with my hands. Three feet down I came upon a spongy layer of caribou moss, then a sand bed. Carefully removing the braided wire noose from the rabbit's neck, I coiled and placed it in the hole. The still-warm rabbit was laid on top of it, curled as if asleep. I sniffed the lynx lure, noting its musky smell for the last time, and set it between the creature's forelegs. Then I covered the grave with moss and snow, while my heart spoke to the Maker.

That rabbit, the first I had snared in many days, marked a turning point. Within the next two days we caught four. The wind left us for good, and though there were some rough spots still to come that winter, our fortunes seemed dramatically changed for the better. I didn't look back.

7 | Across Lake Winnipeg

Flin Flon to Berens River, Manitoba

The last two months of winter 1978, February 4 through April 4, were a long and relatively uneventful slog—330 miles in all, from La Ronge to the western shore of frozen Lake Winnipeg in Manitoba. Dave and Peter spent three weeks of that time in Flin Flon, taking in such north-country diversions as snow carnivals, dog races, Western Hockey League games, and an annual trappers' festival in The Pas, Manitoba. They met the usual quota of helpful or at least colorful natives, like "Old Keystone," aka Gilbert Stove of Easterville, Manitoba—a half-Cree who was impressed by Dave's enthusiasm for trapping and showed him a few tricks. But mainly they just ground out the monotonous miles along snow-covered roads and lakes.

In the draft of his article for Quest *magazine, Dave recalls, "Game was scarce in the scrubby spruce forests of western Manitoba. Sometimes the only food for the dogs was meager scraps of fish scavenged from the ice around abandoned commercial fishing sites. Whenever we spotted circling ravens, we'd race ahead to reach the fish before it was all devoured. Ki, always first on the scene, would chase the birds away and guard the pile of fish entrails from their diving raids until the rest of us caught up.*

"March's climbing temperatures made travel increasingly miserable. The added friction of pulling over wet snow often exhausted the dogs after just a few miles, forcing us to lighten the load by leaving

food and gear behind. Our feet in waterlogged moccasins strained to lift snowshoes weighted with soggy snow. All winter we had complained of the bitter cold—now we bitched that it was too hot!"

But a final daunting stretch of winter travel loomed just ahead: a 120-mile crossing of Lake Winnipeg, which promised some of the journey's most spectacular sledding. Lake Winnipeg is among Canada's largest—about the size of Lake Erie—and is the remnant of a huge Pleistocene lake called Lake Agassiz. A major resort area in summer, in winter it represented a formidable obstacle, with potentially fierce winds, huge pressure ridges to negotiate, and scant means of resupplying.

These 120 miles would be the last covered by dogsled; on Lake Winnipeg's eastern shore, at the mouth of the Berens River, the expedition would make the transition from canine back to canoe travel. There, too, they would celebrate reaching Mile 2,400—the halfway point of the entire journey. There could be no further dawdling, however; they had to make it across the lake before the spring thaw began in earnest—which could be any time after mid-April.

Last stop before the crossing was the village of Grand Rapids, where Dave and Pete reorganized their supplies for speed, gave a talk to high school students, and were entertained by Royal Canadian Mounted Police Sergeant Dominic French and his Inuit wife, Alice. These two were local celebrities: Alice had published a book about her childhood in the Arctic, and Dom had twice been chosen by the RCMP as royal escort to the visiting queen of England.

April 7, 1978. Dom and Alice French stood on the shore of Lake Winnipeg and waved good-bye. I glanced over my shoulder for a last look at Grand Rapids, then turned to survey an expanse of ice stretching across the horizon and the dogs strung out ahead of the toboggan. Before us lay the last leg of our 1,200-mile winter trek. It was already early April, and time had become critical. Any day now the temperature could rise above freezing and leave us stranded in a sea of slush. Though the ice was still six feet thick, it's nearly impossible to drive a team over wet snow. Both we and the dogs had been reduced to half rations, leaving every spare ounce of food and gear behind in Grand Rapids.

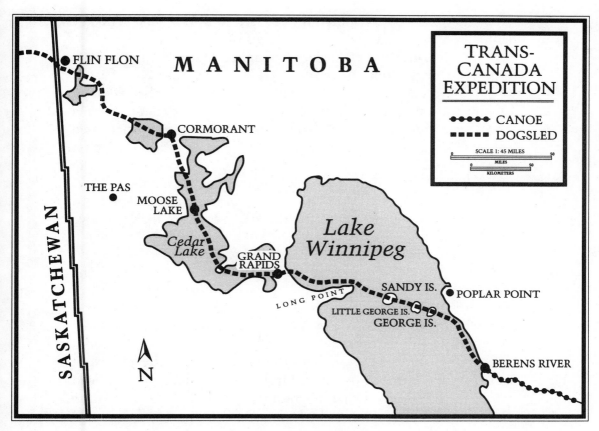

Flin Flon to Berens River, Manitoba, June–July 1978

I doubted we'd make many miles that first day. Pete and I had just recovered from the flu and were quite weak. The dogs were also questionable. Wheels, whom we'd gotten as a pup in La Loche, had sprained a leg two weeks earlier and had to be replaced. We traded him for an expressionless Indian dog, whose strength and uncomplaining nature won him the workhorse wheel position, first harness from the toboggan. He didn't have a name and for weeks we simply referred to him as "the new guy"—so naturally, New Guy became his permanent name. Silver, next in line, had simply played out a few days before Grand Rapids. To run him further in harness would have killed him, so we reluctantly retired him. Lead-dog Whiskey had been left behind in the deep snows of Saskatchewan.

That left only Scotch from our original team. We'd promoted him to lead dog, which suited his inflated ego just fine. For a fourth, we borrowed a bony Irish setter cross named Jack, who looked more at home in front of a fireplace than on a freight team. Yet he turned out to work surprisingly well in harness, and the others accepted him immediately, which is uncommon. Usually a new dog must endure a week of fighting and harassment, at the expense of the master's control, while a new pecking order is established. Ki remained the loafer of the bunch, usually running out in front with Pete, sometimes dropping in line ahead of Scotch to make believe *he* was lead dog.

Conditions were good that day, and we covered a respectable twenty-two miles before stopping to camp at half past seven on the northern shore of Long Point, a huge dagger of land jutting a third of the way out into Lake Winnipeg. Pete began setting up camp in a clump of scrub willows, transforming a snowbank into a living space, while I unharnessed and chained the dogs, tossing each a frozen fish. It always hurt not to have enough to feed the dogs well. Scotch held the frozen fish in his front paws and ate it from head to tail like a Popsicle. Rooting around in the snow for a last crumb and finding nothing more, he looked up at me with a hint of betrayal in his chocolate-brown eyes.

Pete and I splurged on our own supper with grilled cheese sandwiches, enjoying the rare luxury of store-bought bread. We had no tent, but the temperature hung around zero and our goosedown bags on spruce bough beds were warm and comfortable.

After a leisurely breakfast of pancakes, tea, and moose sausage, we set off in the hope of reaching the tip of Long Point, twenty-four miles east, by the end of the day. That afternoon, though, we were pinned down by a whiteout blizzard after covering twenty-one miles and had to set up a hasty camp. As night fell, the temperature rose and the snow changed to rain, which continued all night. I slept little, rolling from one puddle to another and dodging the stream of ice water that trickled through the breath hole in my sleeping bag. Even worse than the physical discomfort was the nightmarish fear of being caught in the spring thaw with no food. That morning we were too cold, wet, and depressed to bother with breakfast.

We'd heard a rumor in Grand Rapids about a few old cabins near the end of Long Point, about four miles from our present camp. This sounded like the most attractive immediate prospect, so we stumbled along the shoreline, squinting through the steady drizzle for a sign of them. I walked stiffly, trying to minimize the chafing of my sodden wool clothes; rain gear was not part of our winter outfit. After six miles we turned around and retraced our steps, then reversed direction again, praying that the cabins were more than a rumor. I shuffled along behind the team, coaxing them on and reminding myself to keep my eyes on the shoreline; finally Pete shouted *"Cabin!"*

Three structures stood (more or less) in an overgrown clearing among the pines. Two had no roofs at all; the best one had three walls and half a roof, which, if braced, could make it a passable shelter. Poking around, we found miscellaneous pieces of burned-out wood stoves, which we jury-rigged into a functioning stove. Set up near the sagging entryway, it sent smoke drifting out where the caved-in roof had been. Firewood came from the walls of an adjoining cabin, and our socks were suspended over the stove to dry and season the stew.

We spent two days huddled in this makeshift lean-to. Our dripping sleeping bags hung near the stove by day, but alas, absorbed more smoke than heat. At night we bedded down on the floor where a pile of rotting fishnets had been. The bags never did dry out. Our town treats were gone, and we fell back on standard fare: two meals a day of split pea, potato, and salt-pork stew. Our only hope of finding more food lay in a lighthouse forty miles out on the lake. The Royal Canadian Mounted Police had given us permission to raid it, but we couldn't always rely on their advice. They had also said there would be fish caches on Long Point for our dogs, and we'd arranged with them for a one-hundred-pound airdrop of fish. We'd found no caches and heard no planes.

Dense fog held us on the point. Our route angled southeast from Long Point, and between us and the Berens River settlement lay fifty-five miles of open ice. There were islands at twenty, thirty, and forty miles out; the Sandy Islands chain would be our next camp. Under ideal conditions, visibility over the ice was ten miles, but for several days it had been almost nil. Proceeding by compass left too much risk of missing the islands altogether. We even considered turning back to Grand Rapids, waiting for break-up, and canoeing across the lake, but I'd heard horrifying tales of canoe travel on this windswept expanse. The chance of succeeding by dogsled this late in the year wasn't great, but I still preferred it to waiting.

Some notes I took while at the cabin detail our predicament:

Journal entry, Monday, April 10, 1978. Woke at 6:30 A.M. Snowed all last night and is still coming strong. Can't snare rabbits as long as it keeps up. Still waiting to make the crossing to Sandy Islands—a few specks of land 20 miles out. Visibility less than half a mile today. God, we'll have to spend another night in this rotting cabin ruin.

Snow continued throughout day. Oatmeal for breakfast, moose stew for lunch, moose sausage for supper. Fed dogs a tiny morsel of moose meat. Dogs are down to quarter rations. The meat and fish will be gone tomorrow and we'll have to feed dogs flour and potatoes.

The lake looks like a mountain range—eight-foot-thick slabs of ice jutting as high as 30 feet into the air along the pressure ridges. It's nearly midnight now. Can't sleep, thinking about tomorrow. Got to make the crossing tomorrow regardless of weather. I'm really worried about food. Fishing season ended April 1, so we won't find any commercial fishermen out. Maybe we'll find somebody poaching. In this weather it could take us another week to reach Berens River. All we have left for two men and four dogs are five pounds moose meat, one pound butter, five pounds potatoes, one pound split peas, one pound oats, two pounds flour. This isn't even enough for us, much less the dogs. Plenty of tea and sugar—at least our bladders will stay full.

Dogs were acting up—just got back from checking on them. Goddamned New Guy slipped his chain and stole two pounds of moose pemmican. As short of food as we are! He'll be so bloated he won't be worth a damn in harness tomorrow. Well, snow or clear, we leave anyway. If we don't make the islands, we'll have to camp on ice. God, I dread that.

The next morning brought temperatures in the 20s and a blessed cloudless sky. After a final check of the compass, I tapped a whip on the toboggan and shouted *"Marsh!"* New Guy waddled off looking like a watermelon in harness, burping off his midnight gorge. Worse, the exercise acted as a laxative, and I suffered the sled driver's curse of his quarter-hourly eruptions.

The pressure ridges were fantastic. Stark, blue-white towers rose over hills and giant slabs of ice. From valleys of glaring, eye-searing snow, sheltered from the wind by ice walls, heat rose in shimmering waves. There was no noise here, not even a whistling wind. We meandered between the ridges, inching along and feeling for hidden holes and crevasses that crisscrossed the surface. The dogs balked in fear of the cracks, jerking back in their harnesses; Scotch refused to lead unless I walked ahead and yanked him along. Despite our caution, a crevasse would sometimes grab us by the legs, the jagged ice leaving our shins bruised and bleeding. While the rest of us struggled along, Ki played pathfinder, leaping from ridge to ridge as if mocking the harnessed dogs.

Eventually we broke free of the pressure ice and gazed to the horizon across a vast tabletop of windblown snow. Somewhere out there, eighteen miles or so farther, was our island. As the day wore on, I began to doubt we would ever find it. It seemed like we had been shuffling across this featureless desert for weeks. Hours went by with no sign of land, and I fell into the dangerous habit of questioning the compass. But we were still cutting across the wind-carved fish-scale pattern in the snow at the same angle. The island *had* to be ahead.

Pete and I both falsely spotted land several times. Each time it turned out to be a low-lying cloud or discolored pressure ridge. Toward midafternoon, though, we sighted three pinpoints that refused to dissolve.

Sledding toward a distant speck of land is agony: Miles go by beneath your feet and still the island appears no closer. We pass the time with self-inflicted torture: Peter guesses the island is eight miles away; I argue seven. Fifteen minutes more, and I wonder if it might now be six and a half miles. I want to stop and ease my leaden feet, but each step takes us a yard farther, and conscience urges us on.

The low-pitched hum of the toboggan sliding over crusted snow, combined with the rhythm of moccasined feet, has a hypnotic effect. If I lag, the brake rope jerks me forward, an insistent reminder to keep the pace. Occasionally I glance ahead to see Pete plodding in front of the team, or behind to make sure that we're keeping a straight course. But mostly my eyes are lowered, watching the snow slide by underfoot. Traveling long distances by dogsled requires a certain mindlessness that takes months to learn. One must remain alert for any of a hundred mishaps that can cripple humans or dogs, yet the monotony can only be endured by shutting off thought and escaping into dreams. The tempo of the dream is sometimes interrupted: The harnesses tangle, and I am jolted back to reality—feet cold, nose needs blowing, body begs for rest. But once the dogs return to their steady pace, the beat resumes and I am back in my dream, warm and content. Thus eight miles become two, hours become minutes, and torturous days become tolerable—even pleasurable.

The sun was now low in the sky, turning our back-trail into a silver ribbon that unrolled to the horizon. Dizzy for a moment, I shook my head, started to stumble, then made myself sit down to keep from falling. I was experiencing vertigo; it happened a few other times on the expedition. The setting sun painted the snow and the sky exactly the same salmon-pink color, producing the weird sensation that there was no up or down, left or right. It looked like the island before us was standing on its head. When the sun dipped lower, the contrast between snow and sky returned and the island fell from space back to the horizon.

Three miles from land, just as we could begin to discern individual trees, the dusk faded to darkness. To our surprise, a beacon began to flash, presumably from the northernmost point of the Sandy Island chain. Hoping to find an occupied cabin there, I headed off north toward the light while Pete drove the dogs on to the main island. If I found no cabin, I would turn south and build a fire on the main island to guide them.

The northern island was deserted, its only structure a fifty-foot steel tower topped with the beacon, which guided summer boaters around the shoals. I jogged back over the ice to find a suitable campsite on the main island, and soon a campfire blaze illuminated the surrounding trees. I gratefully hugged its warmth, letting it saturate my body; the temperature had dropped well below zero and my sweat-soaked clothes had done little to keep out the cold. Soon the dogs' whines drifted in from the darkness as they raced toward the camp, haphazardly bashing the toboggan against ice hummocks. Their frenzied pace abated when they caught my scent and realized this was merely our bare-bones camp, not that of some food-glutted stranger.

We retired early, ate a dinner of watery moose stew in bed, and slept fully clothed, right down to our moccasins. The leaching action of goosedown helps draw moisture out of one's clothes during the night, and the moccasins dry out better too. The only drawback is that one's feet thaw very slowly this way, and as the moccasins dry, they shrink, until it feels like one's toes are caught in a red-hot vise. We would spend the first hour each morning walking stiffly and painfully while our footgear stretched back into shape. Nineteenth-century trappers' journals are peppered with complaints from the victims of shrunken moccasins, such as, "John spent the morning standing in a creek until his moccasins stretched out" (Journals).

Even dressed, I slept poorly, as my sleeping bag was still fairly wet. I spent the night in a shivering ball, my knees drawn up to my chin, and woke to find Pete gone. Bewildered, I got up and followed his tracks through the snow to a small bay on the far side of the island. Six dilapidated cabins dotted a clearing; smoke rose from the one Pete's tracks led to. I found him in front of a massive iron cook stove. Its fire compartment had rusted away, so he had built his fire in the main oven space, after knocking a hole in the back wall.

This appeared to be an abandoned fishing camp. The cabins looked like they hadn't been occupied for twenty years or more. As I browsed around his discovery, Pete explained what had led him there. "I've never been so cold as I was last night. A few hours before sunrise I got up to build a fire, but it was too cold to hold the match. I went back to bed and began to really worry about how cold I was. I dozed for a minute and had a dream: Two men dressed like fishermen walked up to my sleeping bag and looked down at me. One, who called himself Isaac, spoke to me, saying that if I didn't go to the cabins I'd freeze. When they walked away, I woke up and started walking in the same direction they had gone. The dream led me straight to these cabins."

Then he pointed to a spot on the plank wall above the stove where a name and date were carved. The date was 1846 and the name was Isaac.

While Pete brewed up a welcome pail of tea, I sat down by the stove and began making rabbit snares. I had fashioned so many of them over the winter that I'd gotten into assembly-line production. Eyeballing the proper lengths of brass wire, I fed sections across the floor with my right hand while the axe in my left rose and fell in matching rhythm, severing wire at two-foot intervals. I heard an odd-sounding "chop" and looked down at the wire. The end of my thumb, nail and all, lay on the floor. The axe had grazed the corner of the thumb, exposing the bone.

I paced in circles, gripping my hand high in the air and nodding my head up and down, trying to block out the throbbing pain. Like other "nonessentials," the first-aid kit had been left behind to save weight. I pulled my snotty, soot-streaked bandana from my hip pocket and threw it into the brewing tea; then, after packing the wound with salt, I wrapped the bandana tightly around the thumb. I hoped that the salt and the tannic acid from the tea would be enough to overcome any germs.

An hour later we were back on the ice, heading south toward another speck of land on the horizon. This was Little George Island, where, the RCMP had assured us, there was a cabin well stocked with emergency supplies. I held my hand above my head and staggered along behind the dogs, grateful for the numbing cold. Six hours later we reached the island, a deserted, structureless shoal no more than one hundred yards long. We were both exhausted, and my hand throbbed, begging for medication. Anything seemed better than staying here, so we swung back onto the ice and headed for the next island, the sun nearly touching the horizon. It was 2:00 A.M. and we were twenty-two miles from the morning's camp when we rounded the point of George's Island to a welcome sight. Silhouetted against the sky, a line of cabins fronted a lighthouse that cast its cheery beacon in all directions.

We stayed on George's Island for two days, resting the dogs and our own weary bodies. In the lighthouse keeper's home we found the food that the Mounted Police had promised and that we so desperately needed. [*Dave may have confused Little George with George's Island in speaking with the RCMP.*] It was just macaroni, flour, potatoes, and rice, but enough to get us to the Hudson's Bay Company trading post at Berens River. Peter, scrounging through the garbage dump, made a prize find: a loaf of bread that had been thrown out in the fall because of a speck of mold and been preserved through the winter. We found no first-aid kit, but my thumb survived the hot-tea-and-salt treatment.

It was only another twelve miles to Lake Winnipeg's eastern shore, and then another thirty-five miles south to Berens River. The prospect of mild daytime temperatures prompted us to travel the open-lake miles at night, taking advantage of the refrozen surface. The dogs ran surprisingly well on their new diet of potatoes and flour; unfortunately, it left a lasting impression on their digestive systems. Jogging behind, I suffered the brunt of the foul air. I graciously offered to trade places with Pete and lead for a while, but the dogs had been sufficiently audible that he, just as graciously, declined the invitation.

Knowing the dogs were well rested, I allowed myself the luxury of hitching rides now and then. As they marched eastward with Pete trotting ahead, dodging a few crevasses and checking the compass by flashlight, I napped on the toboggan, bounced awake by the occasional large hummock. It was a delight to lie atop the cariole gazing skyward at the pale wash of northern lights; to be lulled to sleep by the soft sound of crunching snow and the gentle sway of the toboggan. Months later, coming acoss this note in Admiral Richard E. Byrd's book *Alone*, I was reminded of that night:

> It was exhilarating to stand on the barrier and contemplate
> the sky and luxuriate in a beauty I did not aspire to possess.
> In the presence of such beauty we are lifted above natural
> crassness. And it was a fine thing, too, to surrender to the
> illusion of intellectual disembodiment, to feel the mind go
> voyaging through space . . . It could travel the universe with
> the audacious mobility of a Wellsian time-space machine.

Long past midnight a skidoo headlight appeared in the distance. We met near shore; the driver and his partner, two young Salteaux Indians, were surprised to see us but were friendly. They were from Poplar River, a few miles from our landfall on the eastern shore, and were heading south to buy bootleg for illegal sale on the "dry" reserves to the north. Assuring us that we were just where our calculations should have brought us, they took our order for a mickey of rye and wished us well on our journey.

The next day we decided to try for Berens River in one push, even though thirty-five miles was twice our daily average. Their bellies full of potatoes, the dogs pulled relentlessly. We met the young smugglers again early in the day, their toboggan sagging under a load of bottles. Though a pint of rye will sell for as much as twenty-five dollars, they refused money for ours. A little later we met a family of Salteaux driving a huge, two-track, heated and enclosed snow machine. After a pleasant chat, they left us with a dozen freshly baked cinnamon rolls. In the warmth of the afternoon sun I lay back on the toboggan, nursing my half of the rye and thumbing through an old *Playboy*, content as a Southern gentleman sipping his mint julep.

Our winter was over. Behind us lay 1,200 miles of snow and ice. As I lazed in the hot tub that night at Jack Clarkson's boarding house on Berens River, I thought about our faithful sled dogs, whom we would now leave behind. They had pulled us all those miles, often going days without food, because it was their nature to pull and to please us. Some were already gone, of course: I thought of Whiskey, lying beside a trail near the Churchill River with a slug in his head; Wheels, probably recovered from his sprained leg and now part of a sled team on a Manitoba reserve; Silver, played out by age and miles, being nursed back to health by an Indian boy in Grand Rapids.

Scotch, who had grown from a goofy pup into a strong and loyal lead dog, would be shipped back to Grand Rapids to become part of an Indian team destined for the traplines, along with New Guy and Jack. Peter and I would fly back to the States for a month or two, to await the break-up of ice on the river and gather the equipment to continue by canoe. Ki was to stay in Berens River while we were gone, looked after by Brother Leach at the Roman Catholic mission. We were sad to leave him, but thought of him as our representative—our link to the trail. It was like leaving part of ourselves in the bush.

8 | Up the Berens River

Lake Winnipeg, Manitoba, to Birch Lake, Ontario

June 3, 1978. The Perimeter Airways Twin Otter banked over the Hudson's Bay Company post and the Catholic mission on its final approach into Berens River. As we taxied down the dirt airstrip cut through scrub spruce, I spotted Peter and Ki waiting by the terminal—a converted motor home. The plane's engines revved, then droned, and Pete strode forward to greet the three people stepping down beside the wing: the pilot, a jovial priest, and me.

They were a grand sight: Peter in a new Gore-Tex rain suit that still smelled of its packing, looking as casually confident as an Ivy Leaguer in Harris tweeds. And Ki, sporting newly sun-bleached fur and his usual smug expression. We set off immediately to see our new gear, which had been shipped to Berens River earlier (most of it donated by a Winnipeg outfitter called The Happy Outdoorsman).

Everything was crisp and clean and shiny; anticipation lay in every smooth surface and sharp crease. Our eighteen-foot Grumman canoe lay keel-up, its hull brilliantly unblemished. The canvas spray cover (to keep our gear dry in rapids and waves) was stiff with factory starch. Empty olive-drab packs stood erect as if still filled with stuffing for a window display. Freshly varnished canoe paddles reflected the sun, fairly begging for the punishment of river rocks. The final 2,300 miles of our journey would be entirely on water, and I

124

Dave hiking on the tracks of the Canadian Pacific Railroad, near Clearwater, British Columbia.

In camp on an island in Lake Mistassini, Quebec, Dave watches a trout cook over the fire.

Prospector Clayton Morris in his cabin in the Coquihalla Valley, British Columbia.

*Ki in a meditative pose,
eastern British Columbia.*

*Canoe and gear strewn on the
riverbank after one of many spills
on the Athabasca River, Alberta.*

Dave and the dog team at sunset, eastern Saskatchewan.

Pete and the dogs relaxing in camp, Lake Winnipeg, Manitoba. Photo by Dave Halsey.

Pete adjusting the canoe's sailing rig,
Albany River, Ontario. Photo by Dave Halsey.

Dave sawing firewood at the Lake River camp, northern Ontario. Photo by Dave Halsey.

Dave with his Cree "family," Mary and Matthew Hookimaw. Photo by Dave Halsey.

Ian Lougheed and the helicopter crew bid the expedition bon voyage from Moosonee, Ontario, with a case of Labatt's ale.

Tough slogging through the tidal flats of James Bay: Dave hauls the canoe and Ki.

The victorious expedition on arrival
in Tadoussac. Photo by Norman Kerr.

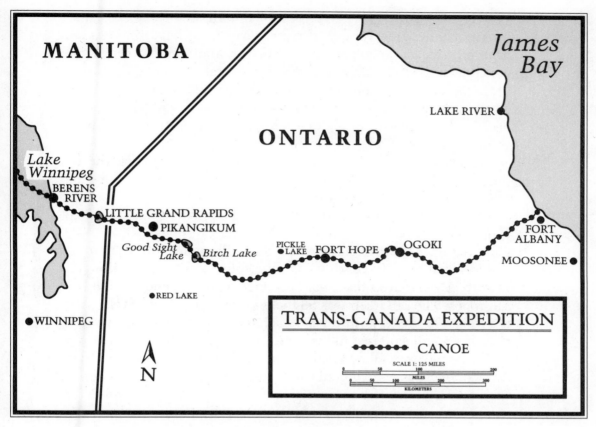

MANITOBA

ONTARIO

James Bay

LAKE RIVER

Lake Winnipeg

BERENS RIVER

LITTLE GRAND RAPIDS

PIKANGIKUM

Good Sight Lake

Birch Lake

PICKLE LAKE

FORT HOPE

OGOKI

FORT ALBANY

MOOSONEE

RED LAKE

WINNIPEG

N

TRANS-CANADA EXPEDITION

CANOE

SCALE 1: 125 MILES

MILES

KILOMETERS

Berens River, Manitoba, to Moosonee, Ontario, July–August 1978

could almost visualize the tattoos those miles would inscribe on our virgin gear.

After seven weeks of watching our bodies soften while waiting for spring break-up, we were eager to resume travel. We had used the time well, though, assembling a canoeing outfit suited to the geography ahead, editing film, and seeing our dog team resettled (Jack Clarkson, who owned the town's only plane, had flown them to Grand Rapids, where they were inherited by a Cree boy). Peter had even gone back to British Columbia to photograph some of the people and places I'd encountered before he joined the expedition.

The next three days were occupied with modifying our canoe for the challenging variety of river travel just ahead. Canoes are primarily meant to be paddled downriver, and that's what we had done on the Athabasca. But here we were starting from the mouth of the Berens River and heading *upstream* to its source, 350 miles away in Ontario. At that point we would cross a watershed and go back to downriver running, following the Albany River system all the way to James Bay.

The most dramatic modification to the Grumman was the addition of a specially designed sailing rig. Commercial canoe sails rely on bulky steering aids such as lee boards and rudders, which were impractical for us. Instead we designed (with the help of The Happy Outdoorsman) a simple square rig that proved surprisingly effective and easy to operate. A ten-foot collapsible aluminum mast rested securely in a steel ring and shoe bolted to the center ribs and thwart. A T-bar atop the mast had rings on either end to hold the sail ropes. The sail itself was 58 inches wide by 90 inches tall, with the lower 30 inches forming a detachable "foot bonnet" for the option of a small sail area in high winds. Horizontal poles at the top and bottom of the sail retained its shape and prevented wind spillage.

Guide rings were bolted to the hull on either side of the mast, with tie-off points (like cleats on a sailboat) directly behind Peter in the bow and me in the stern. With ropes running through the rings on the mast to the tie-off point in the stern, I could quickly raise and lower the sail, while Peter controlled the degree of tack with the ropes running through the lower rings and bow tie-offs. To compensate for the lack of steering apparatus, I threaded a cable through a hole in the stern hull, to which my paddle could be attached with a quick-release ring. With this arrangement I could steer with my left hand while leaning my weight into the paddle to keep us upright, and my right hand remained free to adjust ropes.

Our home on the river was further customized with spray cover hooks bolted to the gunwales and ensolite padding on the seats and stern deck (where I prefer to sit). The bow was painted flat black to reduce the sun's glare; hemp was carefully braided into fore and aft canoe handles. So that our paddle blades might survive their inevitable bashing against rocky river bottoms, we pounded, then bolted thin sheets of aluminum around the tips. Finally, Peter invented an ingenious photographic rig for our underwater camera. We badly wanted to document rapids-running action, yet without a third party it seemed impossible. The split-second timing needed to negotiate rapids would prohibit either of us from dropping a paddle to grab the camera. So Peter installed sets of aluminum brackets, on which a tripod head could be mounted, just behind the bow seat and in front of the stern seat. Thus the camera could be pre-set within easy reach of one of us, framing me in the stern or Peter in the bow. In midrapid, one needed to miss but a single paddle stroke to reach out and click the shutter.

At last we were ready, our supplies purchased and packed, all the gear strewn before us on the beach in front of the mission—the same beach, then covered with snow and ice, that we had sledded across seven weeks earlier. I was apprehensive about embarking on an untested mode of travel; we had no way of knowing whether our system would actually work. But with no further excuses to delay, we swung the bow off Lake Winnipeg and into the river's current.

The Berens River was first explored by William Tomison in 1767 and later named for Joseph Berens, governor of the Hudson's Bay Company from 1812 to 1822. Today, canoe groups regularly make the run down the river, but we would be among the first to paddle up its length since airplanes replaced the old freight brigades in the 1930s. Back then, two Salteaux Indians could ferry more than a thousand pounds of freight upriver 120 miles to Little Grand Rapids, our next destination, in forty-eight hours. I calculated that it would take Peter and me a week to cover the same distance.

For the first 250 miles from its mouth, the Berens is a relatively fast and powerful river, with rocky, forested banks sometimes steepening into canyons, and rapids of all degrees. It flows into and out of lakes all along its course—more frequently after crossing the border into Ontario. Then it gradually narrows and slows as the surrounding country changes, creeping toward its source through a maze of marshy waterways.

We looked forward to challenges aplenty—but the first few days' travel were joyous, sweeping away our ominous expectations. The sail billowed magnificently before steady tailwinds. My view from the stern obstructed by the sail, I did little except steer and roll cigarettes one-handed, while Pete relayed descriptions of river bends and eddies. Ki dozed peacefully on the spray cover as if his canoe lifestyle had never been interrupted by the rigors of winter travel. A few minutes' fishing yielded more pickerel (walleye) and northern pike than we could consume in a day; ducks and geese rose at nearly every bend, promising that we'd never go hungry even if the fish disappeared.

Campsites, too, were luxurious compared to the muddy banks of the Athabasca. Granite slabs of Canadian Shield bedrock—some of the oldest rock in the world—ran cleanly to the river's edge, cushioned with sweet-scented beds of pine needles. Most of our camps were long-abandoned Indian camps, marked by initials and Salteaux symbols blazed on trees. Some of these surely dated back to freight teams at the turn of the century; we found rotting dogsleds and tent poles that crumbled at a touch. The Salteaux symbols we found marking camps or portages were nearly always on the *down-river* side of trees—signposts for the now nonexistent upriver traffic.

Our delight at being back in the bush was marred only by the lack of a few basic items forgotten in our haste: a compass, insect repellent, and toilet paper. We wouldn't need the compass until we reached the confusing channels of the lake country upriver, and woodsmoke and grease could see us through the first few bugs of the season. Toilet paper? Well, there was plenty of moss.

We navigated the various riffles, rapids, and falls we encountered in various ways. Portages around falls were quite simple. Since downriver canoeists also had to portage around these barriers, the trails were well trodden. But rapids that could be run by downstream canoeists or powered through upstream by Indians with outboard motors were another matter. These had long since lost their trails, forcing us to cut our own through the bush.

If a current was too swift to paddle against yet still navigable, we often managed to ascend such quick spots by poling. The poles were stout eight- to ten-foot lengths of spruce. Green wood was essential; a dead, dry pole, though lighter and easier to wield, is not flexible enough to withstand the lateral stress. Some shave the bark off their poles, but we left ours as cut—I prefer the rough bark grip and could never get used to constantly sap-sticky hands.

To advance, we would stand, crouch, or kneel and bring our poles forward, but not too far ahead of our positions. Once the poles were planted firmly on the river bottom we would walk them hand-over-hand to the tip, propelling the canoe in the process. One of us would then lift his pole and secure it in a new forward position, while the other held the canoe in place, and so on. At the end of the rapid we would discard the poles, cutting fresh ones each time. Poling is a dying art, requiring concentration and a "feel" for the river that comes only with long experience. No other canoe skill I know of is as difficult to master, and we never became really adept at it.

Where the riverbank terrain permitted, we preferred to line, or "track," the canoe from shore; the firm granite banks of the Berens were ideal for this technique. Lining does take some skill but is far easier than poling to master. It can be a two-man operation, with ropes tied to bow and stern, or one person can line with the ends of a single rope secured likewise. I generally preferred the latter, because the force of the current often demands split-second reactions, difficult to communicate quickly enough to a partner. As Pete and I had learned on the Athabasca, a moment's hesitation can allow the current's hydraulic action to suck the canoe down.

We used a 150-foot hemp rope; though hemp absorbs water it is much more comfortable in the hands than synthetic rope and holds knots better. Peter would walk ahead to scout the rapid and relay the location of optimum channels. I played out the bow line while holding taut the stern line, allowing the canoe to track to midstream (reversing this process brings the canoe back to shore). If the canoe stays parallel to the current, there is surprisingly little pull on the ropes as you walk the canoe up the rapid. But if the bow slips just a few degrees off course, no amount of strength can overcome the tons of water that will pile against the bow. Fighting to regain the course will invariably swamp the canoe; many craft have been lost by line handlers underestimating the current's power. The only remedy is to slacken the bow line so that the canoe reverses 180 degrees, then the stern line, swinging the bow back into position.

The secret to successful lining is constant attentiveness to the canoe. You skip along shore from boulder to boulder, taking in and playing out the bow and stern ends of the line as needed. You can ease the canoe up narrow chutes, using the ropes like a horse's reins to delicately guide the boat between crags. You must be fast and keep the canoe in motion at all times. Above all, your eyes must never leave the canoe.

Our favorite way to ascend rapids, though, was to cheat by sailing up them. Under a strong enough wind our modest square rig allowed us to inch up rapids that were far too swift and deep to pole against. Of course, we could not sail through large standing waves and deep troughs, but we often claimed victory over swift, narrow chutes. The trick was in the timing. Many rapids rise and fall in evenly spaced surges, and a few minutes' observation of a rapid taught us the timing of these variations in water volume and velocity. At the start of a lull, we would raise sail, lurching from the impact of wind bloating the nylon, and begin to paddle in desperate, body-yanking strokes. The canoe would react drunkenly, charging ahead with each gust of wind, slipping back when the breeze slackened. We judged our progress in feet per minute, praying to reach a slower eddy before the lull ended. The last few feet to the lip of the chute were usually the hardest ground to gain. By then our muscles would be degenerating rapidly, and the river, as if sensing it was about to lose the battle, often chose this untimely moment to launch a new surge.

We won more of these sailing assaults than we lost, however. The wind, no doubt humored by our unorthodox tactics, always seemed to grant us a final solid gust of ammunition. Spent but safe in a back-eddy above the chute, I'd thumb my nose at the river. In all such cases, portaging would have been more logical, but not nearly as much fun.

The river spoke to us through the names of its rapids and falls. Some were historical: English Rapids, where years back an Englishman had drowned; Conjuring Falls, where Salteaux medicine men beat their drums to conjure spirits; Old Fort Rapids and Old Fort Falls, where the Hudson's Bay Company had built a short-lived fort in 1816. Other names described geographic features: Crooked Falls,

Canyon Rapids, Smoothrock Falls, Sharpstone Falls, and Pine Island Rapids, to name a few. The origins of some names were more obscure but intriguing to speculate about: Bladder Rapids, Mending-the-Net Falls, Rattling Rapids, and Moose Dung Rapids.

A few miles before reaching Old Fort Falls, where we were to camp, we stopped at Flag Portage. Here, carved into a granite face as precisely as a tombstone epitaph, was the legend, "A McKay— 1897." We later learned that the region's first Indian agent, Angus McKay, had camped here with his men on their way upriver to pay treaty money to the Salteaux at Little Grand Rapids. It was June 20, 1897, the day of Queen Victoria's Diamond Jubilee, and in honor of his monarch's sixty-year reign over the British Empire, "Mr. McKay gave his men a holiday and hoisted a Union Jack up a tree trimmed for the purpose. His men went for a hunt, killed a moose, and thus provided themselves with several good meals" (Leach, *Indians and Settlers*). Hence, of course, Flag Portage.

The Berens never seemed to rest for long, and our city-softened muscles were no more than a modest match for the relentless current. We tired easily and slept late, reducing our daily average to just under ten miles. Occasionally the river widened, as if to pause before its next onslaught of whitewater; we took advantage of the slackened pace to stretch knotted muscles and reach for a quick handful of raisins. Yet even in the slower current, a one-minute break gave the river a chance to regain ground, and we paid for our rest by paddling the same stretch over again.

The forty-five river miles between our camp at Old Fort Falls and the Salteaux village of Little Grand Rapids challenged us with thirty-four major falls and rapids, plus dozens of uncharted riffles and quick spots. Along one particularly grueling stretch we climbed up and over twenty-four falls and rapids in two twelve-hour days. At many of these the only portage trail was that of the old freight brigades, now lost under fifty years' growth. We spent more time hacking a path with axe and saw than actually portaging.

One trailless portage, where the river tumbled through a sheer granite canyon, nearly proved fatal. From downriver, the only route to safe water was along a narrow, angling ledge fifty feet above the river. In a steady drizzle, we hauled the canoe by ropes to the ledge, then began a cautious carry. Peter eased ahead with the heaviest pack while I followed with the canoe. At a surprised shout from Peter, I rolled the canoe to the ledge and, jogging up, found him sprawled on his back six feet below the ledge. He just lay there, beaming at his luck. Only the heavy canvas pack had saved him from a serious back injury; or worse, had he fallen a few feet to either side he would have missed the shelf and been impaled on the jagged boulders farther down.

On Tuesday, June 13, we set camp half a mile above Big Moose Falls. Six hundred yards downriver, a prehistoric red ochre pictograph dominated the lichen-shrouded granite face of the north bank like the sentry of this stretch of river. The country we were entering contained many such cliff paintings, the brooding record of a vanished Indian culture.

Little remained in our grub box, and Peter, disgusted with his meager dinner ration, announced, "Let's go fishing!" Ki, though subsisting on even smaller rations than us, looked dubious, as was I. "Come on, Dave. You said yourself that bay over there has to be loaded with fish. So let's fish."

Peter was no fisherman. I believe that the sum of his prior experience was one perch from a midwestern lake, many years ago. Perhaps that was why he was undeterred by such things as my broken fishing reel, diagnosed as terminal a few days earlier. Or the fact that I had snapped off the upper third of my rod on the last portage. Pete was hungry. "You've told me about hand lines; let's try it."

I, on the other hand, had been fishing all my life. Trying to suppress my chuckles, I tied a whitehead jig with white bucktail hair (a lead-headed lure that bumps along the river bottom) to my heaviest fishing line. After explaining how one twirls the line overhead while playing it out, then quickly releases the coiled line, I leaned back against the roots of a riverbank spruce to watch and laugh.

On his third cast, Peter landed a fat, two-pound walleye. His fifth cast brought in a second pickerel. At that point I stopped laughing and joined the action. The novice fisherman had taught me a bountiful lesson; I had never dreamed of the riches of such waterways. From then on we provided ourselves with all the fish we could want by hand line, or rather "leg line," fishing from the canoe. Whenever we neared a promising pool beneath a rapid, I threw twenty yards of line over the side. One end was tied to a silvery spoon that fluttered in the current, the other end to my thigh. We often caught two fat pickerel during a fifty-yard paddle to the portage at the head of the pool. Only the largest northern pike, those strong enough to make the line cut into my hands and legs, were lost.

We had one more near-disaster before Little Grand Rapids. By now we had run out of supplies and had been living on unsalted fish and black tea for two days. We made the last portage of the day around Night Owl Falls with empty stomachs and aching muscles, but decided to press on. Peter had not paddled stern since Alberta, and, thinking a change would be distracting, I agreed to switch positions.

At the head of a portage or above a rapid, dangerous crosscurrents often lie hidden beneath a deceptively placid surface. Without strong compensating paddle strokes from the sternman, such swirling currents under the surface can easily drag a canoe back into the whitewater. Peter hadn't paddled from the stern in such a situation before, and as we set off I realized in horror that I had forgotten to warn him about crosscurrents. But it was already too late: We had been sucked into a quick chute and were driving backward toward the lip of a falls.

We paddled like madmen, occasionally glancing at the falls like convicted men at a gallows. Ki understood the danger. He could not will his body off the spray cover, and his eyes had a fixed stare. For the first minute we managed to hold our position 200 feet above the falls. During the second, as the first arrows of pain shot through our biceps and backs, we lost two or three canoe lengths. We retrenched during the third minute and held the canoe 150 feet from the lip of the falls. Few words were spoken. Every cell in our bodies begged to be free of the river's grip.

My anger rose and I began chanting, "Bitch, bitch, bitch, bitch!" in time with my strokes. I envisioned my paddle inflicting more pain to the black water than my muscles were receiving. "Damn you, bitch!" We gained a foot. "Damn you, river!" We gained three more.

At four minutes we broke. Losing a foot per second, we were

quickly 100 feet from the black line where the river ended, with empty space beyond. I started to shout to Peter to leap out before we went over and try to ride the falls feet first, but halted in mid-thought at the sight of a humped white boulder in midstream. Pete veered the canoe broadside, and in three strokes we were upon our stone life raft.

After half an hour of hugging the rock for dear life, we prepared to make a desperate sprint to shore. Once back in the water we would have only seconds before our paddles grabbed open air over the falls. Pete crouched in the bow holding the coiled rope, ready to jump for the nearest tree. From the stern, I released our beloved rock and leaned hard on my paddle. The bow struck the granite riverbank with a concussion that nearly threw me from the canoe; in one fluid movement Peter leaped for a spruce, then held us fast with the bow rope. For the next half an hour we just sat on the bank and watched water cascade over the lip of the falls, no more than forty feet away.

The day after our close call with Night Owl Falls, we pulled the canoe up to the last portage before Little Grand Rapids. More than seventy rapids and falls had left their marks on our clothes and gear, and our faces still carried the tension of our backward run toward the falls the night before. While skipping along the portage trail in anticipation of hot baths and store-bought food, I braked in midstride at the sound of shrill laughter, causing the canoe to sway on my shoulders. We rounded a bend and came face to face with two women who appeared to have just left a picnic in a city park. We exchanged brief stares; then one of them—dressed in polyester slacks, short-sleeved blouse, floppy hat, and sandals—shrieked and turned to flee. It occurred to us belatedly how we must look, and smell, to anyone not used to bush travel.

Their husbands approached cautiously, armed with menacing fishing rods. Peter wasn't carrying his cameras and Ki hadn't yet wagged his tail; I wished I'd had our rusty shotgun to heighten the showdown effect. I advanced with my right hand extended, which they ignored, tightening their grips on those lethal fishing rods and standing their ground. Were we going to rush their women? Pete by now was struggling to keep a straight face.

Five minutes later all six of us were chugging cold Molsons and laughing over the episode. Winnipeg suburbanites, they explained that this was their first experience with the "wilderness." After expressing our appreciation for the beers, Peter and I left, shaking our heads and wondering what tales might be told at the next poker party.

Just before Little Grand Rapids, the Berens River enters wind-swept Family Lake—the last obstacle between us and hot baths. A fierce tailwind bowed our mast as we headed across, leaving Peter in the water as much as out of it, the bow mostly submerged or awash. This was a real road test; never before had we tried our sail design on such a large body of water, in a wind that surpassed the term "unsafe." The mast could snap, the sail could tear, or, without lee boards, the canoe could flip under the stress of a sharp turn.

Peter shouted over the spray that we should drop sail, but that would be too risky in these conditions. In such a high wind, the weight shift needed to lower sail would be more apt to roll the canoe over than the thrust of continuing under full sail. A hundred yards to our port side, two gnarled pines grasped footholds in the cracks of a ten-yard-long island of granite. That seemed the best bet just then, so I yelled, "Take in six inches on the right!" Peter whirled to trim the sail while I heaved against the rudder shaft to make a sharp left-hand turn toward the tiny island.

A four-foot whitecapped wave slammed Pete in the chest. Entirely awash, the canoe lurched indecisively, torn between its desire to maintain forward momentum and the combined instructions of the newly angled sail and rudder to turn left. For a panicky second it seemed to succumb to a trough between waves; then, with unexpected audacity, it shook itself free of foam and charged toward the island. Pete shouted his surprise and I yelled back in exhilaration, "She's got it, Pete! She's really got it!"

Our little canoe and sail had outperformed any expectations. Jubilant, I turned wide of the island and swung the bow back toward Little Grand Rapids on the far shore. Another five miles of heavy sailing and the white frame buildings of the Hudson's Bay Company post appeared like a high-relief etching on the blue horizon—the same sight that had greeted fur and freight brigades for a hundred years, that had greeted Indian agent Angus McKay in 1897.

It's an isolated life for the eight hundred Salteaux and few dozen whites of Little Grand Rapids. During summer, the village can be reached by plane (an hour-and-a-half flight from Winnipeg), by motoring or poling upriver from Lake Winnipeg, or by paddling 130 miles downriver from a dirt bush road in a remote corner of northwestern Ontario. Other than the regular supply plane, outside contact is scanty. Weather permitting, the few residents who own televisions can receive one station; radio reception is equally subject to weather.

There were no telephones in Little Grand Rapids in 1978. If you wanted to talk to a neighbor on the other side of town, you took a walk. If you needed to contact someone outside, the Hudson's Bay Company offered the use of its two-way radio. After an extended search through frequencies, you reached (theoretically) a government radio operator in The Pas, Manitoba, 300 air miles away. The operator took the number you were calling, and then you waited for an open line—sometimes all afternoon. Little Grand Rapids shared two lines with several other villages, the equivalent of two party lines shared by more than a thousand people.

We spent our first night in the settlement with a couple of guys from the HBC post, and the next day we did our usual layover chores: writing, cleaning gear and ourselves, buying supplies. The HBC stocks seemed odd to us: There was no garlic sausage, which we'd been able to buy everywhere since Vancouver, but we found shelves upon shelves of white beans. The Indians buy them by the case, not to eat but to ferment into their famously potent "bean juice." A few days upriver from Little Grand Rapids we would pass a depressing pair of ruined cabins perched above a spongy point of muskeg. These were the "cursed cabins," where two Indians killed each other over a last cup of bean juice. No Salteaux has since stepped upon this land.

The next day, Saturday, June 17, was stormy and windy, so we stayed on. I was lucky to meet a seventy-year-old Salteaux trapper named Walter Moar, who told me a bit about what life used to be like in Little Grand Rapids. "When I was your age I used to haul freight up the river from the Berens River post," he said. "We carried twelve hundred pounds. We made the trip in three days. I lost my job when they started flying supplies in with the airplane. But it's good, 'cause we don't have to wait so long for supplies anymore."

Walter was also willing to talk about traditional Salteaux customs like the ancient "Shaking Tent" or "Conjuring Tent." Apparently the only remaining Salteaux shaman in the region, a man named David Eaglestick, still practiced the ceremony. He and an elder of the tribe would enter a sacred teepee-like pole-and-canvas tent as a crowd gathered outside. Soon wild howls, shrieks, and grunts would erupt from the tent; these were said to be the voices of animal spirits, such as the bear, moose, and beaver, explaining the secrets of the bush to the shaman. The ritual culminated in a violent shaking of the tent, as a mosquito whispered news of the future into the shaman's ear—who would die, who would have a bountiful trapline that season.

Nonbelievers scoffed at the custom, claiming that Eaglestick made the noises and shook the tent himself. Since it was strictly forbidden for anyone outside the tribe to witness the ceremony, the "truth" will probably remain in doubt—but does it matter? It was a belief that went with a way of life, and that way is rapidly disappearing among the Salteaux and most of the northern tribes.

Little Grand Rapids can now be reached by a seven-digit telephone number, as I learned when I tried several years later to call the village via the Hudson's Bay Company radio. Someone found Walter Moar and put him on the line. We talked about the changes. David Eaglestick doesn't do the Shaking Tent anymore, "'cause nobody will come to listen to him. Everybody believes in Jesus. That's okay, though. We still gotta cook our food, get our water, and put wood in the stove when it's cold. It doesn't matter who the god is.

"I'm old now. I can't trap anymore. Watching TV is better than watching your stove," Walter said. "I still like watching my stove sometimes, though."

The mention of stove-watching made me smile. The glow from a trapper's wood stove had often been our evening's entertainment during the first winter of the expedition. You don't really focus on the stove itself. It's just a screen, like a TV set, which serves as a backdrop for a flow of images from memory and visions of the future. We had discovered this bush practice as everyone does: through prolonged solitude.

It is a dying habit now, even for men like Walter, whose early memories are probably of gasping at the wonders of the Shaking Tent and of waiting impatiently by the shore of Family Lake for his father to return with tales of the freight brigades. Now, he only occasionally watches his stove.

Walter told me: "Only three or four people here still believe the old ways. They say they can prove Jesus. I can't prove the Shaking Tent, so I have to believe the new stuff."

————————————

The glistening bodies of a dozen men flash in and out of the campfire's circle of light, while their shadows cavort on the face of a granite cliff. The leader of the hunting party rises from his stooped pose by the fire, cradling an earthenware dish filled with red ochre pigment. He offers it to a wildly costumed shaman, whose grotesque face paintings are highlighted by a popping ember.

Facing the cliff, the shaman pauses to study the rock's contours. He selects a satisfactory location and begins the ritual, dabbing ochre onto the cliff face with a patch of moosehide. The spirit of the moose leaves the piece of hide and mingles with the bloodlike ochre. As the painting takes shape, the moose spirit is captured within its likeness on the stone.

The moose is the most recent addition to an entire mural of images in ochre. Others, painted generations earlier, include an arching line beneath a dozen vertical lines (a party of hunters traveling by canoe) and birds beneath a grid of lines (fowl caught in a trap or net). Still other symbols are more abstract: a stick-man with rays of sun radiating from his head, another with a tail, a rising sun pierced by an arrow.

The shaman turns from his task to face the foaming hills of water in the rapids the group must cross. He begins a prayer to Manitou, the water spirit—a gutteral chant asking the

*spirit's leave to cross safely. As he chants, the hunters pass
single file under the ochre moose. Each leaves the moose spirit
a gift: the talons of an eagle, a favorite smoothly rounded
stone, a string of polished clam shells. The moose spirit has
been compensated for the taking of its meat. The wrath of
Manitou has been appeased by the acknowledgment of his
power. The hunt may now begin.*

Six hundred years later, Peter and I knelt before the same pictograph site as archeologist Vic Pelshea made his own offering to the spirits: tobacco, ammunition, a trinket. Pelshea and his team were documenting this site on Sharpstone Lake, just east of the Ontario border, and Pete and I couldn't resist such a superb photo opportunity. On first witnessing Vic's pre-work ritual, we suspected he'd been in the woods too long, but then we realized that his insistence on ceremony simply expressed a dedicated man's respect for the culture he was studying.

On Friday, June 23, we had crossed the border from Manitoba into Ontario, passing the provincial boundary marker—a sun-bleached skull nailed to a tree—on the north shore of Moar Lake. This followed a frustrating episode of trying to navigate the lake, with its hundreds of islands, without a compass—our first taste of the bewildering lake country ahead. After two days of paddling in circles, we finally gave up and paddled back to the Norse Lodge fishing resort, and Pete bought a compass from a fisherman. I was too embarrassed to show my face there for a third time. It turned out that we had passed our exit channel several times, thinking it a blind bay.

We had heard at Norse Lodge about the archeologists and found them with little trouble. To be truthful, their camp held more attractions than the survey work alone. Supplied by floatplane, it possessed every backwoods luxury imaginable, from outboard motors to cabin-size tents to tables and chairs. Not to mention Vic's assistant, Sheryl Moyer, who had the wildly distracting habit of walking around camp casually topless. The fact that I bashed our bow into a prominent rock upon landing at the camp was pure coincidence, of course. (A hundred miles farther on, Pete and I passed a pictograph site that was apparently undocumented. We sent some sketches on to Vic at the next opportunity, and months later received a response confirming that it was a new site, and adding that Sheryl had named it after us. I wondered what future scholars would make of "The Handsome Adventurers Pictograph Site.")

But the work was fascinating enough. Once the site's dimensions were recorded, along with latitude, longitude, and compass orientation, the pictographs were sponged with water. Ultrathin sheets of rice paper were then spread across the vertical surface; the paper becomes semitransparent when wet, allowing the pictograph to show through in perfect detail. For hours at a time, Vic would painstakingly trace the images onto the rice paper, omitting no detail. If lichen growth obscured some of the image, he would switch from his ochre-colored grease pen to a grey-green shade to indicate the growth. Sheryl acted something like a surgeon's nurse, exchanging pens as needed, remoistening the paper to prolong its adherence, sketching general site illustrations, and hosing down Vic's back when the flies became intolerable. The completed rice-paper murals were spread on the granite shore to dry. An entire site could be documented to the most minute detail in this way, to exact scale and without damage to the paintings.

Two days' travel from Vic's camp found us battling torrential rains and high winds in the middle of another large lake. It seemed imprudent to try for shore, so we holed up on a small island for half an hour while the wind abated slightly. Having more sense than we, Ki had to be carried back down to the canoe as we got ready to dash for shore, then held down until we were too far from the island for him to swim back. As we neared the point of land where the Berens enters the lake, the wind abruptly dropped. The sky hung so low it seemed we could touch the sooty clouds; the waves subsided from vicious whitecaps to syrupy swells. Birds darted silently and erratically over the water.

Rounding the point, we dropped our paddles and stared at a bizarre sight. Spread peacefully on the hillside before us was a midwestern farm straight off a Norman Rockwell canvas: freshly painted barns, neatly tended gardens, fenced pastures. Even stranger than coming on this pastoral scene in the remote wilderness was that it wasn't marked on our recent maps.

An eerie screaming, as if from thousands of birds, led us toward a big barn, and when we opened the door we walked smack into a basketball game! We stood there openmouthed, our bright orange rain gear dripping on the court, while kids darted by in uniforms, referees blew whistles, and an audience of adults in sober black-and-white garb cheered on their teams.

This was our introduction to the Northern Lights Gospel Mission, a Mennonite retreat and Christian boarding school for native children. A classic island of self-sufficiency, its facilities included a gymnasium and baseball diamond, a wood shop, dormitories, and a working farm. Some of the mission's income came from artfully crafted cedar-strip canoes hand-built by twelve- and thirteen-year-olds and exported. Older teenagers milled wood from the surrounding forest and built comfortable frame houses for their teachers. Some food was flown in but most was grown on the farm or harvested from the bush. Dozens of moose and bear quarters, along with pike, walleye, and whitefish, lay packed in slabs of winter-cut lake ice.

Deliberately isolated to avoid outside corruption, the mission nevertheless made us cautiously welcome. We could photograph anything and stay as long as we liked on condition that we followed a few rules: We mustn't talk to the kids about life on the "outside" or consume any of the "drugs" in our packs (coffee, tea, and tobacco) on the premises. Except for my midnight trips behind the icehouse with my tobacco pouch, we honored their wishes.

The first day we were given a strictly regimented tour: One person explained the farm operation, another led us through the construction projects, still others showed off the school, the kitchen, and laundry facilities. Though our own religious beliefs were never questioned, the place seemed nervously repressed. Nearly every tree in the settlement bore a plaque with a biblical inscription. If an unmarried girl, dressed in the standard black skirt and bonnet, approached us to ask a question, her mother would briskly hustle her away.

Apparently we won some kind of approval, though, for things opened up the second day. Buxom women gave our grimy clothes their best laundering since Winnipeg while we wandered about in nothing but our chafing rain gear. Kids demanded piggyback rides, and their elders behaved in a more relaxed way, some inviting us to look in on their lives.

To walk into a home here was to step back into the 1920s: A bearded man in black hat and overalls would greet you at the door, while his wife interrupted her quilting to set an extra place at the table beside the wood stove. The only distraction during dinner might be the ring of a hand-cranked phone, which connected the settlement's buildings. Afterward, the husband would escort you to the parlor for "man talk": perhaps a description of his mare's new foal or of the chipmunk that was eluding his traps. ("Don't tell the wife; she won't leave her flour bin unguarded!") Never would a male guest insult his host by offering to help with the dishes. The evening ended early.

Our third and last day at the mission included a festival featuring volleyball, races, songs, huge vats of potato salad, and hundreds of hot dogs. We were part of the entertainment, too, contributing a short talk about our travels. As we paddled onward the next day, I had conflicting thoughts about the work of the mission. I didn't like the idea that native children were being given no choice about their religion and cultural heritage—every Bible lesson was a step away from the beliefs illustrated by the pictographs. On the other hand, these children were spared the terrible ills that beset so many Indians: alcoholism and its related violence, the lost pride that causes them to desert the traplines for the welfare rolls. Meeting these missionaries left me more respectful of their work yet still concerned about the erosion of native culture.

July 1 found us on giant Lake Pikangikum trying to buy supplies. Since it was the Canada Day holiday, the Hudson's Bay Company post was closed, so we paddled across to the Ojibway settlement of Pikangikum, where there is a store and nursing station. The Ojibway band council called an emergency meeting to decide whether Pete should be allowed to take photographs, and permission was granted. Not only that, he was led around town with an interpreter and met people like Maggie Black, who still makes birch baskets the old way, with spruce roots as lashings, and Helgie Suggashie, who does beadwork on moosehide moccasins. All in all, we were very impressed with this clean, proud settlement.

As we continued to climb the Berens, we grew ever more concerned about our slow pace. Photographic stops had set us back, and a recent lack of tailwinds cut our daily mileage. The crushing blow was the heat, which pushed the temperature into the 80s as July began. It shimmered off the water and sapped our energy; a few times I caught myself falling asleep while paddling. Pete and I found short-lived relief by rolling off the canoe into the icy river, but Ki never swam unless it was a survival issue. He would lie on the steaming spray cover with eyes closed and tongue lolling, his head swaying with the gentle current swells.

The main reason for our schedule worries was that we had an appointment to keep. My father, an avid fisherman and the expedition's "ground control," had arranged to fly north and join us for a week during his vacation. We were due to meet at Pickle Lake, about 350 river miles from Pikangikum, in ten days. The numbers didn't work out: At best we had averaged no more than twenty-one miles of upriver paddling per day. And what would happen to our progress when the river narrowed to a mere creek? Casting around for an alternate rendezvous, I thought of a fishing camp on Birch Lake, a more reasonable 150 miles away, where friends of my father had spent time. The only remaining problem was communicating the change in plans to my father.

July 2 brought another blow. On reaching the far shore of ten-mile-long Berens Lake, we found ourselves in a very different river environment. For 250 miles the Berens had carved a relatively clear path through the solid granite of the Canadian Shield. Only the lakes presented occasional navigation problems. But here the bedrock of the Shield largely gave way to oozing muskeg—a wetland habitat dominated by sphagnum moss, or peat, through which the once-straight river channel twisted and turned in myriad directions. In some places hairpin turns crowded so close together that they weren't even recorded on the map. We had 100 miles of this country yet to cross before reentering the Canadian Shield landscape.

However, on the Fourth of July the now-sluggish Berens River suddenly unfolded into a glistening oasis of open water—Goose Lake. Here we enjoyed a much-needed break at the fly-in fishing camp of Bill and Louise Coppen. The Coppens, in their first year as resort operators, typified the hardy breed who managed to wrest a home and a living from the bush. We felt a strong kinship with such folk, who had spent years chipping a niche in this land. They knew both the dangers and pleasures of the country in a way that their clients never could, and this seemed to give them a special appreciation of our adventures.

As we paddled in, we came upon Louise and her Ojibway helper sinking a crib—a log structure to support a pier. She brushed the hair out of her face and marched us up to the main cabin for freshly baked chocolate chip cookies. When Bill Coppen returned, his float-plane banking over the cabins and leapfrogging the lake waves, we explained our urgent need to reach my father. Bill promptly led us to his two-way radio, and we spent the next hour trying to raise the Red Lake operator. But the chattering static was worse than usual, and we never got through. We left the next morning with Bill's assurance that the next passing aircraft would carry our message and mail out—to deliver to the Coppens' closest neighbor upriver.

The mighty Berens River was rapidly decaying to a syrupy trickle. For a while, the channel remained about twelve feet wide— just enough to pass through without having to part the overhanging branches from the banks. A few miles farther on it narrowed to eight feet, then six. The first twenty miles of the river—the last twenty, for us—squeezed through a channel no more than four feet wide and three feet deep.

Our progress now barely qualified as river travel. The scrub willows lining the banks joined at midstream to form a wickerlike puzzle. Peter rarely paddled in the bow any more; his hands groped forward, parting the branches, while he tucked his scratched face beneath an armpit to avoid further punishment. I poled from the stern, standing or kneeling and scanning the terrain for signs of suitable campsites in the soggy lowland. Between us, Ki lay plastered on the spray cover, torn between his desire to lie low to avoid the tearing branches and his passion to nip every passing blackfly in revenge for his bleeding, bitten ears and belly.

Where we couldn't make any progress poling, we portaged— sometimes through the spongy muskeg but here and there over outcroppings of high, rocky ground. The most interesting feature of this region was its huge moose population; we saw more of them here than anywhere else in Canada. A journal entry describes the contrasts of scenery and our depressed state of mind:

> *July 7, 1978.* Part cloudy, west wind, 75 degrees F, some rain. Pancakes for breakfast. No butter, as a marten raided our camp last night. Ki took care of him, though. We found bits of fur scattered around camp. Poled 50 yards up a quick spot, then portaged 50 miserable yards on south bank through knee-deep muskeg. Saw a cow moose. Caught a half-dozen walleye for supper in only fifteen minutes.
>
> Passed a beautiful lake to the west, which we named "Good Site Lake," it being the only decent cabin site for miles. Ugly country but abundant in fish, game, and fur. I have found no signs of trappers . . . no signs of anybody, in fact. This country is good only for fur—it is so bland that the slightest rock outcropping gets us excited. The only human signs are old Ojibway wild-rice harvesting camps. Their old tent poles collapse upon touch.
>
> Portaged 200 yards on south bank around rapid. . . . Had to first walk it, blazing trees, then "two-man" it (both carrying the canoe) through the bad spots. At one point had to lower the canoe and gear with ropes down a 30-foot cliff.

The terse reference to Good Site Lake in Dave's journal downplays the significance of this place both at that moment in the journey and afterward. Pete Souchuk remembers it as "innocuous, just a small, round lake and not especially attractive. But by that time we had lost track of how far we'd come up the Berens, and we were really worried about falling behind. Finding the lake enabled us to establish our position, and that cheered us up a lot."

When the expedition was over and Dave began talking of homesteading a cabin somewhere in the north, it was Good Site Lake that he talked about most often. "I think its remoteness appealed to Dave . . . the fact that it was so hard to get to," Pete says.

July 8. Exactly one month after we began our 350-mile ascent of the Berens, we entered a small, shallow, unnamed lake—the river's source. Only a half-mile portage lay between us and Shabumeni Lake, the start of the Shabumeni River and nearly 1,000 miles of *downriver* travel on the Albany River system. But this portage proved to be among the Berens' worst. The trail hadn't been used in many years and was so overgrown that we often had to backtrack to look for an axe cut, a paint scrape, any clue that might keep us on track. Poles laid by the Indians to support footsteps through the muskeg had long since rotted away. The blackflies were terrible. Back on high ground we found new obstacles: years of accumulated deadfalls through which we light-footed for more than an hour. In some places we scampered six feet off the ground, dragging the canoe over the branches; in others I crawled beneath the maze of timbers, the canoe rocking on my shoulders.

On a hill partway across the portage we came upon the grave of James Cat Lake, an Ojibway who died in 1943 at the age of twenty-three. Scattered around the grave were rusty trinkets, the gifts of family mourners. The sight stayed in my mind as we finished the portage and took shelter from a drizzle inside the crumbling remains of a trapper's cabin. Munching a raw-potato lunch, I gazed out across the waves slapping the shore of Shabumeni Lake.

Those waves were destined for Hudson Bay. A year later, the rain now drumming on our canoe hull might be part of an ice floe off Baffin Island, trod by a polar bear stalking a herd of dozing seals. Half a mile away, on the other side of the watershed, the rain feeding the current with which we had contended for a month would find its way to Lake Winnipeg, where sailboats cut the cool water. A little boy on a beach outside the city of Winnipeg might cry when his sand castle was washed away by water that had fallen on James Cat Lake's grave.

9 | Fast Times on the Albany River

Birch Lake to Fort Albany, Ontario

At 4:00 A.M. on the morning Maurice Halsey was departing to join his son in the north at Pickle Lake, he got a phone call from a bush pilot informing him of the new rendezvous at Birch Lake. Bill Coppen had managed to get Dave's message through. Maurey Halsey took the change in stride and arranged to be flown in by floatplane, arriving at Jack Green's fishing camp on July 7 with his fishing tackle and as many supplies for the expedition as he could carry.

Two days later he was still alone at the camp. After dinner on Sunday the ninth, he decided to go out for a little more fishing—there wasn't much else to do, and the fine, fat pickerel from the lake would help supplement the grub box. Trolling across a bay as the light was fading, he noticed a canoe moving toward him from the west. The paddles dipped and rose slowly, as if the occupants had been at it all day, and a dog swiveled its head to catch the scent of human habitation. That was the giveaway, and Maurey's vigorous wave was quickly answered by hearty shouts from the canoe.

I had to look twice to recognize my father, the dignified Washington lobbyist, beneath a ridiculous canary-yellow fishing cap and several days' growth of beard. Over celebratory beers at Jack Green's camp, we learned how Dad had been rerouted from Pickle Lake to Birch Lake, and filled him in on our last few days.

We had jumped from lake to lake in the watershed, relying heavily on the compass and portaging when that seemed the quickest route. We were late already and didn't want to add undue worry to my father's undoubted bewilderment. River courses in the country surrounding a watershed behave indecisively in the face of many options. The young stream trying to find its way out of a dead-end valley will investigate every hillside pockmark, eating away at the point of least resistance until it finds a passage through which it can tumble into the next lowland. The result is a tangle of bays and waterways that can confuse even experienced boaters.

Pete and I had had enough of this confusion. Studying the map, I'd noticed that one bay of the lake we were on reached to within 600 yards of Birch Lake. We could portage here—or paddle another fifteen miles by river to get to the same place. A quick scout, marking the way with axe blazes, determined that we could cut a trail, so we portaged over—nearly a full day's travel saved through one hour's work. We then paddled and sailed the remaining ten miles to where we met Dad.

We planned to cover sixty-five miles during his week with us, to a camp on North Bamaji Lake, where he'd instructed his pilot to pick him up. We could have covered the distance more quickly, but this was his vacation from the office—and our vacation from the expedition. Pete and I had been together for more than a year and badly needed a break from each other's sole company. The prospect of a third party gave us both an emotional lift.

Dad had shared his flight in with Karl Koeszur, a seventy-year-old prospector with a homestead on Birch Lake. Before leaving, we paid a visit to Karl and his wife, Polly, an archeologist. Their stamina and zest rival those of people half their age, and their homestead was remarkable. Sipping glasses of Polly's homemade wine, we toured the assorted cabins, one filled with sophisticated prospecting equipment, another with Polly's seventeen-hundred-volume library. Karl had even packed in a cast-iron stove over the lake ice for the main cabin. Their lifestyle might be considered eccentric, but to me it was enviable.

After a hurried breakfast, Peter and I took our usual places in the bow and stern. Dad jostled for space among the packs amidships, and Ki stalked back and forth, irritated at having to relinquish his spot in the canoe to this intruder. Not since our foursome on the Athabasca with C. W. Hughey had we ridden so low in the water. With an extra man as well as extra gear and food, our total weight jumped from an average of 550 pounds to 780 pounds — close to the canoe's listed maximum capacity of 845.

But for the first few days it didn't really matter. We enjoyed a leisurely paddle, taking our time to fish and explore. We encountered only minor rapids, and a more difficult one that Pete and I ran while Dad photographed from shore. Evenings around the campfire were spent gorging on fried fish and tales. After a few drinks, Dad's Navy stories and our bush stories were equally hysterical. For a short time the Trans-Canada Expedition did not exist. We were just three guys on a canoe adventure. Dad's excitement over the country and activities that had become routine to us breathed new life into the trip. And for me there was another reward: Each time he learned something about the bush — how to prepare bannock or how to find a likely pickerel hole — I felt I was repaying one of the thousands of lessons he had taught me throughout my life.

One highlight of his visit was a near-catastrophe on the third day, when our passage to the next lake was blocked by a set of deep rapids. Standing "haystack" waves approached five feet, but still the rapids looked runnable and even fun with a two-man crew and the spray cover. We portaged most of our gear and Peter remained on shore with Ki and Dad's camera while the other two of us made the run.

Dad whooped with delight as one haystack after another slammed into the bow, burying him nearly to his neck. Only one remained between us and the safe eddies below, but the lateral current had swept us too close to the left bank. A "sweeper" — a dead tree hanging over the water — was coming up fast, and I leaned into my paddle to avoid it. We barely missed it, but the correction put our bow at the wrong angle to the next wave; we hit the haystack and rolled.

When my head broke the surface I looked around for Dad, but he wasn't up yet. Seconds ticked by before he finally surfaced on the other side of the canoe. His spray skirt had caught on something, and he spent those seconds wondering if his head would be crushed against a rock as we swept along. Later, though, while we dried our clothes by the fire and drank hot coffee, it seemed as if he had actually appreciated the experience. Pete and I had had similar reactions after a near-miss; once the terror is past, the knowledge of having survived the challenge more than offsets any grim memory.

Saturday, July 15, 1978. At Slate Falls, a tiny Ojibway settlement on North Bamaji Lake, we repacked and relived our vacation while waiting for the plane that would fly Dad out and bring us supplies from Red Lake. We filleted the last of our fish, then packed them in slabs of ice that had been cut from the lake the past winter and stored in icehouse sawdust. Those fish would provide feasts of memories for Dad back in Washington. All too soon the float plane taxied to the dock. The pilot passed us a crate of supplies, then held the pontoon as we three shook hands for the last time. Dad patted Ki's head and stepped onto the pontoon. I would see his smiling face through the window long after the plane slipped over the horizon.

Soon after the Red Lake plane departed, an Ontario Provincial Police aircraft banked over the cabins. The police were returning to Slate Falls to bury the body of an Ojibway man who had fallen off a speedboat and drowned. Word must have gotten out quickly, for within hours overloaded boats of Ojibway families began arriving from outlying camps for the funeral. The visitors milled about, setting up housekeeping camps and chattering with friends. Plump women in calico dresses hefted blankets and pots from the boats; the men seemed content to stand around puffing on pipes and discussing the recent fickle weather.

Slate Falls was rapidly filling up with guests, but Pete and I found lodging for the night with John Reed, a retired railroad man from Pennsylvania who had spent the last thirty summers prospecting for gold in country to the north. (The Red Lake region is a magnet for prospectors.) He was waiting in a rented cabin in Slate Falls for an available boat and guide to transport him and his supplies. As none of the Ojibway wanted to leave the settlement until after the funeral, John was glad of our company. The conversation flowed freely until I touched on the subject of his prospecting success—after all, his grubstake seemed to include quantities of valuable and sophisticated equipment. At this point he clammed up and gave the prospector's typically evasive answer: "Oh, a bit here and a bit there."

We decided to stay for the funeral the next day, and to pass the time until then I paid a visit to the fly-in camp next door. A group from Minnesota made me welcome, and together we watched a party of Georgians clean up after their day's fishing. The senior Georgian discarded an impressive stringer of pickerel, prompting me to remark about the waste of letting fish spoil. One of my hosts corrected my mistaken assumption. "Naw, they're not spoiled. Every day that group comes off the lake with at least twice its limit. They try to give 'em away, but we've all got our limits, so they just throw the extra ones out." I was shocked. "But he just threw away at least thirty pounds of fish! Why don't they give 'em to the Ojibway?" He shook his head. "Guess they don't want to bother with the Indians. Now you know why we don't talk to those guys. They won't even release the extra fish when they catch 'em. They like to take pictures of plenty of fish, to show off to their friends."

My anger rose and I let my voice rise too. "No wonder Americans are hated in a lot of these settlements." The Georgians looked up in surprise, and I went on, staring down the culprit. "If the Ojibway found out, I wouldn't be surprised if somebody slipped in at night and bashed the bastards' heads in. I wouldn't blame 'em, either."

My anger was partly personal. Admittedly Pete and I had occasionally hunted out of season, but only when our supplies ran low in country where the fishing was poor, and it was simply a question of whether to shoot a goose or have no food at all. I thought back to the previous winter, to the times when our sled dogs had literally been starving and the gnawing in our own stomachs had rivaled the bitter cold for discomfort. But I was angrier for the Ojibway of this village, who depended on the contents of their fishnets. In the winter, when the sportsmen from Georgia were showing their slides, the Ojibway would be chopping through several feet of ice to set their nets.

The next day we turned south toward sprawling Lake St. Joseph. The Ojibway funeral of Johnny Loon, Jr., was finished. By tradition, friends of the deceased dug his grave in a peaceful stand of spruce, then lowered the grey pressboard coffin. John Reed was off to look for gold in some obscure northern location; the Minnesotans and Georgians were out on the lake fishing. If my words had had any effect, perhaps the take would be more modest today. And my father was probably about to touch down in Washington, D.C.

Two days later, still paddling down Lake St. Joseph, we paused for a handful of raisins. I swallowed the first mouthful, then glanced down and gagged. "Auggh! Pete, the raisins are full of maggots!" The raisins had been in one of several airtight packages that hadn't been opened since they were packed in Red Lake. I tore open the package of garlic sausage; little white commas crawled through the rancid meat. We had been taken. For Ki it was manna from heaven; for us it was back to fish.

A day's poling up the Doghole River brought us to the tiny village of Doghole Bay, where Ojibway women were smoking fish in preparation for the fall trapping season. We had reached the halfway mark of our 1,100-mile paddle from Lake Winnipeg to James Bay and were about to embark on the rough-and-tumble waters of the upper Albany River. Our canoeing outfit was showing the wear and tear of six weeks in the bush, so we decided to transport it and us to Pickle Lake, the nearest town where we were likely to find hardware for repairs.

An Ontario Provincial Police sergeant obliged us with a lift in his van, and as it accelerated away from the river I realized that we hadn't been in a motorized vehicle since Winnipeg, six weeks earlier. Pickle Lake was also the first town since then that could be reached by automobile from the south. The contrast between our casual, almost crawling pace in the bush and the world racing by through the van windows was mind-blowing.

In Pickle Lake we were put up by the logging company of Charnell & Associates while we stitched tears in clothing and packs and replaced buttons and supplies. The canoe got a face lift too, thanks to aviation mechanic "Trapper" Dick Anderson and his metal-working skill. Its hull and rivets were sound, but some of the aluminum tie-off points had been sheared off by sweepers on the water or branches on portage trails. These he replaced with superior versions made of stainless steel. Bolt holes drilled in the hull were waterproofed with what Dick called "elephant snot"—a green gelatinous gook that soon hardened into a watertight seal when smeared into gaps.

A few days later we hitched back down to the Doghole River where we had left off. From here, a short portage would bring us to the Albany River, a 500-mile highway to James Bay. As forewarned, we found the upper Albany a chaotic snarl of rapids, and the first few whitewater runs were as thrilling as any we had experienced. But after a week or so, the tense business of running serious rapids every day began to take its toll. My journal entries reflected the tension:

Friday, July 28, 1978. Rain, 70 degrees F, north wind. Rapids for the day:
   1. Ran on right.
   2. Ran on right.
   3. Ran down center.
   4. Ran right of center.
   5. *Very tough.* Ran right channel, right of center.
   6. Damn tough—almost dumped. Ran the center of right channel through six-foot drop. Bottomed out twice. That was a poor way to run it. Rapid should have been thoroughly scouted.
   Portaged 600 yards in the rain, on south bank around Kagami Falls and Lower Rapids. Our leather pack straps have rotted through and snapped one by one. We now have to carry the packs in our arms until we can jury-rig new straps. Should have serviced them in Pickle Lake. . . .
   11. Portaged 75 feet on north bank.
   12. Ran down center.
Note: All rapids of upper Albany were run at high water. Rapid strategies may vary greatly during low-water stages. We blazed all portages and marked them with orange loggers' tape. Also marked our campsites with tape as good sites are hard to find.
   Saw two otters playing this afternoon. Camped at a terrible site in the rain, half a mile west of Rarabeck Creek. Macaroni for supper. Covered 25 miles today.

Days like this one, when many rapids had to be run, left us exhausted and edgy. After a particularly tough set of rapids, we would shake from nerves and have to take a ten-minute break to calm ourselves before running the next. We learned that tough rapids shouldn't be run on bright, sunny days; it is easier to read whitewater features under overcast skies. And we found that there were good days and bad days for rapids. On the good days we felt positive: Everything seemed to click, the canoe made turns like a sports car, and rapids became simple. On other days we were mentally down and the canoe handled more like a truck plowing through the water. When we woke in the morning, our first question was about the wind direction, and our second was whether we were "up" for the rapids. If not, we knew we'd see many portages that day.

One evening while setting up camp after an especially bad stretch of rapids, we saw a group of American canoeists passing and flagged them down, always eager for company. In the course of the conversation one of them remarked, "Can you believe all that crap upriver?"

Misunderstanding him, I answered, "Yeah, some of those rapids are pretty nasty."

"No," he corrected me, "I mean those orange ribbons some bastard tied to the trees. I didn't come all the way up here to find that sort of crap in the wilderness. The jerk even left a pair of pants hanging from a tree limb!"

The jerk in question happened to be me, and the encounter was typical of the contrast in attitudes and behavior between those who visited the northern bush for a few weeks and those who lived there. Since Pete and I had been there for quite a while and lived mainly off the land, we tended to identify with the latter and adopt their methods. This group of canoeists was seeking unspoiled wilderness, and the sight of our orange tape marking campsites was enough to spoil it for them. They had removed the tape, the pants I had left behind, even the empty coffee cans filled with our used tea bags and half-smoked cigarettes, left in forks of trees beside old campsites.

Maybe the next group would have felt and behaved likewise. Or maybe they missed a portage and had to cut their own trail, or worse, got swept over Kagami Falls. They may have had to hack out a miserable campsite in the rain because they couldn't find a suitable one, or flipped in a rapid and reached shore with nothing but their waterproof matches. Had they found one of our old camps in such straits, they could have calmed their panic with a coffee can full of hot tea and a relaxing smoke, if they desired it. I've done the same myself at old Indian camps.

Pete and I didn't invent these practices; we imitated those of the Cree, the Salteaux, and the Ojibway. Like us, many of these people have lost everything in a rapid and faced the prospect of walking out without so much as a hot drink. And they don't have much to begin with. Those denim pants that the conscientious campers no doubt burned had been too threadbare for me to bother with yet another patch. But an Ojibway family heading upriver for the wild-rice harvest would have been delighted to find them, and a patient seamstress could have extended their usefulness many months.

In national parks and wilderness areas stateside, I'm all in favor of picking up litter and leaving the place as you found it. It's appropriate in such places, which tend to be heavily used escape areas for city-based outdoor lovers. But it's not necessarily appropriate in a working environment like the northern bush, where you may travel for a month without meeting another soul. John Reed prospects gold for a living, not for his health. And the Ojibway family poling upstream for the dollar a pound the Hudson's Bay Company will pay for their wild rice isn't on vacation. For them, missing a poorly marked portage may mean the loss of half a day's income.

The Indians we met tended to keep their own counsel about the ways of visiting whites, and often they answered canoeists' questions about river conditions and local customs curtly or evasively. They did, however, indulge a penchant for practical jokes in the form of deliberately misleading answers. We occasionally met canoeists who'd been given route directions that would have stranded them in a bog. Earlier in the trek we had fallen prey to such pranks, which are simply a means of judging a stranger. When a *métis* in Saskatchewan convinced me there was a cabin out in the bush "that way," it didn't dawn on me that he was kidding until I had snowshoed six miles without compass or map, through country devoid of landmarks and crisscrossed with deadfalls. If you can decipher the maze and find your own way out, as I did in that case, you have gained respect.

Rather than speaking bluntly, the Indian paints a picture and leaves you to interpret it. The canoeist who has "lost" precious time from his two-week holiday because the Indian failed to connect all the dots has missed the significance of the painting. Part of the Indian's message is that one shouldn't enter the bush without a good understanding of local topography and techniques. Fancy gear, the best maps, even the best advice are ultimately no substitute for self-reliance — that's the gist of the lesson, and too many visitors miss it.

On August 1, we stopped at the head of a portage to scout an ominous-looking set of rapids. An Ojibway family freighting upriver for the wild-rice harvest was there too, getting ready to portage. We exchanged greetings and gave them the remains of an eighteen-pound pike I had caught the day before. While the women set up camp, we helped the men portage their waterlogged Chestnut freight canoe over the trail.

Later we joined them for tea, and the Ojibway shook their heads vigorously on hearing that we planned to run the rapids. They pointed to a wrecked canoe that stood jacknifed in midstream, an inverted V wedged among the rocks. Apparently it had struck a rock with such force that its aluminum hull had cracked beneath the center thwart.

Peter voted to portage but I talked him into running the rapids. With the spray cover on, we could handle deep, powerful rapids with large haystack waves in relative safety. This one, though, was a shallow, sloppy mess: a staircase of drops with scant water cover, littered with unseen rocks. We were likely to encounter similar rapids ahead, and I thought we needed the practice. As a precaution, Ki would ride underneath the spray cover — too many times his scrambling to avoid waves had nearly rolled us over.

Careful scouting didn't provide much encouragement. Four-fifths of the rapids was wholly unnavigable, and the only safe path was an extremely narrow chute on the far side of the river. To reach the chute we would have to cut diagonally across the sloppy upper whitewater. There was a good chance that before we could make it, the current would broadside us into the first stair. The Ojibway family crowded the riverbank as we pushed off.

Less than a dozen paddle strokes into the current I knew I'd made the wrong decision. Judging from our drift, the chance of reaching the chute before the first drop was slim. I wasn't alone in this realization; two of the Ojibway sprinted for their Chestnut.

This was a critical decision point in the rapids, the kind we had come to dread. To turn downriver toward the staircase would guarantee a dump, but at least we would have some control over the spill and might escape with only bruises. On the other hand, if we held our course and failed to reach the chute, the resulting broadside into the staircase could well be fatal. "Downriver?!" I yelled to Pete. He replied with a quick nod, drawing his paddle in to help swing the bow downstream.

We slipped over a modest haystack, then bottomed out on the first shelf of the staircase with a sickening, high-pitched squeal of aluminum on rock. Water began piling up against my back as we strained against our paddle shafts to free the canoe. We broke loose, only to ground out again on the second shelf. On the third, aluminum buckled and the stern began to cave in.

My head broke the surface in time to dodge the rolling canoe. I had difficulty focusing, and put my hand to my face to discover that my glasses had been torn away. Pete shouted from the other side of the canoe and I answered. We tried to fend off the rocks with our legs, but it felt as if they were being beaten with hammers, thrashed and twisted into unnatural positions. Finally the river bottom dropped away and the current began to ease.

The same thought occurred to both of us simultaneously: Ki was still beneath the spray cover! I tore open the stern spray skirt to find a hysterical dog scrabbling to get free of his torture chamber. Then the Ojibway men were pulling us into the Chestnut by our collars and helping retrieve lost paddles and flotsam. Ki would have nothing to do with a canoe; he swam straight for shore.

For the next two days we dried gear, stitched torn clothing, repaired the canoe, and tended our battered bodies. Most of our camera equipment and food was ruined, but the canoe had survived amazing punishment. Though it would always be slightly lopsided, we were able to bash it back to its general shape with hand-held rocks. Ki, except for his terrible fright, was unharmed. Pete and I had lost our boots in the spill, but other than our damaged feet and a few cuts and bruises elsewhere, we were in surprisingly sound shape. The loss of my glasses was more serious. I had only one spare set and their frame was already broken, though a patch job with wire and tape allowed me to see reasonably well.

But in some way this spill took the heart out of us. What began as a slight nagging depression grew to dangerous proportions over the next few weeks. Part of it was feeling psyched-out by the idea of more rapids. Also, the delay forced us to take stock of the expedition's progress, and that was depressing. Vancouver was 3,200 miles behind us, but Tadoussac was still 1,500 miles ahead. We had hoped to make it by the end of this summer, but it was now August, with the first frost only weeks away. We didn't speak of it, but privately we both knew we could never reach the St. Lawrence before freeze-up.

The success of the expedition was never more in jeopardy than here on the Albany. We were sick of it and of each other. Though we never discussed it, I believe we both sincerely wished to quit at this point. And I suspect we would have, if not for the loss of face. I had seriously considered giving up several times while hiking alone in British Columbia, and Pete came dangerously close while dogsledding through Flin Flon. Yet the expedition's success was then still a dream. Ironically, now that we knew for the first time that we *could* reach Tadoussac, the whole thing suddenly seemed pointless.

Undoubtedly the prospect of waiting out another winter and stretching the expedition well into the next year was weighing on us, even if unconsciously. Whatever the reason, we had lost our will to continue. Rather than being in charge, we felt like we were on a dreamlike ride along a predestined course. We were invincible. We knew that we would never be killed—the bush was having too much fun beating us down. Needless to say, this state of mind was extremely dangerous.

To postpone the sight of endless rapids and falls, we escaped into books and often didn't leave the tent before noon. When the lenses of my makeshift goggles fell out and shattered on a rock, I became truly handicapped. My uncorrected vision is terrible, and I could no longer trust my perception of rapids. Peter then became my eyes, shouting back the location of river features, and I simply steered accordingly. The cuts in our feet became infected and blood poisoning further sapped our strength; we limped on swollen feet over the portages.

Strangely, we never argued during this awful period. If you don't care, there's no reason to argue. As at other times, Ki held us together in his blind faith that we would make the right decisions. He sat patiently by the campfire or in the canoe, his only motivation the desire to be with us. [*Peter confirms that both he and Dave were in a terrible state of mind during this time. Dave's depression and sense of invulnerability apparently stemmed from the actual situation rather than from his incipient illness; in fact, Pete believes that, of the two, he himself was more often down and ready to give up the journey. "The whole two and a half years was like a high for Dave."*]

A week after the Indian family had plucked us from the rapids, we stepped ashore at the Ogoki Ojibway settlement. It didn't do much for our spirits: The only empty cabins were owned by the chief, who was far from fond of whites, so we camped in front of the Hudson's Bay post. There was no running water, and we didn't feel like taking bucket baths out in the open—so scratch the baths. A further blow was finding that the post was nearly out of the supplies we'd counted on for our final 250-mile run down to James Bay. The supply plane was due any day, but we came away with just a few armloads of canned food and nonperishables—no meat, vegetables, bread, or dairy products. At least we found some penicillin to combat the blood poisoning.

> *Journal entry, Thursday, August 10, 1978.* Sunny, light west wind, 70 degrees F. Boring, uneventful day. The country is getting increasingly bland and ugly the closer we get to sea level. Steep, 100-foot mud banks—terrible camps. Slow current, no sailing—just boring, mindless, endless paddling. Covered 50 miles today, 802 miles from Berens River. Fried fish for supper.

Though this journal entry still sounds depressed, it does suggest one change for the better: The fierce rapids of the upper Albany were a thing of the past. The next day, things improved still more. After covering thirty-three miles to reach the mouth of the Kenogami River, we spotted tent canvas on the far side of an island that splits the Albany at the river junction. Richard "Top" Foley, a big man with a round face and an ever-present smile, greeted us at the island's dirt landing. His group of half a dozen fishermen from Pittsburgh had flown to this isolated island for a week of trophy fishing; they were scheduled to be picked up by floatplane the next afternoon.

This group had fished remote rivers and lakes throughout northern Canada, and complained that this was one of their least productive trips. They were filleting the day's catch as they spoke: nine pikes that made the table sag under the weight. The largest approached twenty pounds and the smallest was just under ten—a respectable fish by anyone's standards, but prompting Top to apologize that "We don't normally keep anything under ten pounds, but fishing's been so crummy."

Top and his friends provided a cheerful, upbeat atmosphere that gave us a much-needed lift. They liked to rough it and were proficient outdoorsmen, but had decided that one small luxury couldn't hurt—so they had flown in a chef from Montreal. We dined that evening beside a tin wood stove in a tent on a choice of three entrees: I had chicken cordon bleu. I barely knew what to do with the napkin to the left of my salad fork; not since Pickle Lake had we wiped our hands on anything but our pants. Even Ki's dinner put our standard camp fare to shame.

Another pleasant surprise greeted us in the morning: Fifty pounds of unused canned meat and vegetables made up for what we couldn't purchase in Ogoki. None of the fishermen wanted to fly out with the extra food, and I suspect someone had noticed our alarmingly light grub box. We were no longer restricted by freight weight, since the now-sluggish Albany wouldn't require a single portage from here to James Bay, so we eagerly accepted the food.

Our stay with Top and friends seemed to leave us with fresh enthusiasm and luck. A strong tailwind grew as we loaded the canoe, and filled our sail as we set off. I doubt we paddled more than a few dozen strokes all day, yet when we pulled to shore eight and a half hours later, we were seventy-two miles downriver—a new record to add to our "personal bests" of forty-two miles in a day by backpack (a solo mark for which I had paid dearly) and thirty-four miles by dogsled.

We were tempted to continue, calculating that if we traveled until midnight we could break 100 miles. But the wind was shifting, and heavy, charcoal-grey storm clouds were leapfrogging across the horizon. We had reached an abandoned settlement called Ghost River, so we wisely decided to camp there and explore instead. We found no artifacts, but our search was cut short by a drenching downpour. Peter stumbled about trying to erect the tent where the cabins of Ghost River supposedly once stood, fighting to plant stakes against the erratically gusting wind. I hunched over a gravel nest on the riverbank, protecting a wad of birchbark and twigs from the BBs of water.

By the time we finished dinner, the wind had blown itself out and the rain tapered to a drizzle. Peter and I sipped tea beside the spitting fire while Ki preened himself in his nest under an ancient spruce. He wanted little to do with the idiots who had dragged him away from the orgy of food at the fishermen's camp, where he could be dozing in the heat of a wood stove instead of huddling beneath a tree like a wild animal. It was the time of day when individual trees on the opposite shore dissolve into a solid grey saw blade. About 200 yards upriver, a small campfire highlighted an Indian family; while we watched, the parents left their three children in the firelight and paddled toward our camp.

After we'd said our hellos, Peter and I waited for the solemn Ojibway couple to divulge the purpose of their visit. We were already sharing tea, as is customary, but when I reached for the teapail to pour a second round, I saw that their eyes were fixed on the few leftover peas in our dinner pot. They accepted my offer of them and stood there eagerly sharing them in the drizzle. I wondered how hungry their children must be and, without speaking, moved my eyes from the Indians to Pete to the grub box. Pete smiled and nodded his agreement. I walked over to the box and returned with half our food. Broad smiles crossed their faces, and the man uttered the first full sentence we'd heard from them: "We are short on food." Then he led his wife back to their Chestnut canoe. I think Top would have been pleased about how his food was used.

We soon discovered that our record-breaking seventy-two mile day was a fluke. Now only 300 feet above sea level, the Albany's current continued to decrease as the river widened to a shallow expanse. At times our paddles bumped the gravelly bottom in the center of the river. The banks spread out into vast mud and gravel floodplains, bespeaking the river's force in the spring floods after break-up. Steady headwinds further slowed us.

Our travel-weariness reached new lows. At times we even propped open our books with rocks, so we could read as we paddled. Peter was glued to Leon Uris, and I found escape in novels about nineteenth-century southern plantation life. We also devised a form of entertainment we called the "Albany fox hunt"—a practice so foolish I cringe to report it, but this is how bored we were.

The "foxes" were bears, of which we spotted several each day, and Ki was the "hound." When we saw a bear, we put a rope leash on Ki and held his muzzle to keep him from betraying our presence. We silently stalked the animals by canoe: Bears have poor eyesight, and if we stayed downwind and quiet, we could closely approach a feeding bear. A hundred feet from our quarry, Pete would grab the camera and I the shotgun (just in case something went wrong). As soon as the bear detected us, we'd set Ki free and begin the merry chase, following Ki's mad barking until we sooner or later found him carrying on beneath a treed, confused bear.

I hasten to say that these "hunts" always ended safely for all parties, and we gave them up after one episode revealed an unexpected danger. We'd been chasing a cranky old black bear. On reaching the treed bear, I pulled Ki away and was returning to the canoe when a low growl erupted from a clump of bushes ten feet to my left. This was a rather awkward way of discovering that Ki had been chasing *two* bears and had succeeded in treeing only the more intimidated of the pair. The ill-tempered old bear was still squatting in the bushes, ready to revenge the interruption of his afternoon gorge. Though we escaped without seeing him, we swore off the hunts. [*It should also be noted that the creatures involved were black* bears, which nearly always flee humans, and not the dangerously un-predictable grizzly—but the game was nonetheless ill-advised.]

Thirty miles before spilling into James Bay, the Albany fans out into a delta of as many as ten channels. Somewhere in this maze lies a small waterway called Yellow Creek, which leads to the Cree village of Fort Albany—one of the first fur posts established by the Hudson's Bay Company in the seventeenth century and our last stop before James Bay. Peter and I spent much of the afternoon of August 15 wading the canoe over gravel bars, choosing the wrong channel several times. When we did manage to reach Yellow Creek, we were amazed to find a "parking lot" of canoes. More than fifty massive, oceangoing Chestnuts and Peterboroughs—the bush versions of Detroit's big-wheeled cruisers—lay stranded on a tidal mudflat. Each parking spot consisted of four ten-foot posts driven several feet in-to the mud. The rising tide would lift the canoes within their posted spaces, which kept them from drifting free or banging into each other.

When we pulled our compact "import" up to the Fort Albany dock, we were welcomed by Joan Metatawabin, a white school-teacher who had worked in the village for years and had assumed a Cree name. Joan was interested in the expedition and invited us to stay at her home, which spared us the expense of the village board-ing house. While lodging with Joan and her Cree boyfriend, David Hookimaw, we were offered the use of showers and laundry facilities at the nursing station (the village itself had no running water). This we gratefully accepted, and since it was the first time we and our clothes had been clean in a month, I imagine the townspeople were just as grateful.

We again went to work repairing clothing and gear, but our broken pack straps were a problem. We couldn't obtain the kind of leather we needed to fix them and had to make do with straps con-structed of shoulder-pinching hemp. Fortunately our shipping crate of spare supplies, maps, and film had arrived from Pickle Lake, and this solved my eyesight crisis. In the crate was a spare pair of Peter's glasses, and we found that his prescription was close enough to mine that I could wear them.

Our primary task in Fort Albany was to gather information about canoe travel on James Bay, where strong winds, huge tides, and heavy seas would present hazards that we had not yet encountered. It would be much more like coastal ocean travel than river paddling, and we had no experience in this area.

The usual practice of canoeists coming down the Albany was to have their canoes flown out to Moosonee, at the southern tip of James Bay, and then shipped home by rail. If they were determined to travel the bay, they could hire an Indian guide with a twenty-three-foot Chestnut and a fifty-horsepower outboard to take them safely to Moosonee. Our little eighteen footer, the locals warned, would be no match for the unpredictable conditions. The country around James Bay is lowland, and tidal mudflats extend as far as ten miles out from the coast, making camping a tricky business. Some paddlers had lost their boats to the incoming tide and had to walk out through the bush. Others had run out of food after being windbound for weeks. Lives had been lost.

Even allowing for the probability that the tales were embellished by Cree guides with dollar signs in their eyes, the 100-mile paddle to Moosonee sounded less than pleasurable. And our travel on James Bay wouldn't end there; it was another 120 miles from Moosonee to Rupert House on the Quebec shore, where we were to resume river travel.

But we didn't really see a choice. To follow the guides' advice would have meant breaking two cardinal rules of the expedition: Never to travel with the assistance of a guide and never to aid advancement by motor. So we paddled on down the last few miles of the Albany toward James Bay, our mood a mixture of the fascination and fear that a skydiver feels just before his first jump.

10 | James Bay West
Fort Albany to Moosonee, Ontario

After a four-day stopover in Fort Albany, we began the James Bay crossing with a good deal of apprehension. The first day's travel presented no problems; only gentle swells and light breezes greeted our bow. But our first night's camp left us wondering if we should have heeded the guides' advice.

We raced the ebbing tide at sunset to reach shore before the outflow stranded us on the mud. The "shore" wasn't much better: It was an oozing muck of decayed vegetation, with the nearest semblance of trees more than two miles inland—a situation we were unprepared for. Here, dry ground was considered to be anyplace you might step without leaving gurgling puddles in your tracks. We found a campsite on a twenty-by-fifty-foot island of scrub willow in a field of waving grass, and proceeded to our next lesson.

While Pete gathered driftwood for a fire, I walked inland in search of water that was neither salty nor tea-colored. Half a mile inland I filled my bucket from a pond of reasonably fresh water, then turned back toward camp. But where was it? I squinted at the horizon, trying to discern which of a hundred thickets of scrub willow was ours. Retracing the path was out; my trail had twisted and turned during the search for water. Adding to my confusion, the tide was now many miles out and the featureless grass stretched to the horizon.

After a while I yelled, sheepishly at first, and heard Pete's faint answering shout from my right. I walked a few hundred yards in that direction and yelled again. This time his voice came from the left. We played this hide-and-seek game for nearly an hour, until

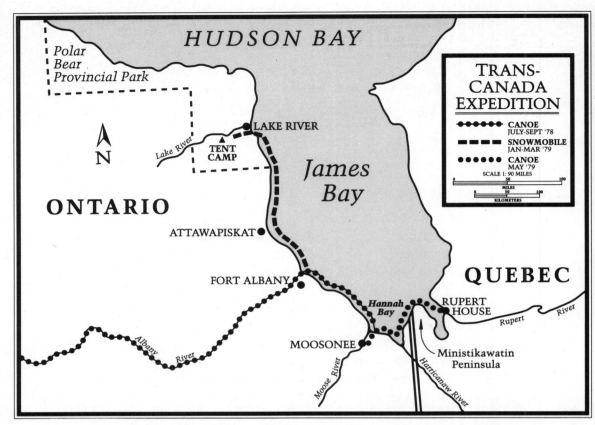

James Bay and the Lake River Camp, Ontario, August 1978–May 1979

finally I spotted a flicker of red in a spot exactly opposite where I expected to find our camp. Peter had stripped off his scarlet long johns and tied them atop a tall pole as a signal flag. It was a good lesson—from then on we didn't venture far across the tidal grasses without leaving prominent marker flags.

A steady rain fell throughout the night. In the morning we learned another lesson in James Bay travel: Never retire without setting the alarm clock if you plan to catch an early tide. (It also helps to know the times of high and low tides, and to understand how wind direction affects them.) Though we were packed and ready to depart by 7:30 A.M., by the time we reached the high-water mark, the tide had left without us. Already the water's edge was more than a mile away and receding fast. There was nothing to do but sit down and wait for the evening tide.

The inevitable next lesson, having to do with all-night paddling in an open canoe, followed promptly. For the first few hours of the evening, the sea rocked us gently and our paddle strokes were quick and eager. But our confidence and strength waned with the setting sun. The orange orb of warmth touched the horizon, then abandoned us, and the temperature took a nosedive. By 10:00 P.M. we were in complete darkness, a black void above us and inky liquid below, our canoe a silver sliver suspended in space.

Our only glimpse of the shoreline was an occasional faint tracing off to starboard. We tried to stay about three miles offshore, to avoid being caught by the nighttime low tide, and the compass assured our direction. But the 28-degree cold and the stinging wind took their toll: As we hunched our shoulders to hide from the wind, our paddle strokes became stiff and awkward. Ki slept in a curled ball between us, apparently having given up trying to comprehend our bewildering actions.

We monitored the falling tide by measuring the water depth with a six-foot pole, and whenever the depth decreased we hustled farther out to sea. Nevertheless, it soon dropped to an alarmingly shallow two feet, and rocks began to surface. The risk of being stranded on a shoal was great, yet we dared not venture farther out — we were already beyond sight of land. We realized our danger suddenly and forcefully. Should a strong wind come up, especially an offshore wind, we could lose our orientation to land and have little hope of saving ourselves if we swamped. [*The canoe's sail was virtually useless during this stretch of travel on James Bay. The rig could exploit only a following wind; here the expedition was heading south, with the prevailing westerlies coming from the side.*]

Slowly the rocks grew into shoals and the shoals multiplied, until we were forced to climb out of the canoe and walk it through channels only inches deep. At midnight we ran out of water completely and just stopped, darker shapes in the darkness, the canoe a shiny speck upon an endless moonscape. We were miserably cold and hungry, so I suggested that we anchor the canoe by its bow rope to a rock, split a can of stew, and catch a few hours of sleep on the shoal. I was certain by now that I could calculate the tidal times and estimated that the tide would regain our shoal at 4:00 A.M. Pete's face, highlighted by the late-rising moon, betrayed his doubt, but he was too tired and cold to argue. I set the alarm for three, allowing an hour's margin for error.

A wave washed over our legs at 2:00 A.M. We were farther offshore than I had thought. We ran in circles around our disintegrating shoal, tossing sodden sleeping bags into the now-floating canoe and groping beneath the slapping waves for any forgotten items. Our clothing soaked through, we dove into the canoe and paddled away from our erstwhile sleeping site. At five that morning we grounded out half a mile off a rocky protrusion called Nomansland Point. We anchored the canoe where we could retrieve it later and stumbled over the flats; by now we were shivering uncontollably. Nearly twelve hours after leaving solid land, we collapsed with our packs beside a high-water wall of driftwood.

We remained on the point that day, and in the afternoon I sat by the campfire, watching the water ripple along the horizon and the first southbound flights of ducks and geese undulate across the sky. Falling into a hypnotic reverie, I began to see a vision: an eighteenth-century fur brigade heading down the coast to the French fort on the Moose River. The voyageurs wore fur tukes (close-fitting helmets with earflaps) on their heads; their red paddle blades danced in the sun's rays. A chanting song drifted over the water. I squinted and turned my head to listen, then glanced over at Pete, who seemed to be having the same dream. We both stared at the phantom craft approaching us, and Ki sat up, his mane bristling.

Nine canoeists paddled into our camp in a twenty-four-foot fiberglass replica of a voyageur's birchbark canoe. Before we could recover enough to speak, one of the "voyageurs" inquired, "Are you Halsey and Souchuk, Trans-Canada?" At our affirmative nods, he then strode forward to introduce his group. "We're Expeditions of North America—ENA. We began in Minnesota, and our destination's Moosonee." Peter asked how they knew of us. "We heard about you in Osnaburgh House, 600 miles up the Albany. You set off on the Albany two days ahead of us. We've been trying to catch up."

The speaker, Chuck Benda, and his fellow leader, Tod Spedding, then explained their trip to us. Both were counselors for a juvenile offenders rehabilitation program in Minnesota. Having learned that the ENA program helped improve attitudes and motivation, the school chose a few of the less troublesome kids to participate each year. This particular group consisted of seven bright and friendly kids ranging in age from sixteen to eighteen.

Both expeditions tried to leave on the next morning's tide at sunrise, but high winds and a heavy, breaking sea stopped us cold. Even the big ENA canoe could make no headway, and Peter and I actually lost ground in our little Grumman. The wind didn't subside until midmorning, long after the tide had peaked. Here was the catch-22 of canoeing James Bay: If we caught the tide before it began to fall, the wind was too strong to paddle against. If wind and waves were light enough to allow progress, the tide was probably ebbing.

We made a few attempts, on other occasions, to catch a falling tide, but they were futile. We'd leave the first load of gear at the waterline, but by the time we returned with the second, the tide would be another 200 yards out. This relay race could continue for miles. The flats were so broad and level that we could watch the tide run off from shore.

Stuck on the peninsula for another day, we joined forces with Chuck and Tod's gang to prepare a major feast of canned chicken and vegetables, soup, fresh-baked bannock, and pie made with ripe gooseberries from a nearby hedge. It was a special treat for the kids after a month on a freeze-dried diet. The next morning brought a gently swelling tide and blessedly light headwinds. Both canoes set off together, though the ENA group soon outdistanced us. Our speed advantage on the Albany had been due mainly to the rapids, most of which we could run while they had to portage. Their brittle, deep-draft fiberglass hull couldn't handle the shallow, rock-littered rapids down which we often bumped and banged, and they had no spray cover to keep them from swamping in deeper rapids. But in the expansive waters of the bay, their craft was ideal. Eight paddle blades flashed in synchrony, while the high-perched sternman ruddered his long, sweeping paddle. They pulled ahead of us with the first few strokes, and slipped beyond the horizon within an hour.

We stayed well off the coast that day, sometimes as many as six miles out. An offshore wind suggested there might be an extra-low tide and we couldn't afford to lose more time hung up on a shoal. Paddling in the deep-water waves was a very different experience than in the short, slapping waves over the flats. Amidst these deep rollers we would glimpse a panoramic view while topping the crests, then descend into the troughs and lose the horizon. Though large, the waves were quite safe, for they never crested. Flocks of scoters—black sea ducks with an odd, whistling call—bobbed between the hills of water.

The wind died as the tide ebbed, and our canoe slipped over the smooth, still deeps beyond the reach of flats and shoals. The only sounds other than our voices were the occasional cries of distant shorebirds. Though there was nothing behind me but the small stern deck, I distinctly heard someone back there say "push," with a soft "p" and an accented "sh" sound. I glanced over my shoulder just in time to see an ivory hump emerge.

"Pete! Pete, look, a whale!"

"Oh, yeah, right, Halsey."

Paddling the calm waters was getting boring, and Peter assumed I was trying to liven up the day with a whale hoax. Then a midsize beluga whale surfaced for air no more than fifty feet from our bow. "Dave, a whale!"

Our escorts remained with us for an hour or so. The white, grey, and mottled belugas, from twelve to thirty feet long, broke the surface as close as twenty feet from the canoe, and never farther than 100 yards away. If we slowed, they slowed. Curious to see how they would react, we stopped paddling altogether. The whales continued to swim southeast very slowly, and then magically paused, as if waiting for us to catch up. From below, our hull was similar to a beluga in shape, size, and color; we wondered whether we might look like an injured whale.

Like dolphins, they surfaced side by side in pairs and threesomes; it was hard to tell how many there were in all. Far from displaying fear of us, they seemed curious, their black eyes, the size of silver dollars, appearing to study us. We were close enough to observe their fascinating breathing technique: first the "push" sound of the exhalation, then a gulp of fresh air. Just prior to the dive, a flap of skin seals the breath hole, making it strongly resemble a giant human navel. Ki was mesmerized throughout the performance. The sight of a bear or a moose made him yap and leap, yet he didn't so much as whine at the whales. He just sat at attention, staring and shaking.

A hummock of water boiled against the hull, and as we watched, a large white beluga passed directly beneath us. This closest encounter may have been a final inspection; in any case, no other whales surfaced again. We were alone on the bay.

Normally we ate lunch in the canoe, the flats presenting a barrier between us and dry land. But the whales had steered us toward a narrow, prominent point that seemed to offer a reasonable anchorage. We beached on the flats and dragged the canoe what we guessed was a safe distance above the waterline. A great heap of driftwood spanned the base of the point, promising the rare luxury of hot tea with our lunch.

Ki interrupted our second mug of tea with an unfortunate success at his latest favorite pastime: He caught a skunk beneath a log somewhere upwind of our lunch site. His concrete sinuses didn't seem to mind, but we preferred the fresh sea breeze and ordered him to stay well behind during our return walk to the canoe.

The coastline was wonderfully serene as we strolled along. Strands of seaweed swayed with the incoming current, shorebirds flitted across the water, and two lumbering cranes heaved their awkward bodies aloft. The scene would have been perfect . . . had it only included an eighteen-foot canoe carrying all our possessions. We gazed around in growing panic, but did not glimpse a hint of metal in any direction. There was a light westerly breeze—an offshore wind, meaning that unless the canoe had caught upon a rock, it was probably headed out to sea. Between us we had the clothes we were wearing, an empty teapail and mugs, a few matches, and a coydog who smelled strong enough to drive away a canoe without any wind. But the real explanation was simpler: We had forgotten to anchor the bow rope.

Pete ran south across what little remained of the flats; I ran north up the coast and continued running through the water after the shoreline dead-ended at a large bay. When the water was at my waist, I climbed onto a gravel shoal that was about to be submerged and searched the horizon, thinking that I would rather see nothing at all than a flash of metal far out to sea. The horizon was empty, but neither was there any sign of the canoe along the shore. Just as I was leaving, a rock about a quarter-mile away began to move. The rock caught and reflected the sun, then pivoted, revealing the profile of a canoe. I closed the distance quickly, but the water was soon to my armpits, and the tidal current swirled against my chest. The rock that held the canoe was steadily shrinking beneath the climbing tide; at any moment, the canoe could find water rather than stone under its hull and skip out to sea on the westerly breeze.

I pushed through the deep water, cursing its drag on my legs. When I was ten yards away, the canoe slipped free, then paused for an instant as if trying to decide whether to escape or stay. I reached out and patted our stray metal steed, then firmly grasped it by the gunwales and hauled myself in. I found Peter stranded on a spit of gravel, having waded channels and crossed shoals as I had. We couldn't see Ki but we could smell him, still off shoal-hopping. Sea water, we sadly discovered, does not reduce skunk odor.

However, Ki's lingering aroma soon became the least of our worries. Over the next four days we gained exactly ten miles. For two of those days we were pinned down by a solid southwesterly wind at a Ministry of Natural Resources (MNR) camp, where a couple of biologists were surveying the trout population in a nearby creek. This was certainly a respite from the rigors of the bay, but we were falling ever further behind schedule. Worse, our supplies were nearly depleted. The MNR employees, Tim and John, couldn't help, as their airdrop was late and they were already rationing food.

By the third day the wind hadn't abated and an angry sea still crashed across the flats. Launching a canoe in such surf was a dangerous business, but our supply situation was critical and we could no longer remain idle. We flipped a coin: heads, we chance the surf; tails, we wait another day. Heads it was, and we launched the canoe on the lee side of a string of boulders. Past this natural breakwater, waves jumped to the sky, the wind shearing off their foamy crests in showers of mist. When we passed the last boulder, the gale struck like fists. No sooner did the spray cover shed the weight of one wave than another put the deck awash.

Ki stood in the center of the canoe, shifting his weight on sea legs as he tried to keep his belly dry. Pete and I learned to sway our hips in time with the canoe's rocking motion. The canoeist riding a heavy sea must keep his body loose and flexible. Simply reacting to the impact of big waves isn't enough—the canoe may swamp unless you anticipate the impact and shift your weight accordingly. By transferring weight from one buttock to the other and leaning the torso in the opposite direction, you improve the canoe's balance and allow the wave to pass beneath the hull rather than sloshing over the top. The canoe should roll with the waves, its gunwales parallel to the surface of the water or the angle of the wave rather than to the horizon. Pete and I danced the hip-sway for three hours, sometimes losing ground, at best gaining less than a mile for each hour's work. Exhausted and defeated, we finally gave up and turned toward shore, making camp a mere two miles from our departure point. The glow from Tim and John's tent was still visible that night.

It was nearly as bad the following day, eight hours of work advancing us no more than six miles. When the wind was too strong to paddle against, we poled laboriously across the shallows. The wind's only benefit was to sweep Ki's noxious odor away from our nostrils. In the space of a week he'd been sprayed by five skunks. Yet his hunting had its benefits, too; one day he stalked and actually caught a fat mallard, providing a nice change in our menu. That same day, perhaps frustrated that we had swiped his kill, he ran down a rabbit and broke its neck in his jaws. This time we didn't have the heart to take it from him.

Daytime high tides were now occurring after noon, and nearly an hour later each day. This meant we couldn't depart until past noon. Even worse, high tide in the wee hours made reaching shore at night an ordeal. We paddled until about 9:00 P.M. and then, when ready to camp, anchored the canoe at the high-water mark and portaged the packs a mile or more to shore across boot-sucking flats. Every 100 yards we left a stake in the mud to mark our trail. From then until high tide, we took hourly turns backtracking to the canoe by flashlight and poling or wading it to the most recent high-water line. Not until long past midnight was the canoe secured on shore.

It was cold, miserable, frightening work. Temperatures were by now regularly dipping into the 20s after dark, and it was a rare night when we didn't get a few bootfuls of seawater. If an onshore wind caused an extra quick tide, submerging our footprints and marker stakes, we might spend an hour or more sloshing through freezing, knee-deep water while playing a dimming flashlight beam over the surface, wondering if it would ever divulge the canoe's location. I have never before or since experienced such intense loneliness as I would feel standing a mile offshore in frigid water, praying to spot the canoe and longing for the warmth and security of our distantly flickering campfire. Once we didn't find the canoe at all until the next morning—and not a minute too soon, as it was shipping water through the spray skirts and had already sunk to the gunwales.

On September 1, we spotted an indentation in the coastline that appeared larger than the usual creek entrances. As we paddled toward it, landmarks fell into place. We had reached Wavy Creek, the shortcut around Ship Sands Island and the quickest route to the Moose River and Moosonee. Our timing was fortunate; the tide was on the rise, counteracting the river's current against our bow. At dusk, eleven days after leaving Fort Albany, we tied up to the dock in front of Moosonee.

Though our bodies, minds, and nerves begged for rest, we intended to spend only one night in Moosonee before pushing on. We hadn't discussed it outright, but we both knew there was no longer any chance of reaching the St. Lawrence before freeze-up—Tadoussac was still 1,000 miles away. Both physically and emotionally we had never been so depleted of strength and will; we were afraid to discuss our doubts and seemed incapable of long-range planning. Our only thought was to push as far into Quebec as the weather would allow and then decide whether to continue overland through the winter or wait for another spring thaw.

Tim and John had sent a message to the Ministry of Natural Resources to expect our arival, and it kindly spared our wallets by providing lodging in a trailer on the outskirts of town. Once we had stowed our gear there, we set off for a long-awaited night in town. Though Moosonee's population is only eighteen hundred, its two hotels and several restaurants qualified it as "big city" for us. With a choice of menus, we bypassed the fine steaks at the Polar Bear Lodge and ordered pizza instead. After months of a bland bush diet, our palates craved spice — washed down by a bottomless pitcher of beer.

Halfway through the pizza, our stomachs began warning us that they weren't prepared for such a culinary jolt. The beer hit equally hard. Finally Pete shook his head and got up to return to the trailer, silent and slightly greenish of hue. An hour later, I pushed aside what was left and weaved my way light-headedly toward the door.

A shortcut, down a trail and across a creek, halved the mile-long walk to our trailer. A steady rain was falling, and my only wish was for bed. Some thoughtful soul had placed a length of sheet metal across the creek, but one step onto the metal sent my feet flying into the air. I landed in the creek, scarcely noticing the water as all sensation focused on the searing pain in my ankle. I tried to stand but the ankle turned to jelly. "Oh, Jesus, I've sprained it," I thought.

I could see the trailer light 100 yards away through the rain and tried to crawl toward it, but altering the position of my ankle nearly made me black out from pain. By dragging myself belly down, however, I found I could keep my ankle fairly flat on the ground. Twenty feet . . . a rest in a mud puddle . . . another twenty feet. Ten feet from the trailer I shouted and threw rocks at the window, but Pete was dead to the world — as I could have been if I'd left the restaurant when he had. I climbed the trailer steps on my belly, stopping at each one to rest.

In the morning the local physician diagnosed my injury as a dislocated ankle and a spiral fracture of the fibula. He explained that at least one operation would be required to put things back together properly and warned that I had little chance of escaping a permanent limp. Meanwhile he tried to relocate the joint; I was pumped full of painkillers, and he twisted and pulled until the bones grated, without success. He then volunteered to perform the operation there in

Moosonee, but what I had seen so far didn't give me great confidence. Clearly there would be no bush travel for me for many months, so I might as well go through the surgery and convalescence back in Washington, D.C., where they knew what they were doing.

Peter's mother, Elinor Souchuk, immediately flew up from Chicago to Moosonee to lend a hand. She played foster mother to me for a few days, helping to arrange my transfer back to the States. My feelings during this time were a black morass of shock, anger, and depression, dominated by guilt. I couldn't face Peter, fearing that my stupid overindulgence had destroyed our chance to complete the expedition. What an ignominious ending, after nearly losing our lives time and again in the bush.

Despite Pete's assurances that he would be ready to start again as soon as I was, my doubts persisted. When he helped me onto the plane back to Washington, I made him promise that if I couldn't continue next spring, he would find a new partner and go the rest of the way to Tadoussac. Ki was accompanying me, caged in the baggage compartment; the Souchuks were flying back to Chicago. As the DC-3 swung out over James Bay before turning south, I wondered whether spring would find me again plying its waters or hobbling along some city street.

11 | In Pursuit of Paradise

Winter at the Lake River Camp, Ontario

From September through December, 1978, Dave Halsey recuperated from his broken ankle at his parents' home outside of Washington. His greatest worry during this time was of losing his acclimatization to bush life. He faced a wait of another four months until late spring, when James Bay and the rivers would be sufficiently ice free to permit water travel again. It loomed like an eternity for Dave, who felt as if he had left the center of his identity in the north. His dream of completing the trans-Canada trip seemed to fade a little more with each day spent in the suburbs.

His concern grew into a resolve to return to James Bay for the remainder of the winter. Even if he couldn't travel, he could resume his bush education by grappling with winter at some remote outpost. Through contacts in Moosonee, he got in touch with the band council at the Swampy Cree settlement of Attawapiskat, on the western shore of James Bay about 175 miles north of Moosonee. A rather vague permission was granted for him to live and work with Cree trappers on the winter traplines at Lake River, an isolated camp 150 miles still farther north. It is doubtful that the Indians believed Dave would actually show up.

Thus began a most extraordinary episode in the expedition—a time in which no "progress" was made in terms of mileage, but one of total and intensive immersion in the experience Dave had come to Canada to find. It is difficult to guess what the Cree made of his motives for wanting to winter over in Lake River—his account contains hints that they considered him more than a little crazy. But if they regarded him with suspicion at first, he eventually won their respect and in some cases affection with his appetite for work, his dedication to learning bushcraft, and his respect for their threatened subsistence lifestyle.

Shortly after his leg cast was removed—luckily, the injury healed completely—Dave flew to Kachechewan, near Fort Albany, and then made his way north to Attawapiskat. There he was introduced to Abraham Paulmartin, an elderly, gruff Cree man who would be his first trapping partner and tutor. Together they traveled north along the edge of frozen James Bay to Lake River, or Lakitusaki, an encampment of cabins located at the mouth of Lake River in Polar Bear Provincial Park.

The partnership began poorly; Dave froze his feet on the snowmobile and lost his toenails, rendering him inactive for several days. Abraham reacted with hostility, probably imagining that he had saddled himself with a useless burden. Furthermore, he apparently convinced himself that Dave was a spy sent north by the Canadian government to monitor the Cree and ordered him back to Attawapiskat to stand trial before the Indian band council. After several days in limbo, with Abraham threatening to run him off the reserve, Dave got a break. A young Indian family named Tookate decided he was being unfairly maligned (Abraham was known among the Cree as a strange and difficult character) and invited him back to Lake River to work on their traplines.

Dave chose a site a mile upriver of the main settlement to build his own cabin and began felling trees, meanwhile sleeping out on 30- and 40-below-zero nights without even a tent. One morning an older Cree couple named Matthew and Mary Hookimaw snowshoed into his camp. They spoke no English and Dave was just beginning to learn scraps of Swampy Cree, but somehow they made it understood that they wanted him to come live with them. The Hookimaws were tearful during this first meeting, and Eli Tookate later explained the reason to a puzzled Dave. Years before, Matthew had found his father frozen to death from sleeping out. He and Mary had no children and seemed eager to adopt the "white boy."

The Indian families and their new apprentice now prepared to move twenty miles inland, to a tent camp that offered quick access to the traplines. Here they would spend the rest of the winter. Mary Hookimaw worked diligently to make sure Dave was properly clothed for work, chewing caribou hide for new moccasins, trimming his parka with fur, and weaving a rabbit-skin blanket for his bed. Matthew became his trapping instructor, giving daily lessons in snaring techniques, beaver skinning, and hide fleshing. In turn Dave supplied them with snare wire, ammunition, and tobacco.

Dave also applied himself to learning to communicate through gestures and phrases in Swampy Cree. Eli Tookate, his wife, Phemi, and their children were the only English-speaking residents of the settlement; at night Eli tutored Dave in the Indians' language and customs, while Dave regaled the children with tales of the city: skyscrapers, restaurants, and traffic jams. After a few weeks, Dave and the two Cree families were developing strong bonds, an intuitive mutual attraction that the language barrier may even have fostered. Only Abraham Paulmartin avoided him and was outraged that the others did not recognize him as just another visitation of evil from the white man.

In the following account, Dave details two typical days at the Lake River tent camp: February 15 and 16, 1979.

As they rose on a particular morning it was snowing hard. One remarked, "It is snowing." Six or more hours passed and it was still snowing. Nothing having been said all day, the other mountaineer remarked, "It is still snowing." The second mountaineer: "I guess we talked that over pretty well yesterday." (Rutstrum, *Paradise Below Zero*)

It being a work day, I wake at 7:00 A.M., about an hour and a half before sunrise. A crescent moon and a faint grey light in the southeast provide just enough light to work without a candle. I move around in my sleeping bag, scrunching as far to the foot end as I can. In this position I slowly come alert, then yank the hood drawstring and am blasted with cold. The might of these northern nights greets me before I even leave my bed. A quarter-inch of hoarfrost has accumulated around the hood, and my hair is matted with ice from my breath. Everything in the tent, from the salt shaker to the calendar, is covered with a thin, milky film of frost. My head brushes the ceiling and I am showered with snowlike crystals.

Early morning is geared toward speed and efficiency. Clad in long underwear and socks, I dance to the tent flap to let Ki out and glance at a clear, crisp sky. The stars are so brilliant it's almost as though there is no atmosphere. On such mornings I feel as if I am standing on the moon, staring out at endless space. Though I have not been out of bed more than ten seconds, the cold has already penetrated my wool underwear. Brushing ice from my hair, I stand next to the stove and urinate into the slop pail. Before me on the spruce-bough floor are three neat piles: one of paper wads and jack-pine slivers, one of finger-sized kindling, and a third of quartered logs. I drop paper and slivers into the stove, taking care to leave a corner of paper protruding from the draft hole. Kindling and logs are then piled on top, with a tablespoon of grimy lard for starter fuel. I strike a match on the stove and touch it to the paper wick. Over the stove-top hole I place the teapail, filled the night before and now a solid block of ice. By now I am aching from the cold, my fingers and toes feeling the first stabs of pain.

I hurriedly brush spruce needles from my stockings and dive for my bed, squirming down in a single movement as far as the narrow mummy bag allows. I check my watch with the flashlight, my usual bed partner (so the batteries won't freeze). To offset the misery of starting the morning fire, I make it a race against time, this morning approaching my record of one minute, fifty seconds. I stay curled in a ball for a few minutes as the goosedown and rabbit skins leach the cold from my body. It's a relief to hear the sputtering of burning lard as the kindling begins to catch. I drift briefly back to sleep to the most beautiful music of the day: the low roar of the draft hole feeding air to a growing blaze. Soon the sides of my oil-drum stove will be glowing red, promising waves of saunalike heat, scalding tea, and hot bannock with melted lard.

Soon the aroma of brewing tea dispels any lingering desire to stall. Though the average temperature in the tent is still only 50 degrees, around the stove is a six-foot circle of luxurious 80-degree heat. I let Ki in and check the outside temperature on a thermometer nailed to a tree. Minus-48—which means it will probably rise to the low 30s or high 20s below zero today. On the coldest mornings the alcohol hangs like red jelly in its glass bubble, as if it had lost its will ever to climb the hatch marks again, like me retreating into my sleeping bag.

At least I have another hour before I need to worry about the cold. Breakfast is my favorite time of day at Lake River. I take a leisurely half-hour, sitting in my underwear at the foot of my bed. The meal usually consists of six or eight mugs of strong tea laced with sugar and powdered milk, and half of a twelve-inch bannock spread with lard and jam—butter is saved for special treats. Most mornings I read a few pages from a novel; this morning *Shogun* is tempting me. I am low on snares, though, so decide to work while I'm eating.

Snare wire is a heavy cable twisted from eighteen individual strands, first cut into two-foot lengths, then separated and retwisted in six-strand sections. The temper must be removed from the tips of the wire by holding the ends in the fire until they glow. With the temper removed, the wire is pliable enough to be shaped. A small loop is twisted into one end, and the other end passes through it to form a noose. Once coiled, fifty such snares can be carried in a coat pocket, while it would take a sled to haul as many traps.

8:30 A.M. As much as I would enjoy a second pot of tea, I must get ready for work. Socks, moccasins, liners, and mitts hang over the stove, thawed and dry. As always, night and day, I am wearing two pairs of ankle-to-neck wool underwear and two pairs of wool socks. Foot insulation is the biggest production: I add liners and insoles to my thin caribou-skin moccasins and put on two more pairs of wool socks, then duffel socks, and finally a homemade pair of rabbit skins. Over all of this go the lined moccasins; over the long underwear go heavy wool pants and shirt, sweater, and scarf.

As the fire dies I fill the thermos with boiling tea and my pack with everything else I will need for the next ten hours: lynx and rabbit snares (ten each); two beaver castors as scent lures; a dozen shotgun shells; spare socks, liners, and moccasins wrapped around the thermos; tea, sugar, lard, and flour; teapail, spoon and cup, spare matches; my lunch (bannock, sardines, and half a rabbit); a frozen fish for bait and two leg-hold traps for fox. In my pockets I carry a few snares, shells, a handkerchief, matches, tobacco, cigarette papers, and toilet paper. I have no need for a map or compass today, as I won't be scouting any new country. Today's trip will take me on a twelve-mile loop to the northeast along one of my three trap-lines. If I have a good day and the wind doesn't pick up, I should be able to check all of my forty lynx snares along the line and set another ten.

Before leaving I tie Ki in front of the tent. I hate to leave him tied, but I cannot take him on the trapline, as his constant bounds through the snow would further confuse the maze of tracks I must decipher. I don a final outer layer of clothing: heavy goosedown parka with fur trim, wool inner mitts, moosehide-and-beaver outer mitts, wool hat. On a rope sling over my shoulder is my shotgun. Since the first mile of trail is packed enough not to require snowshoes, I carry them, too, suspended from my axe handle.

Matthew is much faster at rising than I, and is probably a mile or two south on his own line. Mary, trudging back to her tent with three snowshoe hares slung over her shoulder, waves good morning. Before starting on my line, I make a half-mile semicircle to check my rabbit snares. Four snowshoe hares are neatly snared around the neck and frozen solid; I replace them with new brass snares. Soon I will have to move these eighty or so snares to a new location. Unless we have a heavy snowfall to raise the snow level, the rabbits will eat all the willow bark within reach and move on to other country. When I rejoin the main trail, I leave the rabbits, covered with snow and marked with a stick, to lighten my load. I will retrieve them at the end of the day.

The main trail runs east down the center of the river for about five miles. Every mile or so, a single snowshoe trail angles off to the north or south—Matthew's, Eli's, Eli's father Georgan's, or my own. Like the fingers of a hand, these trails and others along the coast form a network of traplines covering thirty miles east to west and fifty north to south—fifteen hundred square miles for six trappers.

Today I'll work my main line, along Willow Creek. I curse myself, as always, for getting such a late start. At sunrise there is rarely any wind here, but around 9:00 A.M. the wind comes blasting out of the east and funnels down Lake River, right into my face. At 40 below, the texture of a strong headwind changes dramatically. My body feels cold as the wind searches out gaps in my clothing, but the exposed skin on my face feels as if a hot iron is being held against the flesh. Every five minutes or so I raise a mitted hand to relieve the burning and quicken my pace as I near the shelter of Willow Creek. Rarely does the wind penetrate its narrow, winding channel. I pass the halfway point; a few crumbling logs from a trapper's cabin abandoned years ago. Farther along I find the erratic trail of a rabbit ending in the middle of the frozen river, the only sign of its fate the imprint of an owl's wing tips in the snow.

At Willow Creek I stop to put on my snowshoes, roll a cigarette, and enjoy being out of the wind. From here on the clean-swept snow of Lake River is replaced by a profusion of overlapping tracks: mouse, ermine, squirrel, grouse, rabbit, ptarmigan, mink, otter, fox, and lynx tracks crisscross the creek, sometimes following my own trail. For the next five miles my excitement mounts as I envision a frozen lynx in one of my snares. I haven't yet caught a fox or a lynx—the most elusive and most valuable quarry of trappers—yet each time I go out on the lines, I can't help but think that this will be the day.

For the next few hours, I veer off the trail every few hundred yards at set markers. To ensure that drifting snow does not cover my tracks, I have marked the turnoff to each set with a spruce bough stuck in the snow. Many sets are just a few feet off the main trail at key lynx and fox crossings; others are 100 feet or more from the creek. In one such place I drop everything but my axe and struggle up the steep creek bank through a snarl of willows. The snare has not been touched and needs only a slight adjustment. To the left is the discouraging sight of fox tracks leading through a gap in the block fence; I trim a few branches and anchor them in the snow to close the gap. Back on the trail around 10:00 A.M., I kneel down on my snowshoes, roll a cigarette, and enjoy my thermos of tea. The cold seeps in quickly, and I have just enough time to finish my cigarette before I become too chilled.

Half a mile farther down the creek I come to two mink sets. The shredded fish bait has not been touched, and, judging that the sets have been in place long enough, I spring the traps and hang them from my pack. The trail snares haven't been disturbed either, but they can remain. I carefully remove a sapling from the block fence, pass through, and replace it before moving on.

Near the end of my line, about five miles from the creek mouth, I come to six baited lynx sets. Five are untouched, but one has been burglarized. A lynx has managed to slip in and steal the beaver castor without tripping the snare. Annoyed as I am, so many near-misses tell me that at least I'm setting snares in good locations. Before moving on I re-bait the set with a castor and the rabbit from my lunch.

After setting two new fox sets in promising sites, I break for lunch at a sunny spot in a stand of pines. All morning I have been moving constantly to stay ahead of the cold; now, with the temperature up to about 25 below, I can enjoy my surroundings for the first time today. A ring of snow begins to melt around the fire as I cut more wood to feed it. Resting on a pine bough, I relax as the fire's heat bleeds the cold from me. I fill my teapail with crystallized snow from the layer below the surface. This is essential for good tea; the powdery snow on top traps air and melts inefficiently, absorbing woodsmoke and giving the tea a smoky taste. Then I suspend the pail over the fire from a pole stuck diagonally in a snowbank; the sardines and bannock sit next to the fire to thaw and heat. Instead of regular milk-and-sugar tea, I opt for the Cree "tea-plus" recipe, fortified with flour, sugar, and lard. This kind of food goes far in the cold.

I return to the trail half an hour later with a full stomach and refilled thermos. It's already 1:00 P.M., but the day is far from over. I still have ten snares to set and a six-mile hike back to camp. Snare setting is a dreaded chore that I usually put off until the end of the day. The work is painfully cold and full of frustrations. Often after spending half an hour constructing a set, I stand back and eye the design with dissatisfaction, then tear it down to start over.

While checking old sets this morning I took mental notes on likely future locations. Now the job is to choose the best of thirty or forty good sites. A few hundred yards from my lunch spot the creek narrows from its average width of thirty feet to about ten. The banks are steep here, with thick growth on either side—a natural funnel—and lynx and fox sign are good. The idea is to span the gap with an impassable fence, leaving a six- or eight-inch hole to direct the animal into the snare. I cut willow and pine branches and plant them in the snow to form a four-foot fence, interwoven to prevent gaps. Next I anchor a stout four-foot pole vertically on one side of the hole with a bracing pole on the other side and secure the snare to the vertical pole about a foot from the snow. A brass wire hook attached to the bracing holds the noose perpendicular to the trail, and sticks placed carefully above and below the snare prevent the lynx from passing over or under it. After a final adjustment of the noose, I step back to admire the set.

By 6:00 P.M. I have completed nine sets. The sun has just dropped below the trees and the temperature is plummeting. I have worked my way back to within two miles of the tent camp and reluctantly decide there is time to build one more. Like an office worker watching the clock, I am impatiently counting the minutes to sundown, hot tea, and supper. Each set is the "last one" until I round the bend and find another promising group of tracks. But I'm down to my last snare, and it will be dark in an hour. Here I build a teepee-style set to enclose a scene lure, more suitable for the terrain around this part of Willow Creek, where there are fewer defined game trails and you must attract the animal to your snare. At 30 below, my bare hands work clumsily with the stiff wire and lose all sense of feeling after five minutes of exposure. I cannot move my fingers; I must press them against my palm to shape them into a grip. This is nothing unusual: The pushing and prying of fingers may be repeated a dozen times a day, whenever bare hands are needed to set a snare.

In the growing darkness my body throbs from the cold; my muscles are cramped from kneeling in the snow. With a finger over one nostril, I blow through the other to clear it of accumulated ice. Frozen tears have cemented my eyelashes to my cheeks, and for the hundredth time today I wipe my glasses free of snow. I reach the mouth of Willow Creek with a sign of relief. Back on the packed trail, free of the cumbersome snowshoes, I practically skip along in my moccasins. Rounding the last river bend, I stoop to collect the rabbits hidden there that morning and hang them from my axe handle.

Mary's laughter, probably induced by one of Matthew's practical jokes, carries through the still night air. From 200 yards away, my tent glows faintly with candlelight. I am always the last out in the morning and the last in at night, and there's nothing more depressing than coming back to a cold tent and waiting, shivering and exhausted, for the stove to heat up. Mary knows this, and half an hour before I return, she goes to my tent to light a candle, build a fire, fill my water pail with fresh snow, and put the tea on to boil.

Straining against his rope, Ki leaps up to greet me. Once untied, he goes through his nightly ritual of tail wagging and pawing for attention. I find that Mary has left me a surprise tonight: The dirty dishes I left this morning have been washed and stacked, and a fresh spruce-bough floor laid. I collapse on my bed, savoring the aroma of strong tea as the stove's heat pours over me in delicious waves. With the heavily sugared tea I swallow a handful of candy; working in extreme cold produces a ceaseless appetite for sugar and fat.

A pot of leftover rabbit stew thaws on the stove while I peel off layer after layer of clothing and escape back into *Shogun*. Flaked out on the spruce floor with my work moccasins off and my tent moccasins on, the dog at my feet, a metal tea mug and a hand-rolled smoke, I feel like a businessman after a hard day at the office—but content in a way that no office work could ever make me.

I finish my evening chores around 9:00 P.M., except for skinning the four rabbits snared today and two from yesterday. My woodpile is getting low; while I'm outside restocking it, I notice that a light cloud cover hides the stars and the temperature has risen 15 degrees in the last two hours. If the clouds stay all night, tomorrow should be a mild day.

Ki is in a corner of the tent away from the heat, gnawing on a beaver quarter; his dessert will be rabbit heads and guts. To skin the rabbits, I slice through the cartilage and muscle at the base of the ears and along the skull and then peel off the whole skin (except from the paws) inside out like a sweater.

As I'm gutting the rabbits, Eli Tookate shows up for the evening social hour. He helps himself to tea, and five minutes later Matthew comes trudging up. I'm still outside washing rabbit blood from my hands and rolling the carcasses in snow to wipe them clean. I give the rabbit skins to Eli for the blanket that Phemi is making and the dressed rabbits to Matthew for his stewpot.

Matthew begins the nightly tale swapping with an account of his day on the trapline. After he finishes, Eli translates his Cree jabberings for me while Matthew adds graphic gestures. He had a good day today: Not only did he come home with two fat beavers, he found another beaver lodge on a creek to the south. Everyone, he says, will have good beaver meat for supper tomorrow! Eli didn't go out on the traplines, but spent the day cutting firewood and tending his fishnet. Today's net, like the last two, was disappointing: a few suckers, no whitefish, no trout. He is debating moving his net to a better location. "*Muna* [No]." Matthew disagrees. "*Mahsahmaykos paycheinookosow* [Roughly, the trout will come]!" When Eli tires of translating, I must know the subject of conversation and watch Matthew's gestures closely to have any hope of understanding what he says.

By the fourth round of tea and the second bowl of candy, it's time for my trapline tale of the stolen bait. My excuses about near-misses sound to me like fish stories, but Matthew, thinking back to his first year of trapping, gives me a reassuring smile. Then I dig out my map of the region. Scrutinizing it has become a nightly ritual, so that popular areas are greyed from fingerprints and the fold lines are a grid of obliterations. Neither Eli nor Matthew had ever seen a detailed map of the area. All their lives they have navigated by memory, the unseen country around the next river bend remaining a mystery. On the map, such country could be seen. When I explain the topographical symbols, they can determine whether an area is likely to have a good beaver population, for example. While Matthew and Eli ponder the new country, I study the old, their stories of traplines and camps from former years coming to life on paper.

The evening ends with an empty teapail around 11:00 P.M. Ki curls up in bloated bliss, and I let the fire die while I finish a chapter of *Shogun.*

February 16, 1979. The first sound I hear is Mary splitting wood a hundred feet away. I should be up; it's already 8:30 A.M. and I can see the first rays of sun illuminating the tent walls. But the fire can wait this morning, and I'll deal with Mary's dirty looks later. I would rather drift back to my dreams.

Eventually guilt triumphs and I toss off my sleeping bag to start the fire, only to find that I forgot to shave off some pine splinters for the stove last night. Shivering and muttering curses, I grab the axe and whittle a handful of shavings off a piece of split pine. Paper, shavings, kindling, and logs are tossed sloppily into the stove; I'm too cold to bother with the lard. Opening the tent flap to let Ki out, I glance at the thermometer—fifteen below, a warm day after all.

As a stream of smoke pours from my stovepipe, Mary yells, "Hey, hey . . . *kun* [snow]!" Then I hear the sound of a stick whacking canvas and realize what she's yelling about. I hadn't noticed that we got a few inches of new snow last night, and snow must always be brushed off the tent before lighting the stove, to prolong the fabric's life. As the snow begins to melt on the canvas, I yank my pants on and scramble out in my socks, not bothering with moccasins. After a few sweeping circles around the tent, I return to the hot stove for my tea.

This morning, I decide, will be more leisurely than the last. I put on a pot of oatmeal to bubble beside the tea and pull out my Cree dictionary for a little practice. Today I'm working on the food category. My eyes roam the pantry as I repeat the words for sugar, lard, flour, tea, water. I sometimes wonder if I'll ever be able to speak a complete sentence in Cree. So far, any effort of more than a word or two has elicited giggles and corrections.

After cleaning up the tent and constructing some rabbit snares, I turn to woodcutting. With my hand-toboggan loaded with shotgun, axe, saw, and fifty feet of rope, I cross the river to a stand of mixed dead spruce, pine, and tamarack. Passing up the tamarack, whose wood burns too hot for my little stove, I choose three dry thirty-foot pines, each about eight inches in diameter. My bow saw drops one tree after another. While Ki yaps away at his favorite pastime—squirrel chasing—I lop branches from the trunks with the axe and cut the logs into eight-foot lengths. It's fairly tricky work: The axe is constantly swinging, and if, for instance, my snowshoe snags on an unseen branch, the axe head could end up buried in my leg rather than in the wood.

Balancing an eight-foot log on each shoulder, I carry them out to the riverbank and lash nine to the toboggan. I take a few steps back, then dive into the crude rope harness, causing the five-hundred-pound load to lurch down the bank. Halfway down, the toboggan fishtails and topples over in the soft snow beside the trail, and I have to unlash and reload the whole pile. This time I reach the bottom of the bank successfully; eventually the logs will be carried one by one up the far bank and piled in the yard beside the sawhorse.

In the middle of my lunch break, the Tookate kids drop by: James, Madeline, Angela, Linda, and my five-year-old buddy, Patrick. For a while they seem content just to giggle and watch me eat, but I know what they're really here for and finally give in. Each gets a piece of candy, and then my lesson begins, with Linda shouting out the name of an animal in English and me answering in Cree. We go around the circle like this, and I pay for missed words with more candy.

The rest of the afternoon, until 5:00 P.M., I spend back across the river cutting firewood. The day's work yields a good-sized cache, enough for the entire camp if we get socked in by a blizzard. I spend the last hour of daylight splitting and stacking wood in the yard. Not far away, Mary is finishing her own afternoon chore of smoking beaver, four hours of patiently tending a smudge fire. She brings me a perfectly smoked half, the meat black and crusty, just as it should be. She pokes at it, exclaiming in her jumbled accents of Cree, French, and English, "Mmmn, good baby beaver!" She then gestures that she'd like some flour, a request I'm always happy to oblige, as it means that she will be baking some of her delicious bannock.

Tonight, to conserve my store-bought supplies, I'm having one of my less appetizing meals—sucker cakes. Mary brings me a batch of these whenever Matthew gets a bumper crop of sucker fish, and

I always muster some feeble enthusiasm in accepting them. The fish are smoke-dried, powdered, and mixed with lard, water, and a bit of seasoning, then fried in more lard. Tonight I can manage only a few of them before deciding that Ki should share in the bountiful leftovers.

Around 8:00 P.M. Eli and Matthew show up as usual, but with a rare guest. Eli's father, Georgan, is not quite used to having a white man live among his people. He still remembers the earlier part of the century, when the Cree were treated little better than dogs, enduring floods and mass starvation while white residents continued to get regular food shipments from the south. Georgan's harsh life can be read on his face, which is lined and shadowed like seasoned wood in the flickering candlelight.

Georgan leans forward on my bed and, acknowledging no one in the room, begins his stories. His voice is strong but quiet, touched with what sounds like remorse. Many of the younger Cree speak in staccato spurts, but their voices grow more mellow with age. Georgan does not so much speak words as sing a story; I find myself almost swaying to the rhythm of his voice. Eli translates:

My father taught me how to hunt with a bow and arrow. You had to know how to use a bow. The guns broke and could not be fixed. When I was a boy you had to be a good trapper to have a gun. There was no money, just furs to trade. You stacked beaver pelts to the height of your gun. When you had enough pelts you got the gun. The company made the barrels very long so it would take many more beaver pelts to buy a gun.

The flood came in 1935 and killed all the animals. There was no food for two years. Some people starved. Some got sick and died. The trapping was no good. We ate what we could—fox and otter. Nobody eats those today. The young people think they are too good to eat fox.

I used to guide American goose hunters in the 1950s and 1960s. The hunters had a lot of money and paid me well. They paid me better when they were drunk. Sometimes when they went home they even gave me their tents and stoves. They gave me whiskey, too. . . . The hunters are not like that anymore. They never give me whiskey, and they get mad when the geese do not fly.

. . . When everyone became Catholic and abandoned the old ways, Wetigo [the Cree devil] punished us. He drove all the moose and caribou away. There will be little game as long as the priests are here. The people in town do not care. They get welfare money and think everything is so much better. I am the only one left who still uses a dog team. Wetigo will punish them.

The spirits are strong. They can break your traps. If they do not like you, they can break the ice and make you drown. If the people burned the church, the caribou would come back. The church was burned once, but they built a new one.

Georgan breaks off his stream of talk to look at me. He asks my purpose here: Am I another missionary? I explain at length my motives for coming to Lake River, that I am certainly not a missionary and understand his feelings. I talk about my desire to learn the life of his people by living with them. I apologize for not having any whiskey and offer another cup of tea instead. He says nothing, but Matthew and Eli smile slowly as Georgan ceremoniously removes his cap to trade for mine. It is a gesture of acceptance.

It is unseasonably mild tonight, a few degrees above zero as Ki and I sit on the riverbank near the tent. By nearly midnight, the moon has not yet risen, and the northern lights perform with exceptional brilliance. Watching the undulating dance of blue, green, and white lights in the sky and remembering Georgan's talk, I find it hard to picture my life in Virginia. It's as if his visit replaced that life with the image of a life in Lake River. For the first time tonight, I see what these people are giving me. I have caught no fur and cannot keep up with the others. I have better food, clothing, and equipment than anyone here, yet I curse and complain when it's 40 below, or when I have to eat sucker instead of macaroni and cheese. And yet they, even Georgan, have accepted me.

———————

> . . . the mixed smells of conifer gums and woodsmoke,
> of animal fat and scent glands, of prepared scents for luring
> animals, of fish and tobacco and dogs. I recognized it for
> what it was—the heavy, heady incense of the North.
> (Karras, *Face the North Wind*)

Since arriving at the tent camp I had been wanting to make an overnight trapping trip. It seemed so uneconomical to return to camp each night, wasting a quarter of each day just traveling to and from camp, and I was curious to see some new country beyond my traplines. But every time I brought up the idea, Matthew and Eli vetoed it. I had no idea, they said, of the hardships of winter camping without a tent. And what if I broke through the ice while exploring a stretch of river?

They knew nothing about the Trans-Canada Expedition and so had no idea that Pete and I had spent dozens of nights out without a tent the previous winter. I hadn't told them about it because I doubted they would understand. What would be the point, unless you were trapping, of walking and canoeing thousands of miles? Besides, they might not even have believed it, having witnessed firsthand my relative inexperience in the bush.

But finally in late February Matthew agreed to let me make a three-day exploratory trip north. The weather was fine and clear, with moderate temperatures, and he was curious about the fur population, not having trapped that country himself for twenty years. The plan was for me to break a trail eight miles north to a branch of Lake River I hadn't yet seen. There I would make camp and spend a day scouting the area and setting snares, returning to the main camp on day three. Eight miles doesn't sound that far, but when you must break a fresh trail through thigh-deep snow while pulling a toboggan, it's more than enough.

On departure day I loaded my toboggan with two days' worth of food and assorted gear, including a map and compass. Six miles of the proposed route would be on featureless tundra. I had not traveled above the tree line before and was both excited and apprehensive about it. For the first mile I followed Eli's woodcutting trail, the toboggan sliding easily over packed snow. The trail ended where the trees did, and before me, stretching to the horizon, was a white desert of windblown snow. Six-foot stunted skeletons of tamarack dotted the drifts liberally at first, then tapered off to widely scattered clumps. Ptarmigan tracks—and occasionally the trail of an arctic fox—wound around the tamaracks. Now and then the white whir of a ptarmigan rose over the drifts, always out of range of my shotgun. I was losing sight of the trees behind me; since from here on I would have to navigate by compass, I reached into my pocket for it. No compass—I had left it in the tent. I felt a little sick, but as long as the sun stayed out I could use that to navigate. I just prayed that I'd be able to pick up my trail on the way back.

By midafternoon I spotted a telltale line of trees, the oasis along every riverbank above tree line. Ki seemed equally pleased to see it; he'd been rather bored on the tundra with no squirrels to chase. When we reached the trees, though, they proved as much a curse as a blessing. The snow there, hidden from the wind, was soft and slowed the toboggan. Every few paces I had to hew a trail through the dense growth of willow and alder. Finally, two hours before sundown, we reached a narrow, meandering river. The only sign that humans had ever been there was a decades-old axe blaze on a large spruce.

I spent the remaining daylight setting rabbit snares, cutting firewood, and building a shelter. I dug a depression in the snow for a firepit, with a shelf of snow next to it, covered with spruce boughs for seating and sleeping. Around this I built a conical hut from two dozen pine saplings, anchored in the snow and leaning inward to form a windbreak and reflect heat from the fire. My toboggan, resting vertically against the pines, served as a door. With the stove roaring, I could keep the hut a comfortable 40 degrees even after the outside temperature dropped to 20 below. I felt cozy and secure, camped in an island of trees amidst a sea of frozen barrens.

Morning light revealed a low bank of clouds on the horizon, signaling, along with the rising temperature, that a snowstorm was probably on the way. The prospect of traveling open country in poor visibility without a compass briefly forced me to consider delaying my plans and returning to camp before the storm hit. But unseen country is a strong magnet. No matter how far I travel, I hate to turn back without looking around the next river bend. So once again, safety took a back seat to adventure. Leaving Ki tied to the hut, I shouldered my daypack and turned northwest up the river.

Progress was slow over the river's virgin snow, as each step had to be checked with a prodding pole to make sure the ice would support me. Where the pole told me it was unsafe, or where discolored, concave spots indicated thin ice or overflow under the snow, I made wide arcs. After a while I started paying more attention to otter sign than to the ice—not a smart idea, I realized as a four-foot circle of ice gave way beneath my feet. Luckily the snowshoes dispersed my weight, allowing me time to sidestep onto firm ice. Shaken but dry, I stared down into a hole full of gurgling black water.

Otter sign looked better than I'd ever seen, so I set half a dozen snares at den entrances. I was doubtful of any results, though; otters are incredibly strong for their size, and chances were the animal would snap my six-strand lynx wire. Or else its slim, torpedolike body would simply slip through the noose without being snared at all. Beaver sign also looked very good, but since I wasn't carrying an ice auger, I had to leave the lodges undisturbed. [*The procedure for snaring beaver was to drill a good-size hole in the ice and rig the snare underwater.*] However, I had come for lynx and fox, and hadn't seen more than a few tracks all day.

After lunch I constructed eight lynx sets along the meager selection of trails. I was beginning to consider the whole trip a waste of time when I came across a fairly fresh set of moose tracks. Matthew would be excited to hear about this. An even better find appeared on my way back to camp: Under an overhanging ledge on the riverbank, hidden behind an uprooted tree, was the mouth of a black bear's den. Here I thought of Georgan, who, like me, relishes the taste of bear meat. Everyone else at Lake River would rather starve, as Swampy Cree are raised to think bear inedible, but Georgan spent a few years with the Cree of Quebec, where black bear is a delicacy. A good-sized bear with his winter fat could yield two hundred pounds of meat, and Matthew could get forty or fifty dollars for the hide. I inched nervously toward the den. My shotgun was loaded with birdshot, which at close range would be more effective than a slug, but it was too dark inside to see anything. I wasn't about to poke a stick in there, and the smell of damp fur told me all I needed. I stepped back silently and returned to the trail; Matthew and I could come back for the bear.

Back at the hut, I was disappointed to find no rabbits in my snares. If I could catch enough rabbits for food and if the weather held off, I wanted to stay another day to look over more country. I set out another twenty snares and slept peacefully through the night. When I threw the blanket off my head in the morning, I was startled to find myself covered with six inches of new snow that had seeped through gaps in the hut. The snowfall intensified while I gulped down a hurried breakfast, praying "Please don't let there be wind in the open country!" No chance now of staying another day; I was out of food and my snares were all buried—yesterday's work wasted. I had packed light on food in the interest of traveling fast; now I had to think about getting home fast.

I had no trouble finding my trail through the trees, but out in the open the wind had picked up, and there was no sign whatever of my tracks. The seriousness of the situation began to sink in: With no compass and zero visibility, I could end up wandering aimlessly across the barrens. At this point Ki came to the rescue with a creditable imitation of Rin Tin Tin. He trotted on ahead like a homing pigeon, stopping occasionally to sniff around and then strutting cockily onward. Lacking other options, I followed. Every four or five hundred yards, the faint impression of a snowshoe confirmed the accuracy of Ki's nose. Meanwhile the storm had grown into a full-fledged blizzard—the worst I had ever seen, much less traveled in. At times I had to lean into the wind to advance, and anything more than fifty feet away was lost in the swirl of white. Only the thought that Mary and Matthew would be worried sick kept me from turning back to wait it out.

After traveling for hours I wondered why the Lake River trees remained out of sight. Ki was still trotting confidently ahead, but when I looked toward our back-trail, I realized the horrible truth that we had unwittingly been snaking back and forth. Apparently Wonder Nose had lost the trail and was now just roaming around sniffing animal tracks. I sank to my knees and held my head down out of the searing wind as I tried to control the panic welling up

from my stomach. Forcing myself to concentrate, I remembered seeing the last sign of our trail two hours earlier, but in this storm we
could just as easily parallel the river or even go in circles as relocate
the trail. I had to count on the wind; if it hadn't shifted, we were
still heading generally south toward Lake River. Unreliable as it was,
the wind was my only source of direction.

The snow became softer as we went on, until finally I could
no longer break trail and pull the toboggan at the same time. I would
leave the load, snowshoe 100 yards, then backtrack to retrieve the
toboggan. Even in such a short distance, my trail would be nearly
obliterated by the time I came back for the toboggan. Dozens of times
I fell or sank to my thighs, even with snowshoes. The chances of
reaching Lake River before the next day seemed slim. Then in early
afternoon we came to a taller than usual stand of tamarack. Was
this the edge of the heavy timber near the river, or just an island of
scrub in open country? Assuming the latter, I decided it would be
wisest to camp here and continue tomorrow. Browsing around for
a good campsite, I noticed a tree trunk with a gash where the bark
had been rubbed off . . . where my toboggan had bumped into it two
days before! Up ahead I could just make out the faint imprint of my
old trail, and I set off again, marveling at the odds of stumbling onto
it after wandering directionless for hours.

Back in the trees, out of the wind, our speed doubled, and we
raced over Eli's packed woodcutting trail to the banks of Lake River.
I made a beeline for the Tookates' tent, where Eli gave me a casual
hello as he poured my tea. I was rather taken aback: Even in good
weather they had all feared I'd kill myself, so why this unconcern
now? Ice melted from my face as I sipped the gloriously hot tea and
recounted the fur prospects to the north; then Eli explained his lack
of surprise at my safe return. Mary and Matthew had seen the storm
warnings and cried all through my first night out. But the second
night, Matthew had had a dream in which he saw me sleeping safely
and peacefully in my hut. Eli described the hut to me just as Matthew
had dreamed it, and it exactly matched the one I had built — though
I hadn't heard of such a design from anyone, white or Indian. In any
event, the dream had said I was safe, and my friends promptly ceased
worrying.

Mary and Matthew likewise seemed happy but unsurprised to see me. There was scant time for visiting at first, as the entire camp was scurrying around hauling firewood and pulling snares, for fear the blizzard would last another day or more. My eighty rabbit snares could be lost under the snow, so I hurried along the line pulling up the snare sticks and planting them vertically as markers. The lynx sets were well marked as they were. Back at my tent, I hung a flashlight from a tree to light the wood yard while I split an extra supply of firewood. By 8:00 P.M. I was ready; the storm could do as it pleased. With a full barrel of water and a healthy stock of meat I could stay in my tent for days, if necessary. The tent walls shook and the stovepipe rattled with the force of the storm, but I was as cozy as a caterpillar in a cocoon.

February 26, 1979. An eventful day at Lake River. For two hours around noon, James Bay was dimmed by a solar eclipse; at our camp the effect was something like a moonlit night, only the light was more diffuse. The air seemed heavy and grey, and no one spoke for a long time. Today, too, the Hookimaws and the Tookates left on a week's trip into town for socializing and supplies. I stayed behind with Ki to feed the dogs and tend the traplines.

I hadn't been to town in more than a month, yet the prospect of a week's quiet and solitude was more tempting than cold beer and old friends. The peace of Lake River had a dramatic effect on me, and by now Attawapiskat with its yapping Indian dogs and skidoo traffic jams seemed as maddening as the streets of New York. Having the camp to myself, with no noise other than the wind in the treetops and the occasional call of a snowy owl, was much more appealing.

The Tookate clan had already taken off on two skidoos while Matthew finished tinkering with his engine. Now Mary settled into the toboggan amidst rabbit-skin robes and tarps; yelps arose as three small dogs and a cat vied for the warmest spot. After a last round of handshakes, the snowmobile lurched off over the ice, chattering and wheezing.

On the seventh day after their departure, I set off for an inspection of my main trapline, guessing I could get back in time for their imminent return. I had spent most of my time alone cutting wood, and I smiled at the thought of Mary and Matthew's surprise when they found more than three cords of split and stacked wood in their yard. The weather had been fine, sunny and zero or above all week, but for me this was a mixed blessing. Animals respond to good weather just as we do, becoming more active in the sun's warmth, and each day of full sun bleaches a mammal's fur, reducing its value. If it also gets "rubbed"—thinned by snagging brush—the pelt can be nearly worthless.

Three miles out on the line, I stopped in my tracks about 100 yards from one of my lynx fences at a river narrows. The fence was destroyed. I started to shake with excitement as I saw lynx tracks trampling the snow and broken branches, remains of the fence, strewn around. Beneath a scrub willow twenty yards to my left, a lynx lay twisted in the snow, the wire snare and drag pole wrapped around the tree. His paws reached into the air, and his mouth was open, frozen in the last snarl of strangulation. This indicated that in frantically yanking to free himself, he had pulled the noose tight and died quickly.

A lynx! After all those weeks of poorly constructed snares, I had actually set one right. I couldn't wait to show the others. It was a big animal, much bigger than any I had seen caught all winter. When measured, it came to forty-six inches (classified as extra large) and about fifty pounds. The pelt was a near-perfect salt-and-pepper and in good condition for such a late-season catch. It would certainly go for three hundred dollars when Matthew sold his pelts.

Back at camp, I sat and stared at the lynx for hours—one beautiful animal that represented a full month's work. But my eagerness to share my pleasure was frustrated, as the Indians failed to arrive that day, or the next. Still more days passed with no sign of anyone, and a nagging anxiety slowly replaced my sense of peace. My supplies had dwindled to almost nothing. I had finished my last candle on the ninth night and would now have to get by on sardine-tin candles, made by suspending a string in a sardine tin full of lard. Their light was feeble and they smoked terribly, with a rancid odor of burning fat. The last of my powdered milk was gone, and I was down to a quarter-teaspoon ration of sugar per cup.

The quiet began to grind on my nerves. It might seem odd that the solitude affected me so profoundly after only nine days, but you cannot compare, say, a solo camping trip of a few weeks to being alone on the edge of the tundra, 150 miles from the nearest human. It isn't so much frightening as it is a total awakening of the senses. Your body seems to tingle with the crispness of the air, the intensity of the quiet, the thought that you are the only person experiencing *that* particular breeze brushing your cheek. That wind is yours alone; by the time it reaches the next human face it will have changed character a hundred times.

The warming trend continued. Ki spent hours sunbathing on the riverbank, and the springlike weather brought a welcome glut of food. I had my hands full keeping up with the rabbit snares and set a personal record of eleven in a day. This was good news for the dogs, who had been living on oats and lard. For my part, rabbit stew had long since lost its charm, and grouse became the savior of my taste buds. These northern grouse, seldom hunted, are totally unlike the panicked birds of the south; here you don't so much hunt them as harvest them from tree limbs where they sit placidly just above arm's reach.

One still night as I lay in my tent reading, for the twentieth time, a yellowed copy of *Outdoor Life*, I was distracted by an unfamiliar sound—something like the shattering of lightbulb-thin crystal a great distance away. I cautiously slipped out of the tent and gazed upward, where it seemed to come from. An incredibly brilliant display of northern lights rippled across the sky, sheets of color climbing and descending in an intricately precise dance. Every few minutes the colors changed partners and began a new dance; the performance went on for several hours. But the unearthly music lasted only half an hour, during the most elaborate show. To hear the music of the aurora borealis is a once-in-a-lifetime experience; many spend their entire lives in the north without ever hearing it. It moved me the way others are moved by great art, blending sight and sound like a ballet.

I spent the afternoon of the fourteenth day hunting and checking snares, returning to camp to find fresh skidoo tracks running past my tent. Quickly seeing that Matthew and Mary were not back, I raced downriver to the Tookates' tent. There was Eli, unpacking his machine and grinning from ear to ear. His greeting, pronounced with typical Cree stoicism, was "I thought you were dead." It turned out that I hadn't been all alone in the area; Mary had stayed at the Lake River cabins, twenty miles away, to take care of the Tookate kids. Abraham was there, too, and when Eli returned to the cabins from town, he was incensed to learn that Abraham had never come out to visit me. "Even Indians," he said, "check on each other every week or so when they live alone. Too many things can happen."

I assured him I'd been fine, and after presenting me with my long-awaited box of groceries and mail, Eli and Phemi came up to my tent for a pot of tea. As I reached for the teapail, Eli shook his head and smiled. "We thought you would like to help us with this," he said, pulling a quart of Canadian Club from his pocket. For the next several hours our metal mugs remained full as the bottle went around. I quickly ran down the events of the last few weeks, and for the climax, brought forth my lynx. Eli just sat there, grinning hugely. He hadn't caught any lynx himself that winter, so was all the prouder of my accomplishment. "Ha!" he shouted. "Abraham will not believe this. He will think you stole it! Ha!"

Eli did most of the talking from then on, with occasional nods and murmurs from Phemi. With each mug of whiskey, his stories became more personal: He said the Indians in town harassed and abused his family because he refused to take welfare money. Disgust welled up in me as he explained that many were afraid the government would cut off the welfare funds if it saw that a family could, in fact, live well off a trapline. Eli, it seemed, was setting a poor example. He also mentioned that I was referred to in town as "David Tookate," which I found tremendously flattering, even when Eli explained the motive behind it. The name Tookate was quickly becoming synonymous with "crazy." If Eli wasn't crazy, why would he and his family choose the rigors of the bush over the easier life in Attawapiskat? And why would a white man from the city live at Lake River, eating wild meat when he could have the best store-bought food? He must be another Tookate!

Apparently the other Lake River residents—the Hookimaws, Abraham Paulmartin, another man named Eli Metawabin—were tolerated because they were Christians. Eli, Phemi, and the senior

Tookates were among the dwindling few who clung to the old beliefs. So they, and by association I, were outcasts. The bottle was nearly empty now, and Eli was getting groggy. He began telling bizarre stories, usually leaving them unfinished, and recited old Cree spells and incantations. This drew glares from Phemi, who clearly felt that he was saying too much. Though I was fascinated, it made me uncomfortable too, given my past experiences with Wetigo magic.

As Eli rambled on, he revealed that Abraham, far from being a devout Christian, was actually using the new religion as a cover to avoid persecution. According to Eli, he was one of the most powerful and feared practitioners of the old ways on the coast:

"My father and I are having a war with Abraham. Abraham is afraid of you. No white has ever lived here before. So he is trying to cause trouble to drive you away. . . . My father and I have joined together to fight Abraham. Abraham knows this. Three weeks ago I was on my trapline. I knew that Abraham's spirit was behind me, following me. I looked back and saw him many times, but then he was always gone. My father and I said a curse and all of Abraham's traps were broken. Ha! He tells people that wolves did it! Last week Abraham was to the north, hunting caribou. I was in town, but in my dream I went to see him. I found him in his tent. When he saw me he pulled his blanket up over his head and told me to go away. He was very afraid. He will not bother us anymore."

That night Eli and Phemi decided that it was time to end the trapping season, which had been poor for them, and return to town. My eyes filled with tears as I realized this was the beginning of the end of my life at Lake River. As I watched them pack, I thought of our first days together in January, of our late-night conversations around the oil-drum stove, fantasizing bumper hauls of beaver and scheming over new lynx-set designs. Now they were leaving. After several yanks on the starting cord of his recalcitrant skidoo, Eli turned and embraced me, saying he had never had a closer friend. We would have to trap together one day.

Out cutting wood on the sixteenth day, I heard the faint rev, choke, and race of a vintage skidoo. It could only have been Matthew's, and I dashed back to my tent to restore some kind of order to my bachelor existence. It was a joyful reunion, with Matthew nearly speechless, clapping me on the back and repeating, "Heh, heh!" and Mary babbling incoherently. In a cascade of rabbit pelts and bewildered pets, she hoisted her two-hundred-plus-pound frame from the toboggan and began gesturing for this box and that to be unloaded.

Matthew pointed to one apparently important box and signaled for a warm-up around my stove. Over tea, I opened the parcel, their gift to me of a cornucopia of store food: pork sausage, chicken, doughnuts, cheese, factory-made cigarettes, and canned stew that contained not a scrap of rabbit. Then it was time for my gift to the Hookimaws; I presented the lynx with a flourish as Mary clapped and cheered and Matthew launched another round of "Heh, heh!" He puffed up like a dean addressing his graduating class and seemed especially pleased that the animal had been properly snared around the neck, rather than in a fur-damaging body snare.

From now to spring there would be just the three of us. To celebrate our reunion, I proposed a dinner party in my tent. Promptly at 6:00 P.M. Mary and Matthew arrived in formal dress. Mary had combed out her hair and, carrying her purse, walked daintily down the trail in her finest calico dress and moccasins, Matthew strutting beside her in a clean white shirt with all the original buttons. I had laid a new pine-bough floor in my tent for the occasion and covered my bench with a towel. Silverware wrapped in freshly laundered bandanas lent an air of elegance. A heaping bowl of Spanish rice kept warm by the stove as chicken sizzled in the skillet.

We were a little stiff over the grape juice cocktails, preoccupied with table etiquette. While serving dinner I began sniffing the air, trying to place an unfamiliar scent. As Matthew sat up prim and proud and Mary broke into giggles, I recognized it as after-shave, and we laughed through the rest of the evening. The dinner cemented my already close bonds with the Hookimaws, yet our laughter from then on was partly a way to escape the knowledge that we would soon be parting.

Activity at the camp tapered off over the next couple of weeks, and toward the end of March we began pulling up traps and snares in preparation for returning to the cabins. Matthew and I retraced my journey north, but found all my snares empty and the den of the hibernating bear vacant. With little else to do, we spent much of the time stockpiling wood for the spring beaver camp: In June, Matthew and Mary would come back to the tents to hunt beaver by shotgun from a canoe. Matthew would see the long-awaited break-up of ice on the Lakitusaki and hunt among the endless surge of spring Canada, snow, and blue geese — but not I. I would be watching the same flights a week earlier and 300 miles farther south. His snowshoes would be hung from the rafters until next winter, while mine were destined for the customs office, a plane, and finally a garage in the Virginia suburbs. It was time to return to the reality of the expedition.

March 23, the day before we left for the cabins, I went out to pull up the last of my snares, taking Ki with me this time as it no longer mattered if he messed up the tracks. It was painful to erase all those weeks of agonizing work. I vividly remembered setting each snare and building the original sets in February's bitter cold. It didn't seem fair that I had to leave just as I was mastering the art of trapping.

After two months in a tent, cabin life was not as pleasant as I remembered. Without the ventilation of canvas walls, the air was stale and heavy with the accumulated smells of smoke, beaver grease, dogs, gasoline, and human bodies. Small, clouded windows let in little of the morning light, making it too easy to roll over and sleep in. The plywood floor was never really clean, no matter how much I swept, and I thought back fondly to my spruce-bough floor, always clean and fresh smelling.

There were a few chores to complete before returning to town: packing gear, washing clothes, fleshing and drying the last beaver pelts. Matthew spent exasperating hours trying to piece together a working carburetor for his skidoo from pieces of a dozen defunct ones, but finally Abraham had to bring him a new model from town. He brought Matthew another gift in that toboggan-load as well: two mickeys of whiskey. This was reason enough for an impromptu party. Mary brought out the old eight-track tape player and four D-cell batteries she had been hoarding all winter, and rummaged through a shoe box for her favorite tapes — Dolly Parton and Loretta Lynn. We were well into the second pint before the batteries wore down and the music started to slow; Mary wedged matchbooks between the tape and the machine to keep the speed up.

Abraham would have been furious if he'd known the Hookimaws were sharing his whiskey with me, but these evenings brought us even closer. They showed me snapshots of their wedding and their relatives in town, while I tried with sketches and gestures to describe my family and our life. Mary would not touch the liquor herself and Matthew never offered her any; it was the custom that women would never indulge in such a luxury unless all the men had had their fill. Sometimes I would sneak cigarettes to Mary, as Matthew, like other Cree trappers, considered it a waste of money to spoil women with tobacco. It saddened me, but I was not about to challenge local customs openly.

During our last few days together I sometimes walked into their cabin to find Mary sobbing and Matthew wiping his cheek. They didn't seem to understand why I had to leave, why I could not remain as one of the family. In a very real sense, they had become second parents to me, and I was haunted by the thought that I was abandoning them.

One morning shortly before we would make the trip to town, we woke to find wolf tracks—the first we had seen all winter. This was bad news, for our game snares as well as for our dogs, the wolves' favorite food. For the next five nights their howling began just after dark and continued long into the night. Mary, wide-eyed with fright, would dash outside at the first sound and herd the dogs inside like a mother hen. Matthew and I, on the other hand, would grin, grab our shotguns, and unleash a five-minute salvo on the pretense of protecting our homes and property—when in reality it was just an excuse to raise a little hell and waste ammunition without getting a scolding from Mary. We never saw the wolves and certainly never came close to hitting any, though in recounting our heroic deeds to Mary, their snapping jaws were always mere inches from our gun barrels.

The books say that wolves, unless threatened or rabid, won't harm humans, which I tend to believe. The only stories of wolf attacks I've heard personally were from Crees whose friend knew a guy whose wife was related to a man who was once mauled by a wolf, and so on. But I disagree with the books that say a wolf will avoid man at all costs; my experience in Lake River (as well as in

Saskatchewan and Manitoba) suggests that wolves will sniff your toes out of curiosity if they think they can get away with it.

The number and variety of tracks outside our cabins led us to estimate this pack at a population of six or seven. Apparently they weren't looking for trouble; they seemed to be just checking out the situation and hunting for scraps of food. We were more ambitious: at sixty to eighty dollars a pelt, Matthew saw the potential for income, and we hustled to block every wolf trail with an extra-sturdy snare. Traps would have been better, but we had none big enough. The snares remained empty, though, as the animals always found a new route through the bush to bypass the booby-trapped trail.

If the old belief of the Cree and other tribes is true—that all forms of life are spiritually related—then I would guess that wolves and men have a lot in common. One evening after supper, as a large moon rose over the spruce and the wolves began their nightly chorus, I left the cabin and settled in among the willows along the river-bank. This spot gave me a wide view of the river, lit by the moon; with the wind in my favor and a bit of luck, I hoped to catch a glimpse of the pack. My shotgun lay in my lap, mostly for the illusion of comfort, as it was loaded only with birdshot. Occasionally a howl would drift down the valley, to be answered by a lazy chord.

I heard them before I saw them. A pant and a whine, the faint sound of crystallized snow compacting underfoot. Three shapes slipped out of the trees and down onto the frozen river, great graceful hulks in the dim light.

In the States, the wolf is an endangered species, a symbol, a creature to be studied and protected. In many parts of Canada, it is a hated thief of fur and game whose pelt means an extra sixty dollars at the Hudson's Bay post. To me, the three wolves strolling by within a stone's throw represented all that I was seeking to learn at Lake River. In cunning and strength, they are the kings of the fur-bearing animals. They are the embodiment of nature's secrets, and nature had been kind in permitting me to view them at such close range.

Some day I might be granted one of their pelts—not for the sake of tacking it to a wall in pride, but as a reward for learning an animal's habits well. Neither the animal lover who is against trapping nor the hunter who sees animals only through a rifle scope will ever gain this knowledge. The Indian who finds a fur in his snare has not "conquered" the animal. No battle has been won. He has been given the pelt as a reward for his understanding of natural relationships. No human is closer to the animal than that man.

The wolves were nearly out of sight now. I stood up from my nest in the willows, stretched, and gazed up at the sky, then closed my eyes to bring back their images. I walked slowly back to the cabin, somehow convinced that they had been aware of my presence as well.

12 | Breaking the Ice
Moosonee, Ontario, to Rupert House, Quebec

May 15, 1979. After eight months on dry land, the paddle shaft felt awkward in my hands. It would take at least a week of accumulated callouses before the pockmarked handle and ragged shaft would be comfortable again. Our paddle strokes had lost their smooth coordination, and the canoe no longer seemed to steer itself. Still, it felt good to hold a canoe paddle again, to be moving east toward Tadoussac.

When Pete had arrived in Moosonee a week earlier, it was more than a reunion—it was the rebirth of the expedition. Before my broken ankle had intervened, the prognosis for our success had seemed poor. Back in early September, we were near the end of our endurance, with two months of fall travel ahead and another 1,000 miles to our destination. Reaching Tadoussac by the end of 1978 had been virtually impossible, and if we had failed, I doubt we'd have come back for another try.

But the accident that I feared would be a fatal blow had instead given the expedition new life. Pete had enjoyed his time back in the city and worked to raise money for us. I had found my escape in Lake River, where no telephone calls, letters, equipment lists, or budgets could reach me. The delay had left us both rested and eager to return to the trail. Pete had been more disenchanted with bush life than I was, and until I actually saw him in the flesh, I was nagged by the fear that he would change his mind and send word that he wasn't coming back. But my apprehension vanished the second he stepped off the Twin Otter at Moosonee. He looked rugged and ready: no extra inches around his waist, no city-pale complexion.

The remaining 120 miles of James Bay travel to Rupert House would present a new challenge: ice. During spring breakup on the bay, the pack ice recedes from shore, a frontier of open water moving generally west to east, pushed by the prevailing winds. Traveling in the same direction, we would progress as quickly as we could find passage through the ice barrier. The solid pack would split into massive floes and bergs, these ruptures beginning as thin cracks in the pack, or "leads," through which we could pass, depending on luck and timing. [*Dave and Pete got conflicting information from locals about when they should set off. Some said that a mid-May departure would ensure that the lake ice was passable; others advised waiting up to six weeks more. Dave, naturally, preferred the optimistic view.*]

Our room at the Polar Bear Lodge was quickly converted into a command center and storage warehouse—maps strewn on the beds, hip-waders draped over the shower curtain, hundreds of pounds of supplies scattered across the carpet. The expedition overflowed into the lobby, where other guests found us mending sails and sorting paperwork. Word of our plans spread through town, and it seemed everyone wanted to get in on the act. The school donated materials for a new canoe mast; pilots gave us reports on ice conditions in the bay; the local meteorologist, Ian Lougheed, shared statistics on warming trends and wind direction. Rarely did we pass any of the Cree canoe-taxi drivers without receiving some advice on bay travel. For our farewell bash at Ian's, a freight canoe was dispatched across the river to Moose Factory, to recruit the best-looking teachers and nurses.

Mere hours before we pushed off from the dock, the latest updates on weather and ice conditions were ominous. Pilots who had scouted the coast reported solid pack ice clear down into Hannah Bay, at the southernmost tip of James Bay. A narrow lead along the shore had been sighted, but no one knew if it was navigable water or just tidal overflow. The canoe-taxi drivers urged us to postpone our departure until June, past all danger of being stranded by ice. But Ian's forecast of northwest winds to fill our sail was too tempting. What we failed to realize was that those same winds would carry more ice down from the north to form a bottleneck in Hannah Bay.

As we headed toward the mouth of the Moose River, I lashed down the mast ropes and felt the satisfying jolt as our unfurled sail caught the following wind. We turned into a modest tack, and I watched Moosonee shrink and then disappear behind a string of islands. Peter was in the bow, adjusting the tack ropes; Ki napped in his accustomed place on the spray cover. I sat back in the stern with an arm draped over the rudder, smiling at the sun, the billowed sail, and our reunited team.

Great slabs of river ice were jammed up on the banks, but well away from us. Instead, our first obstacle was wood: A logger's boom had burst a few days earlier, sending thirty thousand cords down the river. Pete kept us on a zigzagging course through the "woodbergs," but this was just practice. Near the mouth of the river some ice did block our path, and we began learning the exhilarating game of ice roulette. Sailing at six to eight miles per hour through a four-foot gap between converging ice floes is a trick that leaves little margin for error. To complicate matters, our new sail blocked 90 percent of my forward vision, so Pete had to calculate the degree of turn and update me on our heading. Split-second blind turns through an icy obstacle course proved as stimulating as a difficult rapid.

Ki, in his ignorance, soon grew bored and unexpectedly leaped from the canoe onto a small passing floe, apparently mistaking it for a rock. The ice somersaulted under his weight, dunking one amazed dog. From then on, he did not venture onto any loose ice without first seeing his masters out of the canoe.

As we swung out onto the expanse of James Bay, a helicopter appeared on the horizon. We had arranged for Ian to ride in the hired craft with Peter's cameras and shoot some aerials of us, a photographic vantage we were weak on so far. The copter circled overhead while Peter took light-meter readings and held up signs to tell Ian the correct exposure. When the photo session ended, the crew from above sent down a case of Labatt's ale in a rope sling for a bon voyage toast. The bay nearly claimed the brew when we were blown off target by the copter blades, but we rescued it with the aid of a paddle and raised bottles in salute to our friends in the air.

Our high spirits soon dissipated, however. Fifteen miles from Moosonee, the drifting ice and floes became so thick that we had to lower our sail and pole our way through. Sometimes a half-hour struggle to penetrate the maze would bring us to a dead end, leaving no choice but to turn around and seek a new route. After a few hours, we realized that the ice ahead was not just a denser accumulation of floes; it was solid pack. The only visible path through the mass was a meandering lead three or four miles offshore. It looked inviting, but the Indians had warned us about offshore leads: how the wind can suddenly shift and blow the pack straight out to sea. I imagined clinging to an ice floe far offshore in a sea too rough for our meager canoe, each wave taking another bite from our disintegrating island. It was a powerful deterrent.

The receding tide and impassable ice left us with little choice of campsites. We scanned a moonscape of mud and ice, trying to will a good site into being, but the nearest trees and dry ground were more than a mile inland. Between ice and trees was nothing but the spongy, boot-sucking "goose flats." I like this term better than "tidal flats" because it so well describes the ground underfoot: what looks like thousands of years' accumulation of seaweed and goose droppings.

After staking the canoe at the high-water mark, we began the ritual, familiar from last August, of relaying equipment through the mud and tidal pools to a fifty-foot-square island of semifirm ground. Neither of us felt like walking another mile or so to the nearest creek, so we made do with our five gallons of bottled water from Moosonee. The brackish water of the tidal pools was acceptable for cooking, and the saltier bay water would have been the perfect medium for soaking fresh meat—if we'd had any. We had looked forward to our first camp back on the trail, with town treats, cold beer, a blazing fire. Reality brought an afternoon drizzle that turned to sleet as the temperature dropped into the 20s. Finding little dry wood on the flats, we retreated to the tent with our macaroni and cheese.

In the morning, over a bottle of beer and half a dozen eggs each, we decided our first priority would be to find a good base camp with plenty of firewood and fresh water. From there we could make scouting trips down the coast to determine the extent of the ice, and wait as long as need be for an opening. Natatishee Point, five miles down the coast, seemed a likely spot, but we'd have to portage the whole distance. Walking bareback over the flats was hard enough; we didn't relish the idea of doing it with an eighty-pound canoe and a hundred-pound pack.

Luckily, we didn't have to go that far. As we crossed a creek a mile from camp, we spotted the off-white of a canvas tent, tucked back in the trees about a mile from the coast. Following the creek inland, we found an abandoned Cree goose camp. Dozens of roughly hewn decoys were piled in a corner of the tent along with a collection of foam pads, blankets, and sleeping bags. A family of weasels had moved into that corner, but we took possession of the rest, which looked far more comfortable than our tiny shelter. The freshwater creek was a mere hundred feet away, and driftwood was plentiful.

Portaging over the flats was so miserably slow that we didn't begin to ferry equipment up the creek until the next day. We felt unusually tired when we finished, perhaps due to the fact that we consumed much of our liquid supplies en route, "to save weight." The last few beers we hid in a snowbank, insurance against a protracted stay. The camp was so appealing and the portage so grueling that we weren't inclined to hurry our departure.

The ice remained jammed up for four days. Each day we took turns scouting downcoast for any newly opened leads. But the south winds stayed away, and the ice remained solid. Whenever the frigid air over the pack ice met warmer inland air, we witnessed spectacular illusions: great pillars of cloud climbed hundreds of feet above the ice, and shiplike apparitions rose up on the horizon, then vanished. The pack itself seemed to grow into towering cliffs of ice that shimmered and danced like the northern lights.

There was little else to do but eat and read, and the frustration of being stranded began to wear on our nerves—especially Pete's. The months of quiet at Lake River had trained me to a slower pace, and I welcomed the chance to sit and reflect. I spent some time inventing new creations from our standard fare of salt pork and potatoes, and many hours just viewing an entertaining parade of daydreams. I built my cabin, worked on this book, planned my life year by year up to 2003. Ki seemed to share my philosophy; he was happy enough to doze in the sun, occasionally opening an eye to watch for passing ground squirrels.

Pete, on the other hand, was fresh from the city and more antsy over our lack of progress. Without a book or a chore to attend to, he seemed lost. When his boredom grew intolerable, he decided to walk the four miles to Natatishee Point to check the ice conditions on the other side. He returned in the afternoon with the exciting news that a Cree family had established a large camp on the point. There was bad news, too: The ice was even more solid farther south, and the Indians had advised him there was little chance of reaching the east coast of Hannah Bay before early June. The canoe-taxi drivers in Moosonee had been right. We had no more than a few days' food left, but there were probably other camps farther south, or so the Indians on the point had told Pete. We decided to stay put for the moment and continue when conditions permitted, hoping to find food along the way.

On May 21, a full week after leaving Moosonee, we spotted the family from Natatishee Point canoeing back toward town. We scrambled for our canoe, hoping that the lead would stay open long enough for us to reach the point. It almost did: We got within a mile before being halted by constricting ice and low tide. We left the canoe atop a large floe, marked with the mast, until we could paddle it ashore on the evening tide. The rest of the afternoon we spent portaging equipment to shore through a maze of beached ice. Walking among the grounded floes was unearthly, with cold air currents swirling around ice caves and table-top sculptures.

Our new camp was luxurious—a large winter settlement of a dozen tents and teepees scattered amidst the trees. Each tent had its own cache of equipment, with skidoos mounted on blocks and outboard motors suspended from poles. We chose the best of three canvas tents on the edge of a sand beach. It boasted a straw floor, wood heater, Coleman stove, and lantern; a snowbank supplied us with fresh water and a wall of driftwood provided choice fuel. From a hill on the point we could scan miles around for opening leads. It was an ideal site for planning our new ice strategy.

We scavenged enough food to last us only perhaps another two days, and we couldn't count on finding any Indians on the coast farther south. Our alternatives were to continue down the coast and hope to find food, or to accept the dangers of offshore travel and paddle eighteen miles straight across Hannah Bay to the Quebec border. The latter was our choice, but the danger couldn't be ignored. Waves wouldn't be a problem, as the ice would keep the sea calm, but timing would be critical. Wind and drift, from a running tide, were the key factors.

We plotted our course, examined maps, studied the offshore leads, and noted the fluctuations in wind direction. Our route would take us past three bail-out points where we could abandon the crossing if the wind shifted and the lead we were following closed. The first place was a large, grounded iceberg rising forty feet above the water. From there it was another three and a half miles to a half-mile-long gravel shoal. A cluster of tiny, hundred-yard shoals lay eight miles farther out, with the east coast four miles beyond. If the wind shifted during one of these shoal-hops, and ice bullied us past the shoal, we might never reach land again.

May 22. We spoke little as we paddled toward the first shoal. We had planned as well as we could; the success of the crossing now rode on the luck of the winds. I had left two letters in the Cree tent: one to Toby, the tent's owner, with money for the food and fuel we had used, and another to a potential search party, with a map of our route in case we didn't make the crossing. Every few minutes we heard the distant thunder of massive floes colliding, one buckling up on top of the other. I couldn't erase the vision of a canoe caught between floes in such an encounter. Great hills of water leaped up as top-heavy bergs somersaulted, shearing off slabs of ice. Leads opened and closed within seconds, and we sprinted through the gaps in rhythm to their swelling and constricting.

Four miles offshore we found our first shoal encased in a mile-wide belt of wedged floes—too solid to pass through yet too unstable to climb over—and our plan collapsed before it was barely launched. We headed back to shore, and for two more days waited out the ice in an abandoned trapper's shack. It was far from perfect, but with our sail in place of the missing door and a stove fashioned from discarded sheet-metal, we managed to stay warm and dry. The snow was quickly receding under the late May sun, and the first unwelcome flies of the season appeared.

Late on the second day, two Chestnut canoes slipped in and out of the ice on our horizon, one towing the other. I met them in my hip-waders 400 yards from shore. A man who had been poling off ice raised a hand to greet me; two Cree women with a tarp over their shoulders sat between the men, and children peered over the gunwale. They were leaving their goose camp on the Harricanaw River to purchase supplies in town. During break-up, outlying camps are stranded for up to six weeks, and this was the start of the Indians' spring exodus from bush to town.

They shook their heads in disbelief when I described our shoal-hopping idea. "Even a fool would not make that crossing this time of year," the poler said. "Hannah Bay is open water. Better to stay by the coast. You only have five more miles of ice! But hurry; the lead is bad and it will close with the afternoon tide." He dug his ice-pole into a floe as his partner yanked the starter cord of a battered outboard. They left us with a final tip: "You will probably find Indians with food on the Harricanaw River, around Francis Island."

May 25. It seemed we were destined to hug the coast after all, though our food situation was still dire. As we poled through the ice, the cries of sea ducks echoed off the bergs. The birds were no doubt acceptable eating in an emergency and were dawdling along at a leisurely pace. We dug with our paddles to get within range, and as I yelled *"Fire!"* Pete dove to the bow deck, his ears plugged, to stay beneath the shot pattern. Firing over your bowman is hardly an advisable hunting practice, but sometimes we had to stretch the rules when an empty stew pail threatened. Two ducks lay in the bottom of our canoe by the time the others caught on and took flight.

About halfway through the remaining ice we reached a spot where the floes were packed solidly together. We chose the likeliest looking crack for a test of the canoe's icebreaker potential and built up some speed on the approach. At the last second before the crash, Pete yelled for a slight left turn. It was perfectly timed; the Grumman's double-riveted bow cut into the ice, wedging its nose far enough into the crack to part the floes. We leaned on our paddles, their aluminum shoes cutting into the surface, and drove the canoe farther into the gap. Like a steel wedge splitting a log, the canoe's thrust continued to widen the opening; aluminum ground against the floe with the screech of fingernails on a blackboard. After a thirty-foot struggle, we slipped out from between the floes into the next pool. The test had been a success, and the canoe had suffered no structural damage—only a few cosmetic gouges in its hull.

We continued to make progress through the morning, sometimes lining the canoe in places where the ice was too solid to part but where enough overflow had dribbled onto the surface to float it. Many of the "open" pools were navigable yet not really open; the temperature had dropped into the teens the night before, leaving a skin of new ice. I enjoyed looking back at the pattern traced by our stern's wake through the delicate layer of crystal.

Around midday an odd shimmer caught my eye. I stood up in the canoe and looked out, all the way to the horizon—across open water! Waves licked the suface: waves created by wind unhindered by breakwaters of ice. We dragged the canoe onto a small floe at the edge of the open water for a celebratory lunch. Ki rolled in the snow to scratch his back, then investigated our swaying hundred-foot-square island as Pete and I sprawled on the ice with the last of our garlic sausage and raisins. We lounged a bit too long, though; without the protection of surrounding ice, the floe was being quickly eaten away by growing waves. Then a crack developed beneath the canoe, and we began to list. As waves washed over the ice and lapped our boots, we frantically grabbed the remains of lunch and fastened down the spray cover.

We sailed south for the next ten miles, making good time and marveling at our sudden freedom. Three miles short of the mouth of the Harricanaw, which flows into the south end of Hannah Bay, the wind shifted and rose, throwing waves into us broadside. The waves soon had us outclassed, forcing us to turn back toward the goose flats. Low tide stopped us a mile from shore, so we staked the canoe and started on the familiar hike inland. Our portage took us as close as the stench would permit past the great bloated carcass of a moose that had washed ashore. It seemed ironic that we were so critically low on food, while hundreds of pounds of moose steak lay rotting for the sea gulls.

After an hour of weaving back and forth over the flats and around tidal pools, we reached the "trees"—a few clusters of scrub willow on patches of semidry ground. A nearby swamp offered passable drinking water, better if disguised as tea. While I plucked our sea ducks, Pete left on the three-mile round-trip to the canoe for a second load. At suppertime our first bite of sea duck told us why no one hunted these birds—all in all, a dismal ending to a long day.

Our camps on the goose flats were the most miserable of any in the journey. My journal entry for the next day describes a typical experience:

Saturday, May 26, 1979. East wind much too strong to travel. Spent the morning reading and writing in the tent. Fried garlic sausage for lunch. The last of the salt pork and potatoes for supper. Hunted a while—flushed a few cranes, nothing bagged. Ki got into another skunk, but Pete managed to get him away before he got sprayed. What a depressing camp—so wet that puddles ooze from the ground in our footprints, and leach through the tent floor. And this is the driest ground around! Can't wait for the Harricanaw—trees, fresh water, and food!

On Sunday the wind abated just enough to tempt us into leaving. We missed the tide, and never had I seen mud so sloppy as on our last portage off the flats. Every few dozen steps one of us had to retrieve a rubber boot from the muck. Mud was everywhere—in our boots, on our faces, in our hair. At one point Pete had to drop his pack to rescue me, over my knees in mud with the canoe on my back.

The Harricanaw did provide the longed-for oasis; here, sour seaweed and salt air were replaced by sweet spruce and black earth.

Scouting the west side of Francis Island, at the river's mouth, we found an Indian camp that had been inhabited just days earlier. Was this where we had been told we could buy food? Picking through the garbage pile, I found a mason jar containing a few handfuls of rice. This would be our supper. We searched for the rumored active camp all the next day, finding nothing but the maggot-covered remains of a seal kill. We would have to continue north toward Quebec's Ministikawatin Peninsula and hope that somewhere ahead was food.

May 29. About fifteen miles up the east coast of Hannah Bay we came to the Missisicabi River and another goose camp, hidden back in the trees with only a radio tower sticking up to reveal its presence. This was a well-established camp where American hunters paid for the privilege of roughing it in half a dozen cabins circling a clearing. The cabin doors were locked but the windows, decorated with football team decals, were open. Though we found the radio inoperable, we did get away with some booty: a handful of loose tea, a pound of lard, a few saltines that the mice had overlooked, and a little sugar and macaroni. I was delighted to find an ashtray of half-smoked butts; I hadn't had a cigarette for days.

That evening we had visitors: four Indians in a Chestnut loaded with shotguns and fishnets. They were low on food too, they said, and couldn't afford to sell us any. The spring goose flight had been the worst in decades and the whitefish weren't running. We were more concerned about ice conditions than hunting prospects, but they could not tell us the extent of the ice farther north. They wished us luck and, as they pushed off from shore, tossed us a freshly killed goose. We declared the evening a minivacation and lounged on foam mattresses reading dog-eared copies of *Playboy* while picking goose meat from our teeth.

Our luck seemed to be improving. Our grub box was growing heavier rather than lighter; when we stopped to help some Indians dislodge their scow from a sandbar, we were rewarded with cans of bacon, beef stew, and peaches—the best food we had seen since Moosonee. We passed more ice as we worked our way north, but never as much as we had battled on the west coast. Every time we thought we were running into pack ice, a new lead would open up and allow us through. Far offshore, aircraft carriers of ice, towering up to twenty feet above the water, cruised by in defiance of the warm sun. Grey and white beluga whales surfaced between the floes, sometimes as close as fifty feet from our canoe, and seals dozed on the ice.

May 31. Our last day in Ontario. As we completed the three-mile crossing of Gull Bay, we entered the tidal waters of Quebec. We were still only halfway to Rupert House, and our food would last only a day, two if we rationed. But it was hard to complain on such a spectacular day. A light, quartering headwind sent ripples across the bow, and I stripped to my underwear in the 70-degree heat. We were paddling two miles offshore to avoid shoals, marveling at the variety of passing ice formations, when we heard the drone of an airplane. After several passes, the plane circled and buzzed us, then turned into the wind to land on the water. Eagerly speculating that it might be a newspaper or television crew who had tracked us down for a story, Pete and I sat up from our slouch and dug deep with our paddles, trying to look as macho as possible.

But no cameras clicked from the windows; no microphone was proffered. Instead, an officer of the Ontario Provincial Police stepped down onto the pontoon, and I greeted him with a feeble joke about not having seen any speed limits posted. "You boys okay?" the officer rejoined laconically. We assured him that we were fine, if a bit hungry. Neither he nor the pilot had thought to bring so much as a candy bar. They had been dispatched from South Porcupine, Ontario, after getting a radio report from Moosonee that Indian hunters had spotted us caught in the ice. They offered to return with food, but I proudly declined (and would kick myself for it afterward). After bringing us up to date on the news—Canada had a new prime minister, Joe Clark—the officer promised to phone our parents and climbed back into the plane.

Our first camp in Quebec, on Pointe Méscanonane, was among the most beautiful we had seen. Almost exactly at the Quebec border, the hellish tidal flats of James Bay's west coast gave way to the magnificent country of the eastern shore. Instead of miles-wide flats, clean sand-and-gravel shores rose rapidly from the water. The land was higher and drier here, reflecting the reemergence of Canadian Shield geology. Grassy knolls backed by tall spruce replaced the dreary swamp landscape. The country around here reminded me of California's Big Sur coast; it even has its own version of the "witch tree," a gnarled, centuries-old spruce clinging to a rocky point.

June 1. Though we cherished every hour of travel through this pleasant country, we still had forty miles to go and there seemed little chance of reaching Rupert House with full bellies. On James Bay, a headwind can drag on for days, stretching a two-day paddle into a week. Our luck held, though, and the modest headwind soon changed to a substantial tailwind. With the sail up, we practically flew along the coast, at one point covering four miles in twenty-five minutes, without paddling! We were about to round the Ministikawatin Peninsula, where our heading would change from northeast to east-southeast, and I feared that our rig wouldn't handle the new tack. But again the wind shifted in our favor as we made the turn.

Near a place inappropriately called Consolation Point, the lively weather turned suddenly fierce, and rain hammered our backs as we raced past granite cliffs. We had a decision to make: turn south at the point and hug the coast for safety, or cross the open water of Rupert Bay to Stag Island, eight miles out. The latter route could save a day's travel, and our growling stomachs made the decision. The instant we passed the point we were committed. The wind shifted again to the southwest and lashed out with new strength. Its force snapped the sail taut and jolted the canoe nearly onto its side. I had to lean all my weight against the rudder paddle to keep us from flipping over; both of us, in fact, were leaning far out over the water, yet still we rode at a forty-five-degree angle. I wondered if our inadequate craft could withstand an ill-timed wave.

Our speed slowed on this difficult tack; after half an hour we had covered only four miles—halfway to the island. My hands ached and my arms were cramped from gripping the rudder; my jaws hurt from clenching my teeth. The rain stung our skin, and I began to doubt we could take another thirty minutes of this punishment. We had forgotten to put on life jackets, but it hardly mattered: In water just a few degrees above freezing, we wouldn't last more than a few minutes, with or without them.

The wind shifted even more to the south. We were sliding too far north; we would miss the island! As we adjusted ropes to compensate, I suddenly lunged sideways and nearly fell from the canoe; the rudder lashings had snapped under the increased pressure. Seconds later a rope-guide ring bolted to the hull broke free with a metallic twang. The sail flapped wildly as Peter climbed from his spray skirt and inched along the deck to grab the whipping rope. Ki began to panic and run back and forth on the deck to escape the waves breaking over him; Pete held the loose rope in one hand and pounded Ki with the other to keep him down and prevent his shifting weight from toppling us.

It's hard to sail a canoe in a wind much over twenty miles per hour. Later we learned that the winds that day reached forty — strong enough to keep many bush pilots on the ground. The waves were close to six feet, black walls of water towering over us and burying our bow much of the time. After a while I couldn't look away from the waves and began to hallucinate. Directions became meaningless; once I was sure we were sailing backward. Finally, I grew so dizzy I couldn't hold the rudder, and as the bow veered off course, Pete screamed at me to look away from the waves, keep my eyes on the sail.

This helped, and the bow swung back toward the island. But now we were sailing at uncontrollable speed toward a wall of rock surrounded by tremendous breaking surf. Just as it seemed we must crash, we glimpsed a sand beach tucked between massive boulders. At this critical moment, our canoe performed brilliantly. Instead of wallowing in the surf, she rode the tops of the waves as gracefully as a surfboard and we coasted in safely. Tears of relief filled my eyes as we jumped out and pulled her up on the beach.

June 3. Two days later, after inching the rest of the way across Rupert Bay against strong headwinds, we landed in front of a cluster of Cree cabins and tents. Dogs charged through camp to announce our arrival, and a huge Indian stepped from a tent. Six children hid behind him, sneaking peeks at us around and through his legs. This was Roderick Stevens, a trapper from Rupert House. Our arrival was timely, since his table was already crowded with food, but he grunted to his wife for even more. Our meals for the last two days had consisted of water, oats, and onion broth, and the spread nearly overwhelmed us. We ate smoked whitefish, "spork" (Spam) sandwiches, potatoes, bread, and fruit cocktail, and drank quarts of tea with sugar and canned milk — and then we ate some more, until Roderick was satisfied that we were in obvious discomfort.

We declined his offer to stay the night. Rupert House was only ten miles away, a three- or four-hour paddle, and I was eager to turn our bow into the Rupert River and bid farewell to James Bay. The bay had done its best to beat us: to sink, starve, freeze, or drown us. But the battle was over and we had survived it.

13 | Rivers to the Sea

Rupert House to Tadoussac, Quebec

June 8, 1979

Dear Mom, Dad, Steve & Sara,

Well, in a few hours we'll start up the Rupert. Rupert House [aka Fort Rupert] is the oldest HBC post in Canada—est. 1668. It's sure going to be hard to leave this place. We've never had a reception like we've had here. They're closing the school for 15 minutes to let the kids watch us go (we gave a talk to the kids yesterday). John Pearson, the Hudson's Bay manager, is going ahead of us to the first rapid, to photograph us coming in. . . .

No one in recent memory had paddled a small canoe from Moosonee to Rupert House, so our arrival provoked much curiosity. Before docking, Peter and I slicked our hair down and jammed our shirttails into our pants to give an impression of casual competence, but I doubt anyone was fooled. Our strained faces, torn clothing, chafed skin, and sunken cheeks were giveaways. Apparently a rumor had reached town that we were lost on the bay and had probably perished in the ice; it was hard to tell whether the Cree men who crowded around our canoe were pleased or disappointed by the fact of our safe arrival. They poked the spray cover and sail and asked ques-

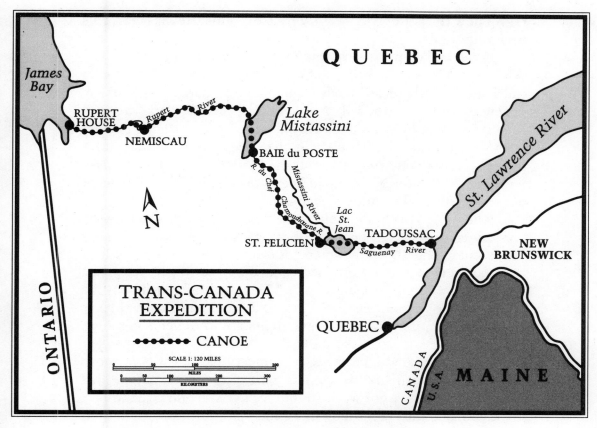

Rupert House to Tadoussac, Quebec, June–August 1979

tions faster than we could answer them, but their expressions were noncommittal.

There were no reservations, though, in the welcome we got from John and Hazel Pearson. They immediately sat us down to a fortifying dinner of shepherd's pie and beer from John's prized stash. Childhood sweethearts from the Shetland Islands, off Scotland's north coast, they had worked at Hudson's Bay Company posts all over Canada. John was a bluff, blond, bearded Viking type with a vocabulary to match. He entertained us over dinner with the salty tale of how the police had recently tried to confiscate his beer. (This was a dry reserve.)

In general, John wasn't impressed with his current posting. While speaking of the beauty of his native Shetlands ("Don't ever call a Shetland Islander a bloody Scotsman!"), he glanced out the window with disdain and added, "Not at all like this dung pile they call Rupert House. I been assigned HBC posts on Baffin Island, Belcher Island, and Pond Inlet, to name some. They were all beautiful— none a these bloody trees to spoil the bloody view." This remark rendered Pete and me, who had been craving the sight and scent of spruce for weeks, quite speechless.

John evinced a child's excitement about our journey and eagerly pressed us for details. The next morning, as we reviewed plans for our ascent up the Rupert, he shook his head over his Cream of Wheat and commented that no one had canoed *up* the Rupert for years. "You do have some work ahead a ye." Then he brightened: "Say, La Sarre Airways flies all the [HBC] freight for me. The bloody thieves charge enough, they owe me a few flights. Tell 'em Pearson said to fly you upriver to scout the rapids."

Thus originated a network of connections that was to prove invaluable throughout this difficult part of the trip. As John had warned, we did have our work cut out for us. Ascending the Rupert made going up the Berens look like child's play. A few statistics tell the tale: The Berens gains elevation at a modest 1.4 feet per mile, while on the Rupert we would climb an average of 2.75 feet per mile throughout our 450-mile ascent from sea level to 1,230 feet. And along the river's first 100 miles, that average would shoot up to 8 feet per mile. Walking along a trail, this elevation gain would be too slight to notice, but on the water it's a very different story. Even a single foot of altitude per mile is a struggle.

We met pilot Georges Boucher at the La Sarre Airways trailer, and he happily agreed to help with the aerial scouting. In fact, he was just on his way to Carroll Lake to pick up supplies, and we were welcome to ride along. Carroll Lake, about ninety miles east of Rupert House, lies on the region's only north-south road, about fifteen miles south of where it bridges the Rupert River. Trucks on their way north leave supplies there for Rupert House, and Georges flew the round-trip from town six times daily. So not only could he take us on recon flights, but he could easily track our progress once we set off on the river.

Carroll Lake was also known as NBR II, one of a string of construction sites for the largest hydroelectric project in history—the massive James Bay Hydro project. At this time, the major rivers of James Bay's eastern watershed were being dammed or rerouted to provide power for lower Quebec and New York City. *NBR* was a site designation standing for the *N*ottaway, *B*roadback, and *R*upert rivers. The road was built to service the hydro teams, and we found much other evidence of the project's impact on the country—both positive and negative.

Pete wanted to photograph around town, so I drew the first flight with Georges. It was an interesting trip. I didn't learn the identity of the supplies we were to pick up (twenty-three-hundred pounds of bagged cement) until Boucher's obnoxiously loud, rattling, single-prop Beaver landed on the lake. The forklift on hand was a primitive model (the two-armed, sore-back design)—so much for my free ride. Once the stuff was loaded, Georges taxied the length of the lake and ordered me into the back. In response to my puzzled look, he said as an afterthought, "Oh, I forgot to mention: This plane's maximum cargo capacity is eighteen-hundred pounds. I'll need you back there to adjust the load till we fly level."

The lake was nearly a mile long, and our pontoons left the water no more than 200 yards from the far shore. Once airborne (if our gasping, treetop-scraping progress deserved that term), I dove for the rear and began shifting bags of cement until Georges shouted the okay. I expected him to fly at a safe 1,000 feet or so on the way back, but he obviously wanted to give me a close-up view of the rapids and we followed the Rupert at about 100 feet most of the way, sometimes as low as 20 feet. Georges held the plane tightly to the river course, banking at each bend like a sports car carving up a country road. This wasn't just showing off; if we had veered from the river channel, we would have struck trees. I tried to take notes on the whitewater, but from this perspective most of the rapids defied navigation, and I was reduced to noting possible portage routes.

By June 9 Peter and I were ready to get going. From here to Tadoussac we would be on rivers all the way, except for a few lakes and innumerable portages. True to their word, John and Hazel, along with a few friends, met us at the first rapids, two miles from town, for a final farewell party, preceding us upstream in their outboard-powered rubber boat. Aside from this, day one on the Rupert was a total disaster. The current was about half again as fast as it had been on the lower Berens, and we failed in our attempt to line and wade up that first mile-long set of rapids. The rapids would have presented no problem for canoeists heading downstream or for natives going upriver under power, but as on the Berens, we found that upriver travel by pole, line, and paddle is nearly extinct, and we were again forced to blaze our own trail through a maze of brush. We camped the first night on an island only six miles from town.

New problems arose as we struggled on. Whereas we were used to paddling through stretches between rapids on the Berens, on the lower Rupert even the "slack" current flowed with steady force, and the "flat" water was too swift for us to make progress by paddling. Other options were equally limited: The water was often too deep to advance by poling, and the banks were either sheer rock covered by matted growth or else choked with dense brush, both impractical for lining from shore.

Most often we resorted to a method we called "willow walking," which we'd developed on the Berens (and which I'm sure is widely used by bush travelers, though we'd never heard of it). Scrub willow in the northern bush is beloved by rabbits but passionately cursed by humans, who are too big to slip under its intertwining snarls. We found one way to take advantage of it, though. Willow walking is simply pulling oneself hand over hand by overhanging branches, while remaining in the canoe. Pete describes how it worked for us:

> I would lean with my chest over the bow plate and grab at the dense foliage growing alongside the river, as Dave kept

the stern away from shore with his paddle blade. I passed
the branches over my head; usually they would clear Ki, but
when they were too big or just the wrong height, he would
move reluctantly out of the way, with an exaggerated slow-
motion effort.

It was a painfully slow form of progress, our gains measured in scant
yards per hour, and the willow exacted its price in countless slashes
across arms and cheeks.

*The week following the expedition's departure from Rupert House was
one of exhausting river travel. They had committed themselves to a
schedule that would put them in Tadoussac on August 17, and plans
had been set in motion for their arrival celebration. Meanwhile, though,
it was a terrible grind, and Dave's account of specifics is limited to
terse journal entries such as these:*

June 10. Tough, lining day—quick current.
June 11. 2 mi. portage, camp on pond, Georges flies over.
June 14. Terrible 2 mi. port.—many cutlines [from the hydro
     survey], lost

*In some places they could take advantage of pulsations in the river
current, as they did on the Berens. Pete Souchuk contributes further
notes on paddling the Rupert:*

We timed our frenzied canoe rushes upriver when the water
was in its low-surge mode. We usually stayed near the shore
and hopped from back-eddy to back-eddy. [Eddies are
patches of reverse current that allow one to rest now and
then.] Sometimes we even crossed the river to utilize attractive back-eddies or a piece of shoreline that looked
especially conducive to willow walking.
    Often during our all-out bursts of paddling to overcome
small stretches of whitewater, we would fix on a tree on shore
to gauge our movement upriver. Sometimes we moved only
two to three inches in as many minutes, and one botched

paddle stroke would end our forward momentum, shooting us downriver. We took turns calling out the cadence for beating up such rapids, like a coxswain in a race. After fifteen minutes of hard stroking, our voices grew hoarse, and our labored breathing supplied the synchronization.

On June 17, five miles before reaching the Rupert River Bridge, the team had a pleasant surprise. As Dave relates in a letter home,

[a] plane circled and landed on the river, and out jumped 6 of our friends from Rupert House—John and Hazel, HBC clerk Paul Wicks, Georges Boucher, a nurse, and a teacher. We all climbed onto a beaver lodge, tied up the plane and canoe, and had quite a party with the goodies they brought. . . . Pete and I were in shock! Paul decided to join us for the 5 mi. paddle to the bridge; he'll fly back tomorrow. Poor Paul. The last 5 miles were some of the worst, with 3 rapids and no portage trails. With the blackflies, it was living hell heaving the canoe through the bush and wading to our waists. . . .

To sum up the Rupert in one word—it's a bitch. But at least the worst stuff is over. To give you an idea, we've come 80 river miles (270 to go), and climbed 700 feet—more than in the whole 350 miles of the Berens R. The bad thing about the Rupert is that the rapids are long and drawn-out. Before this, our longest portage *ever* was ¾ mile. So far we've had 2 two-mile portages, 1 three-mile, and 1 four-mile portage—that one took us 12 hours!

What makes the portages worse is the blackflies. Dad, in comparison it seems we had no bugs last summer. They come in clouds—getting into your eyes, ears, and hair. You inhale them when you breathe & swallow them when you open your mouth. Repellent has no effect. The only respite is to light a smudge fire and sit in the smoke.

The other problem with portages is that the g.d. hydro project has wiped out the trails. They've got cutlines crisscrossing the bush, wiping out trails with fallen timber. Cutting our own trails has cost us days. I used to think the Indians were just complaining about the dams. But now I see the incompetence and damn lack of consideration and I'm dead against the project. With the trails gone, the trappers will have no way of getting to their lines. I'm in favor of developing the north, but blind destruction is ridiculous.

The James Bay project, incidentally, was a major environmental issue in both Canada and the United States before it was pushed through. Dave, whose bush experiences often left him unsympathetic to the concerns of wilderness enthusiasts, whom he called "two-weekers," seems to have joined with them in this case.

Dave's letter concludes with some comments that express his complicated response to hardship:

I feel like an old man. I hate to say it, but there's little joy in the trip anymore. I guess we've gone too many miles. In order to have some leisure time on the Saguenay, we're going 7 days a week, 10–12 hours a day. I never have time to fish anymore. We don't really enjoy camps — just light a smudge fire, wolf down dinner, read in the tent for half an hour, and collapse. The really long portages are the worst — by the end of the day we're shaky and nauseous with exhaustion. I really feel like crying sometimes. We feel like we've paid our dues and don't deserve such a schedule. But the thought of missing Aug. 17 is overwhelming — we just can't take a chance. I don't think I'll ever be able to convey the pain and misery. You can describe the physical but not the mental. But it's certainly been more than worth it and I know I'll be counting the days to the next trip.

At times I've stood atop a granite ridge overlooking the river. I'd look up at the sky and across the rock, over the trees and down into the water. And I'd want to scream. I'd feel superhuman with a strength derived from the elements. Each time we've gone hungry or dumped in a rapid or writhed under the intense cold we've learned a little more and grown a bit stronger. The elements always seem to be waiting to pull you down and defeat you. They wait until you're off guard and then jump in with both heels in your face. And when you beat them, it's beautiful.

Navigating the remainder of the Rupert would take close to another month, though the difficulty of travel eased in the later miles. As they approached Lake Mistassini—a large lake almost dead center in Quebec between James Bay and the Atlantic coast—the landscape flattened out and the Rupert widened into a system of narrow lakelets and connecting channels. Here the tough portages and rapids were interspersed with sections where they could make good time with the sail up or by paddle.

They also acquired new friends to look after their progress; helicopter pilots with the NBR II project kept an eye on them after they were out of Georges Boucher's range. Occasionally their pontoon-equipped machines would land near the team, at future dam sites along the river, to deposit a geologist or pick up remote field-testing equipment. Once or twice they even talked Dave and Peter into flying back to one of their base camps for dinner and drinks.

Lake Mistassini was the turning point of the Quebec travel. On exiting it, they would be heading downriver the rest of the way to the St. Lawrence. But finding their way through the headwaters of the Rupert and into the lake posed a navigation risk because they were without the proper maps. A package containing all the large-scale maps for the last leg of the journey had been lost in transit from Moosonee to Rupert House. All they had left were two small-scale (one inch to eight miles) maps of the Rupert donated by Georges Boucher, and none at all for the country beyond.

Dave's original plan called for them to proceed east from Lake Mistassini and pick up the Mistassini River, which flowed south several hundred miles to Lac St.-Jean and the Saguenay. This involved some particularly tricky route finding, for which they needed maps scaled at one inch to the mile. Dave's letter home from Rupert River Bridge concluded with an urgent request for a duplicate set of maps for the upper Rupert and Mistassini regions to be sent via John Pearson. Maurey Halsey bought the maps and shipped them by air to Boston—just the first leg of a roundabout route by which they reached their destination. From Boston they were flown to Montreal, then forwarded by smaller carrier west to Val d'Or, Quebec, and by ground transportation to La Sarre, near the Ontario border. Here La Sarre Airways and Georges Boucher took over, flying them to Rupert House, where they were picked up by Randy Blake, one of the NBR helicopter jockeys who'd gotten to know Dave and Pete.

On July 6, Randy flew up the Rupert and spotted the Trans-Canada crew staked out at an abandoned goose-hunting camp. He was just in time: This was the limit of the copter's range, and another day's travel would have put the expedition out of reach. It was too windy to land, Peter recalls, and "with his copilot standing on the chopper's skid, Randy maneuvered as close to the rocky shore as the helo's rotors would allow. The copilot heaved the heavy tube of maps into our camp, and they were off. That was the last we saw of them."

One of the charts in the tube contained an affectionate and worried message from Jean Halsey, and on another Maurey had noted his proposed routing of the maps as well as some cautions about the Mistassini River travel Dave was contemplating. The Mistassini, a beautiful wilderness river, was an eagerly anticipated highlight of the trip. But its remote, southerly course was packed with rapid after challenging rapid, and Maurey's carefully penned note questioned the wisdom of tackling it, given their commitment to an arrival date in Tadoussac.

Dave was already worried about the Mistassini route. First, though, they had to wend their way through the complex lake-river system of the Rupert's headwaters. Pete Souchuk attributes their success here, as in the many route-finding challenges the expedition faced, to Dave's facility with charts. "His ability to visualize three-dimensional landforms on a two-dimensional map was inspiring, if not aggravating. One of the keys to Trans-Canada's success was Dave's meticulous pre-expedition planning at the National Geographic Society's cartographic department. I imagine his skill was a combination of tips he had learned from his father's training as a navigator in the Navy and an innate talent that successful navigators seem to possess."

On reaching Lake Mistassini, they encountered stiff easterly winds and decided the best way to make progress was by paddling at night. Peter recounts:

On a beautifully cold, clear evening [July 17], we paddled east-southeast toward the horizon and Ile Dablon, fifteen miles distant. As we approached the little island several hours later, I remember thinking how the tall spruce trees looked like witches standing before the rising moon.

The next day we paddled south to Ile Marie Victorin and remained there windbound for two days. Dave caught a huge lake trout and meticulously smoked it over the fire— indescribably delicious! Heading south again toward Baie du Poste (at the southern end of the lake), we were very aware that less than a month remained to reach Tadoussac. Talk became serious as we met with the Baie du Poste Indians to work out an alternate route to Lac St.-Jean.

Originally Dave had planned to enter the Riviere Té-miscamie at its headwaters, and via several lakes enter the Mistassini River. He had talked about that river for more than a year. We calculated the number of rapids we had to negotiate on the Mistassini and, much to Dave's disappoint-ment, concluded that we simply couldn't travel this river safely in the allotted time.

Dave went back to his charts and worked out a new plan for reaching Lac St.-Jean that economized on time but also offered beautiful wilderness canoeing. This took them from Baie du Poste a short distance north on the Birch River—another upstream haul with a steep elevation gain. From there on, however, it was all downhill: on the Chilfour River to File-Axe Lake, thence to Lac Carbonneau and the Riviere du Chef.

Another six days on the Chef brought them, on August 2, to its junction with the Chamouchouane River, their highway to the good-sized town of St. Félicien on Lac St.-Jean, one of Quebec's largest lakes. But the Chamouchouane (or Ashuapmuchuan, in the Indian spelling) was anything but a smooth ride. Its upper reaches for some twenty-odd miles were thick with rapids; among Dave's last detailed journal entries is a description of one in particular.

August 3, 1979. We're camped on a one-and-a-half-mile portage around a gorge where the river drops more than a hundred feet. As usual we're low on food (and fishing is lousy). . . . Hours ago we experienced a pair of the most traumatic incidents of the expedition.

Everything had been going well: so well that we'll have plenty of time in the last 100 miles to the St. Lawrence to relax, sip wine, drift with the river, and enjoy the women. That's been our conversation for weeks, including last night, when we approached a set of five consecutive rapids. Our blood was running — we were in the mood for rapids. Our spirits were high after running the first, but as we neared the second, we started having bad feelings. I suddenly realized that the stage was ideally set for a dump: We were feeling cocky and bold (willing to run unscouted water), light was fading, we were tired and hungry, and a steady drizzle kept visibility to a minimum.

Our uneasiness grew as half a dozen nighthawks appeared, circling and diving as close as a paddle's length from the canoe. I had never seen birds act like this. None could be seen upriver or down — only around our heads. The water had turned inky black, sluggish and shiny in the dim light. I remember the water of the Athabasca looking the same when we had our serious accident two years ago. As we neared the second rapid, that whole sickening, gut-wrenching sensation of the Athabasca returned.

Of course, the Indians would say that the nighthawks and slick water were signs of nature, warnings of danger. They would never, under any circumstances, travel another foot after seeing such signs. But we are white men and knew such things were foolish. We should have learned our lesson by now — from the *métis* in Saskatchewan who gave me the caribou medicine pouch and the subsequent exorcism of Wetigo. And from other things I couldn't explain, like Matthew dreaming in perfect detail of my winter camp north of Lake River, or the Tookates' ongoing war of spell-casting with Abe Paulmartin.

But apparently we hadn't learned enough. We flared the canoe, turning the bow upstream to stand and scout the rapid. It seemed to present no problems — a fairly safe run through a chute to the right. We forgot our nervousness and turned into the fast water. When we got to within fifty feet of the rapid, the view was quite different: Instead of a chute, there was a "lip" (a small falls), meaning certain disaster. We swung the bow toward shore and made a frantic leap, literally skimming the edge of the falls, and reached shore less than a canoe's length from the drop. The nighthawks were gone.

What happened next strengthened the lesson twofold. It was a warm, breezy, shirtless afternoon, a day for suntans, Tang, and making miles. As usual, the talk revolved around wine, women, and Tadoussac.

We had just run a big, deep rapid. It was one of our best runs of the season — perfect maneuvers through five or six consecutive four-foot standing waves. The second rapid of the set looked much tougher but still runnable. We grounded out on a white sand beach to scout, munching blueberries as we walked up and down the shore.

My decision was to run it; it looked tough but fun and not too dangerous. But Peter flat-out refused. I couldn't understand his objection, and though we talked the rapid through, turn by turn and rock by rock, it was still no go. He agreed that he saw nothing radical enough to justify his fears, but insisted that he had never on the whole journey had such a terrible feeling of disaster lurking in a rapid. Finally, though, he conceded to my wish, and we agreed it would be safe enough to take Ki along without his being washed overboard.

It was the kind of rapid I most enjoy: deep standing waves mixed with quick, critical turns. Fifty feet into the only navigable route, the current slammed into a rock wall, slipped around a jagged corner, and disappeared in an avalanche of cascading white. If we didn't cut that turn perfectly, we wouldn't see the rest of the rapid — or anything else beyond. Once around the turn, though, we simply had to keep the bow into the deep stuff and maintain pressure on the rudder to keep the canoe from rolling in crosscurrents. It was my job to "feel" the constantly shifting current. In a big rapid it can change direction three or four times in as many seconds, and without immediate opposing pressure on the rudder, the canoe will roll. Pete's job was, if anything, more nerve-wracking; he had to keep our speed up to prevent the canoe from settling and floundering in the wave troughs, even when he couldn't see through the whitewater. For all the bowman knows, there may not be anyone in the stern, yet he must keep digging.

We cleared the rock face beautifully, with room to spare. The canoe leaned into the turn and we hit the first wave perfectly, taking a little wash over the spray cover. Ki suddenly rolled off; I would almost say he jumped off intentionally, which would indeed be a first. We lost sight of him behind rock and spray but soon spotted him dashing along the shore rocks after us.

So Ki was safe and we had only three or four big waves to go. We plowed into the first, and as we began the descent down its slide (backside), we got our first full view of the next wave. What had appeared from shore to be just another four-foot wave loomed now, less than a paddle stroke away, as a ten-foot fang of white and grey. This was because the base of the wave was a black hole six feet beneath the surface, invisible unless you were looking right into it.

Deep holes in rivers are sometimes called recirculating holes, referring to their greatest danger. The combined pressure of the current and the height of the wave behind it can trap an object—a canoe, for instance—so that it never breaks free of the hole, endlessly climbing and descending the same wave. There was no way our eighteen-foot canoe would survive a head-on collision with a ten-foot wall of water without upending in a spectacular somersault. Yet there was no time to avoid it; any attempt would have taken us into the hole broadside—in which case our bodies and the canoe would probably recirculate until ice from next spring's break-up forced us out.

My thinking hadn't progressed this far when we began our descent into the hole. At such times I imagine that thoughts are crowded out of the mind by sheer awe. Probably in the last second I shouted some vital instruction to the bow, such as "Ohhh, shit!"

The fact that we hesitated probably saved us. Earlier, I would have said that speed might be one's only chance to clear such a rapid, but in this case a spurt of speed would have been just the thing to complete the somersault and leave us keel up. As the bow rose and cleared the crest, the canoe stood nearly vertical. We couldn't climb over it, nor did the wave have quite enough force to flip us. So we compromised by sliding backward into the hole. At the bottom, the stern slammed into the rock from which the wave originated. The rear third of the canoe, where I sat looking up at Pete, was underwater, as was I from the rib cage down. Then we rebounded and began to climb the wave a second time, without any help from our paddles. Again the bow cleared the crest, and again we slid back into the "death hole"—the name that came soonest to mind. There is no feeling more revolting and gut-wrenching than to slide backward into the bowels of a rapid.

As we slammed into the rock a second time I screamed to Pete, *"Paddle! For God's sake, paddle!!"* This seemed to rouse Pete from his paralysis and he dug for life. Later he told me he thought the hull had been pierced and we were taking in gallons of water; he had begun tearing at the spray skirt to leap from the canoe. In two short paddle strokes it was almost over; we emerged back into the life-giving sunlight and out of the wave. We were still too busy with "Hard left!" and "Taking on water!" to celebrate, but within seconds we had cleared the last waves, veered into a back-eddy, and ground ashore, as if we had imagined the whole thing.

We ran upriver shouting for Ki and found him on a small beach, searching the river with his eyes and ears. He bounded toward us joyfully, coughing a few times to clear water from his lungs. The canoe was basically sound, too, and after a short calm-down session we paddled back into the river and through a last minor rapid.

All I could think of was how beautiful everything was. Each tree, each passing rock, each paddle stroke was full of unspeakable beauty. I kept thinking that we shouldn't be seeing these things— we should still be in the hole. My skin was beautiful; the wind was an art form. The sky was a deeper blue than I had ever seen.

The remainder of the trip down the Chamouchouane was relatively uneventful, and the deep wilderness gradually began to show signs of civilization—the occasional road or rail track. About twenty-five miles from St. Félicien, the two camped at a series of waterfalls: the Rapide des Roches and the Grand and Petite Chutes a l'Ours (Bear Falls). They were unprepared for the sights that greeted them there: several families fishing and picnicking, children playing games. The parking lot was filled with cars and garbage cans overflowed. "In the middle of this chaos," Pete remembers, "grew millions of sweet wild blueberries. We feasted on gourmet blueberry pancakes Dave concocted and reluctantly accepted the fact that our trip was nearing its end."

August 6 and 7 were spent in St. Félicien. Now just ten days from their scheduled completion date, Dave phoned home to alert the Halseys that it was time to leave for Canada. The family would arrive in Tadoussac a few days early, to coordinate the landing celebration. Then the expedition embarked on its last major lake crossing. Lac St.-Jean, some four hundred square miles, was a formidable challenge, with giant ore boats to dodge and high winds to contend with. Setting out straight across the lake, they made about five miles under sail and then flipped in a strong wind. Making a right-angle turn south, they barely paddled to shore at a spot called Pointe Bleue, and a few days later made a successful thirteen-mile crossing to a landfall near Pointe a la Savane on the eastern shore.

Sailing parallel to the lake's northeastern shore, they continued on to camp at Ile Beemer at the mouth of the Saguenay River (known as the Grande Decharge), just below the town of Alma. Coming into Alma, they had the unique experience of portaging the canoe down the face of a dam that provides hydroelectric power for aluminum processing. The urban influence continued along this upper part of the Saguenay, through the towns of Arvida and Chicoutimi—the biggest city along their route since Kamloops, British Columbia. Two more dams were portaged around. They were now less than 100 miles from the end of the journey.

Before it joins the St. Lawrence, the lower half of the Saguenay turns wild again. As their canoe sailed down this majestically broad stretch of river, between high cliffs on both sides, Dave had plenty of leisure for daydreaming and fantasizing. But it seems to have fallen short of being the joyful, self-congratulatory time he had imagined in earlier, more stressful days. Peter was by now counting the hours to Tadoussac ("I'd lie in the tent each night thinking 'One day closer'"), while Dave withdrew into himself. They spoke little during the last two weeks.

What conversation there was centered on the future and what lay ahead after the trip, rather than on reminiscences. Dave occasion-

ally brought up the idea of another Canadian expedition—this time going east to west, and farther north—but Pete couldn't muster any enthusiasm and Dave stopped mentioning it. They talked about the article they hoped the National Geographic would publish and the possibility of making a movie about the journey. Dave spoke of attempting a sailing adventure, and maybe writing a book about hoboes. They didn't talk about their families, except of their mothers' impending relief at the whole thing being over.

Both families, meanwhile, were camped out in the Tadoussac Hotel. Excitement in the little town was building, and the Halseys were kept busy on the phone with the Canadian media, local officials, and representatives from Labatt's, which was donating quantities of beer for the arrival celebration. On the day before the expedition's scheduled landing, Maurey and Steve Halsey, along with reporter Don Dutton from the Toronto Star, went upriver by motorboat to spend the evening with Dave and Peter at their last campsite. This was at a spot about ten miles above Tadoussac where there was a small settlement and a pier. They brought a bottle of champagne, discussed final arrangements for the ceremony, took some photos. Maurey Halsey thought Dave seemed slightly depressed.

When Jacques Cartier explored up the St. Lawrence seaway around 1540, there was an Indian village on the site of present-day Tadoussac. Its location, on the north bank of the St. Lawrence just at its confluence with the Saguenay, was strategically superb. It soon became a trading station for furs and fish, and later, in 1600, the first French Canadian settlement. Today Tadoussac boasts a full-time population of only about a thousand, but is a popular summer resort and proud of its place in the history of Canadian exploration.

Whales travel up the salty St. Lawrence to the Saguenay and beyond, and whale-watching excursions are a popular tourist diversion in Tadoussac. Around midday on August 17, 1979, one of the excursion boats headed up the Saguenay in search of a different quarry: the eighteen-foot canoe of the Trans-Canada Expedition, due to land on a small beach in Tadoussac at 2:00 P.M. A few other craft—rowboats, kayaks, canoes—joined it to form a small flotilla. From his vantage point on a breakwater extending out into the river junction, Maurice Halsey watched them through binoculars as they moved slowly up-river.

After covering half the distance between their last camp and Tadoussac, Dave, Peter, and Ki stopped behind a prominent, cliffy point of land called Cap de la Boule, remaining out of sight of town until it was time for the last paddle to the beach. As they rounded the point and came into sight, Canadian and U.S. flags flying from bow and stern, a foghorn on the south bank tooted in greeting, and the escorting boats crowded around to offer advance congratulations and refreshments. When they came abreast of his jetty, Maurey Halsey returned to the beach and switched on his tape recorder to capture a cacophonous welcome from the waiting crowd of close to five hundred.

"The first thing I saw as we turned the point was some friends holding up a huge sign that read, 'Welcome to Vancouver,'" Peter recalls. "Boats of all sizes were coming near to offer drinks and salud. *As we came close to the beach, the water got shallow and our paddle tips were scraping bottom, so I turned around and touched Ki and just looked at Dave. We were both smiling. I wanted to hug him, but he was too far away. When we hit land, we both stood up slowly and Ki hopped out first. Dave motioned for me to get out, but I thought he should go first; I can't remember now which of us went ahead. Cameras clicked as we hugged our families and each other, posed for photos, yelled for Ki, shook hands, drank champagne, and moved through the crowd wearing silly grins, feeling really high."*

Not much of Dave and Pete's excited reunion with their families is intelligible on the tape, and when the celebration later moved up to the Tadoussac Hotel, the party grew very merry indeed—thanks in part to the generous donation of beer from Labatt's. The mayor of Tadoussac, Octave Caron, made a speech of welcome in French and English, and presented Dave and Pete with plaques hand carved by a local artisan commemorating their journey. Each of the teammates took the microphone briefly to thank the citizens of Tadoussac; their families, friends, and supporters back in the States; and all the Canadians who had befriended them along the trail. Ki posed graciously for innumerable photographs. The national Canadian media weren't on hand as expected, due to the sudden death of former Prime Minister John Diefenbaker, but they were hardly missed.

A banquet followed the party, and festivities at the hotel and the youth hostel continued for some time. Two days later there was another excuse for a party: The Expeditions of North America canoeists, whom Dave and Pete had met on James Bay, showed up to add their congratulations. The young "voyageurs" had planned to make the official arrival ceremony, but fell behind schedule. Fortunately, the Halseys had remained in Tadoussac, so a belated celebration was in order.

It was an emotional time for Dave's family, compounded of relief, excitement, pride, and a vicarious sense of triumph. They, especially Maurice and Jean Halsey, had shared the journey almost mile by mile, and certainly their support had more than once kept the expedition going when it might have faltered. Steve and Sara were happy for their big brother; the siblings were closer than most and Dave had reliably shared in their ups and downs. They had worried about him when he was restless in college and when he had embarked on this extraordinary, puzzling journey, and they rejoiced for him now.

Pete thinks that, while he and Dave shared in the general jubilance, they were also suffering from a certain amount of posttraumatic stress. The events in Tadoussac—the parties, speeches, dinners—unfolded for him as though in a kind of fog. He remembers this feeling lasting for a long time.

Dave, in his taped remarks to the celebrating crowd, sounds strongly moved and almost disbelieving about his success. There were so many times during the journey, he recalled, when reaching Tadoussac had seemed impossible. He wrote in his final newsletter to supporters that, while the parties were going on, he thought about particular people who had contributed in important ways to the expedition. He mentions Joe and Carolina Camp in Fort McMurray, Alberta trapper Baxter Gillingham, his Cree friends at Lake River. And others who were anonymous but helped nonetheless: "The hardships of the trail were often put aside while we enjoyed a cup of coffee with a prairie farmer, or shared a hot meal and a glass of rum at a Hudson's Bay Company post."

People were a big part of the journey for Dave, and the gregarious part of his character responded freely and warmly to the human side of the experience. People who lived in the bush, especially, won his interest and admiration. A celebration is intrinsically a "people" event, so it's natural that Dave's public thoughts were of his social encounters on the trail.

His private thoughts are harder to know. Perhaps there was some sense of anticlimax, or perhaps that had already come and gone somewhere back on the Saguenay—or even earlier. Those close to Dave noted a marked contrast between his social side—the hail-fellow who could strike up instant friendships in a bar or persuade strangers to support his schemes—and the solo adventurer, who was happiest in a one-on-one embrace with wild country and challenging circumstances. The more solitary Dave may not have been at the Tadoussac Hotel at all, but in any one of countless places that would live in a different part of his memory: on a windblown ridgetop in British Columbia, at a campsite on the Athabasca, in a snow shelter near a branch of Lake River, or somewhere on James Bay, diving with the beluga.

And perhaps his feelings at the journey's end were not so different from those that led him to begin it. One of Dave's favorite writers was Jack London. His copy of **The Sea-Wolf** *contains several highlighted passages that, while depicting London's characters, clearly had personal meaning for Dave. This one goes to the heart of the impulse behind the Trans-Canada Expedition:*

> It struck me that he was joyous, in a ferocious sort of way;
> that he was glad there was an impending struggle; that he
> was thrilled and upborne with the knowledge that one of
> the great moments of living, when the tide of life surges up
> in flood, was upon him.

Epilogue

Good Sight Lake

And now my tales are done.

And as I wrote, I wonder if the actors in them did not come back from out of the Past, and live again, and play their parts once more. And as I told of them and what they thought, and what they said or did, who can say but that they gathered there, around the Empty Cabin and listened, in that silent and enchanted grove of pine trees.

Perhaps the grove was no more silent, but was filled with all the voices of those whose tales were told here, long ago. And maybe the Cabin was not empty, but was filled again with movement, while its door stood wide in welcome and its window glowed with light, and its fire was burning brightly and it woke from all its dreaming, when those who once had lived here, lived again.

Grey Owl
Tales of an Empty Cabin

Both Dave and Pete read Grey Owl's classic tale of bush life (the author's Cree name is Wa-Sha-Quon-Asin) during the expedition. Pete still has the copy given to him by the Taylors of Besnard Lake, Saskatchewan. To Dave, a cabin in the wilderness represented the best kind of shelter in the world—a refuge from bitter cold nights on the trail, like the cabins they had found throughout Canada, but also a kind of refuge from the chill winds of life as he experienced it when the expedition was over. He was making plans to build his own cabin in the bush, and had a site picked out, when he died in the summer of 1983.

Things did not go well for Dave in the months and years following Trans-Canada. Anyone might be expected to suffer a certain amount of postachievement letdown after such a long, intensely focused effort. But in addition, fate dealt him some major disappointments and he took them hard, as always. *National Geographic*, which had supported the expedition both financially and with verbal encouragement all along, declined to feature an article about it in the magazine. Dave's literary agent, Julian Bach, found a publisher for the book Dave had begun to write, but then the publisher unexpectedly backed out of the contract. Dave did publish some articles about the trip elsewhere, and Sierra Club Books soon picked up the rights to the book—but the ego blows took their toll.

Less than four months after Dave returned to McLean, Virginia, taking Ki with him, Ki was killed by a car on the road near the Halseys' home. As Jean Halsey has remarked, the handsome coyote-dog was in some ways the spirit and backbone of the expedition, and Dave often credited him with keeping the team together when troubles arose. He demonstrated the classic canine gifts—loyalty and trust, courage, a flair for clowning—and they made a difference when it counted. Dave wanted to dedicate an epilogue in his book to Ki, and though this isn't the epilogue Dave would have written, we can still give Ki his due.

There wasn't much of a living in writing articles and grinding out a book manuscript, and Dave's worries were compounded by growing guilt about being dependent on his parents. He'd missed out on the college experience and degree while educating himself in bush survival; he thought he might make a career as a writer but meanwhile felt that people were expecting more of him—that he was failing to "take his place in the world."

This concern isn't exactly rare among young men in their early twenties, and none of Dave's problems, taken alone, seems overwhelming. But his reaction to his situation began to cause his family alarm; he grew increasingly depressed, drank too much, had great difficulty managing money, spoke of future plans and prospects in grandiose and unrealistic terms.

Pete and Dave kept in touch only intermittently during this time—Pete had reentry problems of his own to cope with, but he recalls that a few times Dave phoned him in the middle of the night and rambled on for several hours. The calls had a nightmarish quality for Peter, not so much due to their content—Dave seemed to be apologizing for the expedition being a commercial failure—but because Dave's voice was so subdued, an uninflected monotone. He might have been drunk or just depressed; in any case, it was a shocking contrast with the animated manner Pete was accustomed to. His own attempts at reassurance seemed to go unheard.

Early in 1983 Dave began seeing a psychiatrist and undergoing lithium treatment for manic-depression. It was in some ways a relief to him and his parents to identify the syndrome he had apparently been suffering from for several years—yet Dave still resisted the idea of being ill and the need for medication. It was hard for him to reconcile the person who had planned and carried out a noteworthy expedition with the person who now needed help to function.

This is typical of the illness: Its victims very often are hyper-competent and unusually creative in the "high" mode. Dave's appetite for the mounds of detail involved in route planning, his extraordinary persuasiveness with potential supporters and team members, his sense of invulnerability to wilderness perils—these could, in retrospect, be attributed to a mildly manic state. People who manifest such well-organized energy usually function very effectively in business or other areas, so those who suffer from moodswing don't see their highs as part of an illness. The expedition also seems to have smoothed out or masked the downside of Dave's condition, with his day-to-day environment providing both a comforting routine and challenges he was largely capable of handling. The fact that he adapted so well to bush life probably delayed his diagnosis.

At the same time he was being treated with lithium and antidepressants—with some success, apparently—Dave was prescribing for himself a kind of therapy that he had more faith in. The idea of getting back to Canada, to the bush, was a constant underlying refrain that grew ever more urgent. He began making fairly elaborate plans to return on his own, to homestead a cabin and get by however he could. The place he had in mind was an unnamed lake on the upper Berens that he and Pete had discovered in early June 1978, on the way to their rendezvous with Maurice Halsey (see chapter 8). Though it was unnamed officially, Dave called it Good Sight Lake (or "Good Site"; his notes vary but both names are meaningful). His description of the surrounding landscape wasn't glowing, but the country had all the features most important to him: It was "abundant in fish, game, and fur" and as isolated as one could wish for.

Dave's resources were slender, but his planning was meticulous: driving routes, maps, supply lists, sketches for his cabin and canoe, down to the last detail. Since he would be far from any pharmacy, he persuaded his doctor to prescribe a large enough supply of his current medications to last several months. This included, besides lithium, a relatively new and little-tested antidepressant with potentially toxic side effects. He never got the chance, however, to try out this regimen of an ancient lifestyle combined with modern medicine. One night in McLean, the treacherous combination of depression and a car wreck led him to take all the drugs he had on hand; by the time he found his way home and then to the hospital, his time had run out.

———————————

The chartered plane circled above the marshy flatlands of central Ontario, then set down on a small but lovely lake, still unnamed on the pilot's map. Dave Halsey had told his parents about Good Sight Lake, and after his death they had found his plans and notes about making it his home. Maurice and Jean Halsey decided to carry out their son's wish, and Dave's marked-up chart from the expedition made it easy to find the lake again.

They spread his ashes on the mossy rocks and scattered them on the quiet water. They walked along the shore a little way and tried to imagine where Dave would have sited his cabin. They stayed a few hours and then flew back to Virginia, by way of Red Lake. The following year they returned with a plain brass plaque bearing Dave's name and a few lines about the Trans-Canada Expedition. It was cemented to the mossy rocks, and they have visited the spot a few times since.

We can only speculate about whether Dave could have made his life work in a hand-built cabin on Good Sight Lake—or perhaps found some healing influence there that would have allowed him to survive the pressures of young adulthood and come back to a more "integrated" lifestyle. Social and family ties drew him strongly, but wilderness seemed to exert an even more powerful pull. The bush was an immediate, palpable reality, whether comforting, hostile, exalting, or exhausting; it could be embraced or grappled with directly, unlike the more abstract challenges of civilization.

Dave's views on the appropriate uses of wilderness and humankind's place in it may have diverged from those accepted by most environmentalists—and probably he wouldn't have called himself one of "them." But, as Pete points out, he and Dave had lived close to the land for more than two years, and both emerged with a keen concern for its fate, not limited to the wild places they had traveled through but for how people around the globe will sustain themselves and their environments, now and in the future. Certainly Dave would have wanted others to have the opportunity he enjoyed: in Pete's words, "to walk in the footsteps of yesterday's explorers."

Dave was unique both in his achievement and in his problems, but he was also representative of a breed of modern-day explorers who, with the planet's geography a settled issue, feel compelled to find new challenges in nature, devise goals as yet unattained. Will Steger, making his landmark treks to the poles, is one of these, as is Tim Severin, who sailed an open curragh from western Ireland to Newfoundland in an attempt to show that Irish monks could have discovered the New World in the sixth century, and Japanese polar explorer and mountaineer Naomi Uemura.

Scores of mountaineers still pioneer new routes in the Himalaya, Patagonia, and other great ranges; kayak descents of fearsome river headwaters take place around the globe every year. The motives of the adventurers may differ, but the need for physical challenge in isolated surroundings is a shared theme. Bill Graves of *National Geographic* compares Dave, in character and purpose, to the young British explorer Robert Swan, who in 1986 at age twenty-nine followed in the tracks of Sir Robert Scott to the South Pole, on foot and without dogs or radio, and in 1989 reached the North Pole as well. Graves adds:

> Had Dave lived, I think he would have gone on to do significant things and to make a contribution to the science and the skill of exploration. He was already on his way and one couldn't help admire him and wish him the very best, for he earned it the only real way, the hard way.

But Dave turned out to be a little different from other adventurers who move through the wilderness, experiencing it as a more-or-less temporary antidote to life in an industrialized society. His urge was to inhabit it, to be at home in it—this was the aim of all his hard-learned bushcraft and the source of his admiration for both Indian and white residents of the Canadian bush. It was also why the idea of a cabin beckoned to him. The image of lighted windows and a welcoming fire spoke strongly of all that he'd found good: the best in human nature, the meeting place of his contrary desires for society and solitude, the refuge from cold nights. A home that he could make for himself, yet one that echoed with many voices.

Acknowledgments

Dave Halsey, we think, would have wanted to thank everyone who helped him concerning the Trans-Canada Expedition, beginning with his parents, his brother Steve and sister Sara, his partner Peter Souchuk, Peter's parents, Elinor and Dan Souchuk, and his short-term partner in Alberta, C. W. Hughey. He would have gratefully acknowledged the support of the National Geographic Society, especially Editor Bill Graves and Photography Editor Bruce McElfresh, as well as Barry C. Bishop and Andy Brown. Dave would have expressed his gratitude to Britches Outdoors, Grumman Aerospace, the Happy Outdoorsman, and the North Face for the equipment they donated, as well as to everyone else who donated money, time, and supplies or made other contributions to the expedition. He would have reserved special thanks for the officials and citizens of Canada — many of whom are mentioned by name in the text — who broke trail, opened doors, provided food and shelter, shared bush craft, and gave their interest and encouragement.

Some he would surely have mentioned by name include Joe and Carolina Camp, Derek Tripp, Gary Hughes, Rita Ford, Mike Jones, Randy and Donna Davis, Baxter Gillingham, Ron McCormick, George Malbuth, Don and Dan Ehman, Dick Naumann, Roger and Danielle Léger, Jim Perry, the Northern Lights Gospel Mission, Bill and Louise Coppen, Joan Metatawabin, George Frederick, Tobe Lemaige, Archie Janvier, Dominic and Alice French, John and Hazel Pearson, pilots Georges Boucher, Randy Blake, Jim Gerlach and Tim Kielman, Brother Leach, Moses Daniel Flett, "Trapper Dick" Anderson, Ian Lougheed, Vic Pelshea, Roy Turner, Abraham Paulmartin, David Coon, Don Dutton, Clayton Morris, Angus Phillips, Ruth and Ivan Stepnich, CBC Radio, the National Wildlife Federation, Mayor Octave Caron and the citizens of Tadoussac, and especially Eli Tookate and Matthew and Mary Hookimaw of the Lake River Cree.

Dave might also have acknowledged those who supported his efforts to write about the expedition, notably his agent, Julian Bach, and including the editors of *Quest* and *International Wildlife* magazines and the staff of Sierra Club Books.

His cowriter wishes to thank, above all, Jean and Maurice Halsey for their unfailing assistance, patience, courage, and hospitality during the months and years it took to prepare this book for publication. Several days spent in their home outside Chicago, reviewing the vast archive of material from the expedition they have so meticulously organized and maintained, served as the foundation for the work that needed to be done in stitching the story together. More than anything else, it has been their love, will, and faith that have carried this book along since Dave's death.

Peter Souchuk, Dave's partner and friend and the photographer of the Trans-Canada Expedition, was exceedingly generous with his time and memories, contributing many insights and clarifications where needed in the manuscript, as well as the splendid photographs that bring the places, people, and events Dave described to life.

I am grateful to my former colleagues at Sierra Club Books, especially Publisher Jon Beckmann, who saw the promise in Dave's early manuscript and exercised his usual good judgment, tolerance, and faith as the project crept toward publication. And to Editor David Spinner for his enthusiasm and excellent work in fine-tuning the manuscript, along with Copy Editor Barbara Fuller.

Bill Graves of *National Geographic* read relevant parts of the manuscript and corrected several errors of fact and interpretation, for which I am indebted to him.

It is probably a bit unusual for an editor or collaborating writer to acknowledge the author in print, but many circumstances of this book have been unusual. So I want to thank David Halsey, whom I never met except by telephone but whom I have come to know and admire through his tale, for daring to dream of the expedition, for making it happen, for seeing so much and describing it so well, and for giving me the opportunity to do some exploring of a more sedentary kind.

Bibliography

Bauer, George W. *Tales from the Cree.* Ontario, Canada: Highway Book Shop, 1978.

Burns, Bob. *The Manitoba Trappers' Guide to Better Quality Fur.* Manitoba, Canada: Department of Renewable Resources and Transportation Services, 1976.

Byrd, Richard E. *Alone.* New York: G.P. Putnam's Sons, 1938. Reprint. New York: Avon Books, 1968.

Comfort, Darlene J. *Ribbon of Water and Steamboats North: A History of Fort McMurray, Alberta, 1870–1898.* Canada. 1974.

Grey Owl. *Tales of an Empty Cabin.* Toronto, Canada: Macmillan, 1936. First Laurentian Library Edition, 1975.

Journals of Smith, Jackson, and Sublette fur brigade, 1828–29. N.p., n.d.

Karras, A. L. *Face the North Wind.* Ontario, Canada: Burns & MacEachern, 1978.

Leach, Brother Frederick. *59 Years with Indians and Settlers on Lake Winnipeg.* Winnipeg, Canada, 1976.

London, Jack. *The Sea-Wolf.* New York: Macmillan, 1904.

London, Jack. *The Unabridged Jack London.* Edited by Lawrence Teacher and Richard E. Nicholls. Philadelphia: Running Press, 1981.

Rutstrum, Calvin. *Paradise Below Zero.* New York: Macmillan, 1968. Collier Books Edition, 1972.

Turner, Daisy. *Moose Factory Cree.* Ontario, Canada: Highway Book Store, 1975.

Wallace, W. S., ed. *Sir Henry LeFroy's Journal to the Northwest in 1843–44.* Transactions of the Royal Society of Canada, 1938.

Wolfart, H. Christoph, and Janet F. Carrol. *Meet Cree, A Practical Guide to the Cree Language.* Alberta, Canada: University of Alberta Press, 1973.

Index of Place Names

Kamloops, B.C., 20, 29–30, 31, 237
Kenogami River, 160
Knee Lake, 101

Lac Carbonneau, 232
Lac La Loche, 90
Lac La Ronge, 108
Lac St.-Jean, 230, 232, 237
Lake Agassiz, 112
Lake Mistassini, 230, 231–32
Lake of the Woods, 20
Lake Pikangikum, 142
Lake River, Ont., 166, 177–206, 207, 211, 240
Lake St. Joseph, 151–52
Lake Winnipeg, 111–27
Lakitusaki, Ont., 178, 203
La Loche, Sask., 85–101
La Ronge, Sask., 35, 101, 107–11
Little Fort, B.C., 31
Little George Island, 120, 121
Little Grand Rapids, Man., 131, 134, 135–38
Long Point, Man., 114–15
Lower Wells, Alta., 43
Lynn Canyon Park, 14

McClure Ferry, 31
Manitoba, 16, 72, 111–39, 244–45
Merritt, B.C., 22, 27–29
Methy Portage, 46, 65
Ministikawatin Peninsula, 217, 219
Missisicabi River, 217
Mistassini River, 230, 231, 232
Moar Lake, 139
Moose Factory, 208
Moose River, 174, 209
Moosonee, Ont., 125, 164, 174–77, 207–10
Morin Lake Reserve, 107

Natatishee Point, 211, 212
Nicola Lake, 29
Night Owl Falls, 133–34
Nomansland Point, 168
Norrish Creek, 16–19
North Bamaji Lake, 148, 150
North Thompson River, 30, 31–32
Nottaway River, 225

Ogoki, Ont., 159
Ontario, 125, 126, 127, 139–218

Patuanak, Sask., 101, 103
Pelican Point, Alta., 43
Peter Pond Lake, 85
Pickle Lake, Ont., 143, 147, 152
Pikangikum, Ont., 142

Pinehouse Lake, 101, 102, 103, 105, 106–7
Pine River, 103, 105
Pointe a la Savane, 237
Pointe Bleue, 237
Pointe Méscanonane, 218–19
Polar Bear Provincial Park, 178
Poplar River, 122
Post Creek, Sask., 101

Quebec, 1, 164, 174, 213, 217, 218–41. See also Tadoussac

Rarabeck Creek, 153
Red Lake, Ont., 150
Riviere du Chef, 232
Riviere Témiscamie, 232
Rupert Bay, 219–20
Rupert House, Que., 164, 208, 218–31; route from (illustrated), 223
Rupert River, 221, 222–23, 224–31

Saguenay River, 8, 229, 230, 237, 238, 241
St. Félicien, 232, 236–37
St. Lawrence River, 8, 158, 174, 230, 233, 237, 238–39
Sanderson Lake, 107
Sandy Islands, 115–16, 118–19
Saskatchewan, 34, 68, 72, 77, 81–110
Saskatoon, 101
Senyk Lake, 103, 105, 106
Shabumeni Lake and River, 146
Sharpstone Lake, 139
Shetland Islands, 223, 224
Ship Sands Island, 174
Sikachu Lake, 107
Slate Falls, Ont., 150–52
Smith, Alta., 37
South Thompson River, 30
Stag Island, 219–20
Stanley Park, 14

Tadoussac, Que., 1, 8, 158, 174, 207, 227, 231, 232, 237–41; route to (illustrated), 223
Tekarra, Alta., 35
Turnaround Lake, 104

Upper Wells, Alta., 42, 43

Vancouver, B.C., 2, 6, 13, 14, 158
Vega, Alta., 35–36

Wapawekka Lake, 108
Wavy Creek, 174
Willow Creek, 183, 186

Yellow Creek, 163